Reclaiming Pakistan Imran Khan's Quest for Freedom

BY

Mansoor Sarwar Khan

Copyright © **Mansoor Sarwar Khan**

All rights reserved. No part of this publication may be reproduced, distributed, or transmitted in any form or by any means, including photocopying, recording, or other electronic or mechanical methods, without the prior written permission of the publisher, except in the case of brief quotations embodied in critical reviews and certain other noncommercial uses permitted by copyright law.

Acknowledgments

I dedicate this book to the indomitable spirit of Imran Khan, whose unwavering resolve and courage have inspired countless Pakistanis to dream of a better future. His vision for a just and prosperous Pakistan has been a guiding light, even in the darkest of times. Through his relentless efforts, he has awakened a sense of hope and purpose in the hearts of a nation.

I also wish to honor the memory of the fallen workers of Pakistan Tehreek-e-Insaf, who made the ultimate sacrifice during the peaceful march to Islamabad on November 26th, 2024. These brave souls, driven by their commitment to truth, justice, and democracy, exemplified the spirit of resistance against oppression. Their sacrifices remind us that the struggle for freedom and dignity is never in vain.

To every supporter who walked alongside us, faced adversity with courage, and stood firm in the face of tyranny, this book is a tribute to your resilience. You are the unsung heroes of a movement that seeks to restore the soul of our nation. Your dedication will forever be etched in the annals of history.

May this work serve as a small token of gratitude and a reminder of the enduring fight for justice, equality, and freedom. Together, we shall continue to march forward, undeterred and unbroken.

Tribute to True Warriors

In Pakistan's most turbulent times, when speaking the truth was an act of defiance, I find immense inspiration in the bravery of fearless journalists. Although I have never had the privilege of meeting them, their courage echoes deeply within me.

Moeed Pirzada, Sabir Shakir, Aleema Khan and Imran Riaz Khan— your steadfast commitment to truth and justice stands as a beacon of hope in the face of darkness. Your voices, rising against the tide of censorship and intimidation, have ignited a spirit of resilience among the people of Pakistan.

To the late Arshad Sharif, who paid the ultimate price for his unyielding dedication to journalistic integrity, your sacrifice will never fade from memory. Your pen, more potent than the sharpest sword, etched a legacy that will continue to inspire generations to come.

These warriors faced difficult and testing times, proving that truth cannot be silenced. Their indomitable spirit is a testament to the transformative power of journalism and the unbreakable strength of the human will.

May their sacrifices remind us that the pursuit of justice is a noble cause worth every risk. May their legacy guide us in the ongoing struggle for freedom and integrity, and may they be blessed with boundless health, prosperity, and recognition as paragons of bravery.

Dedication

This book is a heartfelt tribute to the unwavering love, sacrifices, and timeless legacy of my family.

To my beloved mother, who left this world far too soon at the tender age of 30—your radiant smile, gentle touch, and endless love remain etched in my soul. Though your time with us was brief, your impact on my life has been eternal.

To my illustrious father, Ch Muhammad Sarwar Khan of Rupochak, the longest-serving parliamentarian in Pakistan's history—your life was a testament to unshakeable integrity and selfless public service. Your unwavering dedication to the people continues to inspire me, and your legacy lives on in the countless lives you touched.

To my grandfather, Chaudhry Qasim Khan—a man of vision, strength, and boundless determination. Your sacrifices and legacy as a pillar of our family history remind me of the values of resilience and courage that flow through our veins.

May Allah, in His infinite mercy, bless my parents and grandfather from eternity to eternity. May their sacrifices, wisdom, and love continue to guide me as I strive to honour their memory with every word, every action, and every breath.

This book is my humble effort to live up to their enduring legacy. In the words of the poet:

"The smallest act of kindness is worth more than the grandest intention." Through their selfless acts of love and kindness, my parents and great-grandfather have been my guiding light. I hope this work makes them proud and contributes to the principles they held dear.

Tu shaheen hai, parwaz hai kaam tera,

Tere samne aasman aur bhi hain.

O Imran, you are the Shaheen of Iqbal's dream,
Soaring beyond horizons, where freedom gleams.
Inspired by Allama Iqbal

Disclaimer

This book is an exploration of Pakistan's political, social, and institutional history, with a focus on constructive analysis aimed at fostering dialogue and understanding. It is not the intention of the author to malign, disrespect, or unjustly criticize any state institution, political party, or individual. Instead, the narrative seeks to present a balanced perspective that highlights challenges while celebrating achievements and resilience.

Every institution, including the judiciary, military, parliament, and civilian government, plays a vital role in Pakistan's progress and stability. This book acknowledges that these pillars of state are interconnected and must work in harmony for the nation to thrive. The constructive criticism presented herein is rooted in a spirit of optimism and a desire for national betterment.

The opinions expressed in this book are those of the author and are not intended to provoke animosity or undermine respect for any entity. The goal is to encourage dialogue that contributes to Pakistan's future as a strong, just, and prosperous state. Long live Pakistan!

Commitment to Ethical Standards, Data Privacy and Source Attribution.

This book contains references, excerpts, and quotes from various sources, which have been utilized under the principles of fair use. The intent of their inclusion is to enhance understanding, provide context, and promote discussion on the topics covered. Efforts have been made to credit all authors, publications, and sources appropriately. Where permissions were necessary, reasonable steps were taken to obtain them. Any omissions or errors in citations are unintentional, and the author welcomes communication to address such issues promptly.

No part of this work intends to infringe upon copyrights or intellectual property rights of any individual or organization. The author firmly believes that all referenced material contributes to the educational and analytical objectives of this publication

The aim of this book is to promote informed dialogue.

This book is based on publicly available information, personal experiences, and interpretations intended solely for informational and educational purposes. Every effort has been made to ensure accuracy and fairness, with no intention to compromise the privacy or confidentiality of any individual, organization, or institution mentioned.

No unauthorized access to private or classified information was used in creating this book. References to specific entities, events, or individuals are drawn from open sources and have been handled with respect and responsibility.

The author upholds the principles of data privacy and confidentiality, emphasizing that the inclusion of names, incidents, or quotes is neither an endorsement nor a critique beyond what is in the public domain. This content is presented to foster constructive discourse while adhering to ethical standards.

Table of Contents

Chapter 1: Origins Of Resolve: The Journey Into Pakistan's Political Crossroads 12

Chapter 2: Loyalty, Leadership, And Legacy: Navigating The Crossroads Of Political Integrity 20

Chapter 3: A Grassroots Revolution: Pti's Intra-Party Elections And The Dawn Of Democratic Transformation 25

Chapter 4: Democratic Struggles: Lessons From The Past And Hope For The Future 39

Chapter 5: Shadows Over Sovereignty: Pakistan's Civil-Military Imbalance 60

Chapter 6: For Pakistan To Move Forward 82

Chapter 7: Imran Khan's Spiritual Journey 99

Chapter 8: Imran Khan's Rise To Power 106

Chapter 9: Profiles Of Courageous Leaders 133

Chapter 10: Imran Khan's Tenure As Prime Minister Of Pakistan 143

Chapter 11: The Unintended Missteps Of Imran Khan 164

Chapter 12: Imran's Struggle In The Cultural Context 173

Chapter 13: Imran Khan's Future 180

Chapter 14: Future Of Pakistan 193

Chapter 15 Future Roadmap Of Pakistan 211

Chapter 16: My Farming Policy And Challenges In International Frontier 239

Chapter 17: A Journey Of Resilience, Unity, And Progress 275

Chapter 18: Conclusion And Objective Of The Book 287

Chapter 1: Origins of Resolve: The Journey into Pakistan's Political Crossroads

On March 9, 2009, I received a call from Ahsan Rashid, the then-President of PTI Punjab, inviting me to join a meeting with Imran Khan at Liberty Chowk. The goal of this meeting was to persuade former PPP minister Rana Shakur to align with the PTI. At that time, PTI was still a small political entity striving to make a mark in Pakistan's political landscape.

Upon arrival, I was introduced to Imran Khan, who greeted me warmly an uncommon gesture for a public figure in Pakistan. This meeting marked the beginning of an intriguing political journey. Our convoy departed for Sahiwal, with Ahsan Rashid narrating my academic achievements and political background to Imran Khan. Despite his initial skepticism about convincing Rana Shakur, I emphasized the importance of perseverance and strategic negotiation. Imran Khan smiled and decided to give it a try.

The journey was a mix of informal camaraderie and serious political discourse. During the drive, I reflected on a piece of advice from the book *Leaders* by President Nixon, which emphasized the value of understanding human behavior in politics. Midway, we stopped for a simple meal at a roadside tandoor. This down-to-earth gesture was quintessentially Imran Khan, showcasing his connection with ordinary people. Encouraged by my suggestion, he acknowledged the crowd that had gathered, leaving a positive impression.

Upon meeting Rana Shakur, I leveraged my knowledge of his background and shared history with my father to engage him in meaningful dialogue. The interaction highlighted the importance of humility and persistence in politics—a lesson that would resonate throughout my tenure with PTI.

Despite facing adversity, including jail sentences, financial losses, and being denied an NA ticket in my ancestral constituency in 2018 and 2024, my dedication to PTI under Imran Khan's leadership has remained unwavering. His exceptional leadership, vision, and commitment to a prosperous and just Pakistan have been a constant source of inspiration. Though internal party politics and external pressures, including the influence of establishment-backed figures, created obstacles, Imran Khan's integrity and courage in the face of challenges reaffirmed my belief in his ability to lead Pakistan toward a brighter future with dignity, prosperity, and unity for all citizens.

Imran Khan's leadership embodies unwavering principles, selflessness, and resilience, prioritizing Pakistan's progress over personal gain. Influenced by Imam Ali's teachings, his theological depth highlights faith as "Al-Haqq" (The Truth), reflecting confidence and integrity. Pakistan, a diverse nation shaped by Indo-Aryan, Iranian, Turkic, and Arab influences, blends tradition and modernity. With strong community values and resilience, it requires exceptional leadership to navigate its multifaceted identity and challenges.

Pakistan is a civilizational state with a rich history shaped by cultural, linguistic, and genetic exchanges. Its people represent a blend of diverse ethnic groups, including Indo-Aryans, Iranians, Turks, Arabs, Central Asians, and Dravidians, reflecting influences from ancient civilizations and empires. As a multi-ethnic federation with a shared Islamic heritage, Pakistan is defined by its linguistic unity in Urdu, strong community and family values, and a unique fusion of tradition and modernity. Its resilience and cultural wealth, encompassing music, art, literature, and cuisine, highlight the complexity and richness of its national identity. Leading such a nation demands exceptional vision and leadership to navigate its diversity and challenges.

The Harappa Civilization, as ancient as Mesopotamia, originated in Sahiwal and extended to Mohenjo-Daro, encompassing much of present-day Pakistan. Earlier still, the 7,000-year-old Mehargarh civilization flourished along the Bolan River in Balochistan. These civilizations were primarily composed of local Dravidian peoples. Over time, the arrival of the Aryans from Central Asia brought significant cultural and genetic exchange, as they gradually settled in Pakistan and intermarried with the Dravidians. This blending of populations laid the foundation for the region's rich historical and cultural complexity.

The Dravidian people, whose exact origins remain debated, are believed to have emerged from the Indian subcontinent, with ties to the Indus Valley Civilization. Their migration to southern India likely resulted from climate changes and agricultural expansion around 3,000 BCE. The Dravidian language family, approximately 4,500 years old, reflects this history of cultural exchange and adaptation. Despite their concentration in southern India today, their genetic and cultural footprint, including contributions from Iranian farmer DNA, underscores their integral role in shaping South Asia's ancient civilizations.

Pakistan's history and culture are rooted in ancient civilizations, including the Harappa and Mehargarh settlements, which thrived along the Indus and Bolan rivers. The region's inhabitants were primarily Dravidians, later intermingling with Aryans who migrated from Central Asia. This blend of populations contributed to the region's diverse genetic and cultural identity, with Dravidians influencing southern India and Aryans shaping the linguistic and social framework of the subcontinent.

Sindh, home to the ancient Indus Valley Civilization, reflects a fusion of Dravidian and Indo-Aryan elements. Its cultural legacy includes Islamic influences, rich storytelling traditions, Sufi poetry, and unique cuisine like Sindhi biryani. With a history spanning Persian, Islamic, and colonial rule, Sindh stands out for its strong sense of community and tolerance. Its geographical and cultural uniqueness makes it a vital part of Pakistan's identity.

Punjab, the "land of five rivers," showcases a vibrant history marked by the Indus Valley Civilization, Mughal Empire, and Sikh rule. Its cultural fabric is enriched by its diverse heritage, encompassing music, dance, folklore, and cuisine. The people of Punjab are known for their warmth, hospitality, and shared traditions, reflecting a blend of ancient influences and modern diversity.

Khyber Pakhtunkhwa and Baluchistan each bring distinct flavors to Pakistan's cultural mosaic. KPK, with its Pashtunwali code and tribal traditions, reflects resilience shaped by its mountainous terrain and strategic location. Baluchistan, Pakistan's largest province, boasts a heritage influenced by the Indus Valley, Persian, and Islamic empires. Both regions showcase the strength and adaptability of their people, preserving tribal customs while embracing modernity.

Baluchistan's cultural and genetic distinctiveness stems from its unique tribal traditions, geographical isolation, and a history shaped by migrations and invasions. The province's rich heritage, blending Balochi culture, Sufi traditions, and Islamic influences, stands apart from other regions in Pakistan. Its minimal exposure to British colonial rule further preserved its distinct customs and identity, emphasizing the need for strong, visionary leadership to navigate its challenges.

Pakistan's political landscape, marred by military interference, fragile democracy, and systemic corruption, contrasts sharply with India's democratic stability. The ongoing tensions between civilian leadership and the military have undermined trust in institutions, fueling public frustration and disillusionment. Addressing these issues requires a robust commitment to dialogue, reform, and strengthening democratic norms to ensure a progressive future for Pakistan.

Amidst this turmoil, Imran Khan emerges as a symbol of principled leadership and political integrity. His unwavering commitment to democratic ideals, rule of law, and resilience against political persecution sets him apart from leaders like Nawaz Sharif and Asif Ali Zardari, whose pragmatism and alleged corruption have prioritized personal gain over national interest. Imran's vision and courage offer hope for a Pakistan that upholds justice, democracy, and prosperity, standing as a counterbalance to the military's overreach and systemic decay.

The evening at Rana Shakur's residence was filled with warmth and hospitality. Imran Khan engaged in light-hearted discussions while Ahsan Rashid and I convinced Rana, a seasoned politician, to join PTI. Rana admired my courage in leaving dynastic politics for PTI, which I believed offered a promising alternative for Pakistan under Imran Khan's leadership. His decision to join PTI delighted Khan, who joined us at dinner, his charm and wit winning everyone over. Despite his genial nature, Khan's leadership style raised questions. Could he be tough enough to counter Pakistan's entrenched corrupt systems, political mafias, and interventionist military forces?

Imran Khan's journey echoes historical figures like De Gaulle, navigating exile in his own country while shaping a vision for Pakistan's revival. His belief in politics as an "act of the willed" over mere pragmatism reflects his commitment to reform. He embodies a man engaged in a great enterprise: reclaiming Pakistan from dynastic elites and military overreach to return it to its people. This mission aligns with his deep understanding of leadership, balancing idealism with pragmatism while remaining a beacon of hope in the turbulent landscape of Pakistani politics.

Pakistan's history is marred by recurring crises, stemming from systemic military interference, fragile democratic institutions, and entrenched corruption. Parallels to 1971, when military dominance led to the secession of East Pakistan, are striking. Imran Khan's political struggle against military overreach mirrors Mujib-ur-Rehman's challenge to power structures of his time. The outcomes remain uncertain, with possibilities ranging from political instability and violence to democratic reform through dialogue and negotiation. To avoid catastrophic consequences, Pakistan's leadership and civil society must prioritize democratic principles and national interests over personal gain.

Imran Khan envisions a Pakistan where justice, equality, and the rule of law prevail. His speeches resonate with the masses, painting a vivid picture of a nation free from corruption and oppression. His call to empower youth, women, and minorities strikes a chord with those disillusioned by the status quo. Khan's movement is more than political; it is a revolution of the soul, fostering unity among Pakistan's diverse population. However, achieving this vision requires addressing the systemic flaws that have long plagued the country, including the military's interference and the stranglehold of dynastic politics.

Khan's leadership is marked by resilience and charisma, yet his tendency to exclude strong-willed individuals from his inner circle often weakens his team in moments of crisis. This policy has allowed sycophants to thrive while sidelining loyal, principled supporters. Betrayals by easy-going associates during turbulent times highlight the risks of prioritizing harmony over diversity of opinion. To build a resilient and effective team, Khan must recognize that loyalty and strength of character outweigh convenience and flattery.

Despite his flaws, Imran Khan's resilience sets him apart. Like Napoleon returning from exile or Lincoln overcoming repeated failures, Khan has the rare ability to transform adversity into opportunity. This tenacity allows him to rise stronger after setbacks, embodying the spirit of a leader determined to achieve greatness. His vision for Pakistan is one of justice and equality, challenging deeply rooted power structures while inspiring hope for a brighter future.

Pakistan's moral decay stems from historical subjugation and the psychological scars of colonialism. Societies shaped by slavery or foreign rule often prioritize survival over principles, leading to mediocrity and fear-driven governance. This toxic cycle perpetuates sycophancy and suppresses potential. To break free, Pakistan must nurture courage, character, and talent, fostering an environment where excellence thrives.

The cultural richness of Pakistan's provinces further highlights the complexities of governance. Sindh, Punjab, Khyber Pakhtunkhwa (KPK), and Baluchistan each contribute unique traditions and histories to the national identity. From Sindh's Sufi heritage and Punjab's vibrant folklore to KPK's tribal traditions and Baluchistan's geographical isolation, these regions reflect the diversity and resilience of Pakistan's people. Governing such a multifaceted nation demands exceptional leadership capable of uniting disparate elements under a shared vision of progress and inclusion.

To navigate Pakistan's challenges, Imran Khan must focus on key principles: cultivating a strong, loyal support base, embracing transparency, and empowering marginalized voices. By forging alliances and leading by example, he can counter the entrenched systems that undermine democracy. Khan's journey also serves as a reminder of the lessons of history. The struggles of figures like Imam Ali illustrate the perils of power and the importance of maintaining integrity in the face of adversity.

For Pakistan to move forward, it must address the root causes of its political instability. This includes reducing military interference, fostering dialogue between stakeholders, and prioritizing education and reform. The international community can support these efforts by encouraging political stability and promoting democratic values. Ultimately, Pakistan's future depends on its ability to embrace change, unify its people, and uphold the principles of justice and equality.

Imran Khan's vision for Pakistan resonates deeply with those yearning for change. His belief in the power of the people and his determination to challenge the status quo offer a path toward a more just and democratic society. However, realizing this vision requires overcoming significant obstacles, including internal party dynamics and external resistance. By learning from history and embracing inclusive leadership, Khan can pave the way for a Pakistan that fulfills its potential as a land of dignity and opportunity for all.

Chapter 2: Loyalty, Leadership, and Legacy: Navigating the Crossroads of Political Integrity

Nicolaus Dansforth astutely observes that political loyalties are rare commodities, transcending national identities in ways leaders would do well to realize. Throughout history, loyalty, goodness, and obedience have been the cornerstones of successful leadership. In ancient Greece, Alexander the Great's unwavering loyalty to his companions earned him their devotion, while Julius Caesar's deep commitment to his legions propelled his rise to power in Rome. More recently, Nelson Mandela's steadfast dedication to his comrades during the anti-apartheid struggle in South Africa exemplifies the transformative power of loyalty. These figures, revered for their alignment with values of loyalty and justice, demonstrate how leaders who embody these virtues inspire followers and achieve greatness.

However, history also warns of leaders who, by prioritizing self-interest and forsaking loyalty, invite their downfall. In the modern era, celebrities and icons, often consumed by their quest for personal success, risk falling into this trap. For a figure like Imran Khan, whose journey from cricketing hero to political leader is unprecedented, understanding the value of loyalty in politics is crucial. The stakes are high, and the path is fraught with challenges.

Pakistan's political landscape, marred by sectarian divisions, political rivalries, institutional mistrust, and pervasive corruption, presents a uniquely complex challenge for any leader. These challenges demand not just vision but also wisdom, the ability to inspire loyalty while fostering a culture of meritocracy, accountability, and justice. True loyalty is earned by empowering individuals who share a leader's vision and values while cultivating trust and openness. Imran Khan's success depends on his ability to navigate these treacherous waters and distinguish genuine loyalty from sycophancy.

History offers a wealth of lessons on the interplay between loyalty and leadership. Abraham Lincoln stood by his loyalists even under intense criticism, inspiring trust and admiration. Mahatma Gandhi's ability to empower his followers to take ownership of India's freedom movement exemplifies how leaders cultivate loyalty by creating a shared sense of purpose. Lee Kuan Yew's visionary leadership transformed Singapore into a global economic powerhouse by fostering a culture of meritocracy and loyalty. In contrast, leaders like Nicolae Ceaușescu and Saddam Hussein, who prioritized sycophancy over genuine loyalty, ultimately faced ruin.

Imran Khan finds himself at a crossroads. His charisma and authenticity have garnered him a loyal following, but his leadership is tested by the need to build a sustainable institution. Pakistan Tehreek-e-Insaf (PTI), his political party, must evolve into a robust political force capable of withstanding adversity. This requires more than personal charisma; it demands a focus on organizational strength, internal democracy, and merit-based leadership. For Khan, the challenge lies in transitioning from a personality-driven movement to an institutionalized party that embodies justice, accountability, and equality.

Islamic philosophy offers timeless guidance on governance and leadership. The principles of justice, equality, and accountability that once defined Islamic civilization propelled it to unparalleled heights. Scholars like Ibn Khaldun emphasized that justice is the cornerstone of societal prosperity, while Imam Ali's commitment to fairness serves as a model for leaders. Ibn Rushd (Averroes) highlighted the importance of accountability in governance, noting that states are judged by their actions in this world. These principles remain as relevant today as they were centuries ago, offering a blueprint for leaders like Imran Khan to navigate the complexities of modern governance.

Pakistan's political history, marked by repeated military interventions, highlights the consequences of abandoning these principles. The military's disproportionate influence, coupled with the corrupt practices of successive civilian governments, has stifled democratic growth and institutional integrity. Nawaz Sharif's appeasement of the military and Zulfikar Ali Bhutto's compromises exemplify the perils of prioritizing short-term gains over long-term stability. These failures have left Pakistan grappling with economic stagnation, institutional decay, and a crisis of public trust.

Addressing these systemic challenges requires visionary leadership. Imran Khan's authenticity and commitment to reform offer hope, but his leadership must evolve to address the demands of the moment. Building a strong political institution entails fostering internal democracy, promoting transparency, and cultivating a culture of meritocracy. Without these foundations, PTI risks becoming a transient force rather than a sustainable vehicle for change.

Leadership, however, is not without its pitfalls. Sycophancy, a universal phenomenon across civilizations, has often undermined great leaders. Historical examples abound, from Emperor Qin Shi Huang of China to King Louis XVI of France, whose reliance on flattery led to poor decision-making and eventual ruin. In the Islamic world, Caliph Al-Hakim bi-Amr Allah's governance suffered from his preference for yes-men, while Sultan Selim III's inability to build a loyal and capable team contributed to the decline of the Ottoman Empire. These examples underscore the importance of surrounding oneself with individuals who prioritize integrity and constructive criticism over personal gain.

Imran Khan faces similar challenges within PTI. The party's candidate selection process has often been criticized for favoritism and the inclusion of controversial figures. Instances of tickets being awarded to individuals with questionable loyalties or track records reflect the depth of this issue. The rise of factions within PTI, fueled by personal ambitions rather than shared values, further undermines its organizational integrity. For PTI to thrive, it must embrace transparency and merit-based governance, ensuring that its leaders and representatives reflect its mission.

The principles of justice and accountability, deeply rooted in Islamic philosophy, remain critical to Pakistan's future. Imam Ali's guidance on governance, emphasizing fairness and the rule of law, serves as a timeless reminder of the responsibilities of leadership. Western nations' success in adopting these ideals demonstrates their universal applicability and enduring relevance. For Imran Khan, embodying these principles is essential not only to address Pakistan's immediate challenges but also to build a legacy of enduring reform.

Imran Khan's leadership, marked by his resilience and authenticity, holds the potential to transform Pakistan. His ability to inspire trust and mobilize people, as demonstrated during his flood relief efforts, reflects his unique capacity to connect with ordinary Pakistanis. However, leadership is not merely about vision; it is about execution. For Khan, this means addressing systemic inequities, fostering accountability, and building a culture of excellence within PTI.

The broader challenges facing Pakistan demand more than political reform. Economic stagnation, institutional decay, and widespread inequality require a holistic approach to governance. Imran Khan must lead a national movement that prioritizes education, health, and economic development while addressing the entrenched influence of the military and elite. This requires courage, foresight, and an unwavering commitment to justice.

The lessons of history are clear: leaders who prioritize principles over personal gain inspire not only their contemporaries but also future generations. Figures like Nelson Mandela, who chose reconciliation over revenge, and Abraham Lincoln, who navigated the United States through its darkest hours, exemplify the transformative power of principled leadership. For Imran Khan, the opportunity lies in building a legacy rooted in these values, transcending the limitations of personality-driven politics.

In the crucible of politics, where power and principles often collide, true leadership is defined by the ability to navigate complexity with integrity and wisdom. Imran Khan's journey, marked by challenges and triumphs, offers a microcosm of Pakistan's broader struggles. By embracing the principles of justice, equality, and accountability, he can transcend the limitations of personality-driven politics and build a legacy rooted in enduring values. The stakes are high, but the opportunity for transformative leadership is within reach.

With courage and determination, Imran Khan can guide Pakistan toward a brighter, more equitable future. The task is daunting, but the rewards are immense. By drawing on the lessons of history, the wisdom of Islamic philosophy, and the resilience of the Pakistani people, Khan has the potential to lead a movement that not only addresses Pakistan's immediate challenges but also sets the stage for a more just and prosperous nation.

Chapter 3: A Grassroots Revolution: PTI's Intra-Party Elections and the Dawn of Democratic Transformation

Imran Khan had always envisioned transforming PTI into an institutionalized political party resembling those in the UK. The establishment of intra-party elections by Pakistan Tehreek-e-Insaf (PTI) marked a watershed moment in South Asian politics, distinguishing it from the traditional norms of political parties in the region. South Asian political culture has long been dominated by dynastic politics and centralized decision-making, with party hierarchies often reflecting familial or regional loyalties rather than democratic processes. In this context, PTI's initiative to hold transparent intra-party elections was not only unprecedented but also a bold step toward institutionalizing democracy within Pakistan's political landscape.

Intra-party elections, a hallmark of Western liberal democracies, symbolize internal accountability, grassroots engagement, and a culture of merit-based leadership. By adopting this model, PTI challenged the entrenched norms of patronage-driven politics in South Asia. The elections provided a platform for ordinary party members to have a voice in choosing their leadership, breaking away from the tradition of top-down nominations that have historically sidelined grassroots workers. This commitment to democratic values within the party resonated deeply with the public, particularly the youth, who saw in PTI a vehicle for systemic change and empowerment.

The process itself was a logistical and organizational triumph, involving millions of registered party members across Pakistan. PTI implemented a robust system to ensure transparency, with independent oversight mechanisms and technology-driven solutions. Candidates for leadership positions were required to campaign within the party, presenting their vision and policies to party workers. This not only fostered healthy competition but also cultivated a culture of debate and critical engagement—qualities often absent in the rigid structures of traditional political parties.

The significance of this move cannot be overstated. Intra-party elections signal a shift from personality-driven politics to a more institutionalized approach. In the South Asian context, where parties often revolve around charismatic leaders or dynastic families, PTI's model offered a template for how political organizations can function as democratic entities. By empowering its members to shape the party's leadership, PTI laid the groundwork for a more participatory and accountable political culture.

This initiative also underscored Imran Khan's vision of transforming Pakistan's political landscape. Khan, who has consistently advocated for justice, meritocracy, and transparency, saw intra-party elections as a microcosm of the larger democratic ideals he wished to implement at the national level. The exercise reflected his belief that democracy begins within the party structure and that genuine change must be rooted in the values of fairness and inclusion.

The implications of this experiment extend beyond PTI. By demonstrating that intra-party democracy is possible in Pakistan, PTI set a new standard for political engagement in the country. This achievement has the potential to inspire other parties to adopt similar practices, gradually steering South Asia's political culture toward greater internal accountability and inclusivity. Moreover, it strengthens Pakistan's democratic institutions by fostering a new generation of leaders who rise through merit rather than nepotism.

Despite challenges, such as resistance from traditional power brokers and the complexities of managing such a large-scale electoral process, PTI's intra-party elections represent a bold and progressive step in the evolution of South Asian politics. It is a testament to the power of democratic ideals and the vision of leaders committed to meaningful change.

In a bold move, he dissolved all party office bearers and established a caretaker setup comprising retired bureaucrats, politicians, and military personnel. This marked the start of a three-month registration process, engaging Pakistan's population and overseas members. The foreign wing managed registrations abroad, while within Pakistan, individuals like my son, Sufghan Khan, took charge of local efforts.

Sufghan, a student at Bristol University, managed the digital and physical registration drive in our twin home districts of Sialkot and Narowal during his summer break. Meanwhile, I, alongside my dedicated Central Punjab team, launched an intensive grassroots campaign, traversing villages, towns, and fields. The campaign was not just about party registrations but an immersive journey into Pakistan's rich cultural, geographic, and historical tapestry.

Walking through abandoned agricultural fields and witnessing the crumbling infrastructure underscored the impact of water scarcity and government neglect. This journey offered unparalleled insights into the land's deep history and psyche, shaped by ancient civilizations like Harappa and Mohenjo-Daro, and later by colonial exploitation. The colonial legacy, in particular, stood out as a defining tragedy, stripping the subcontinent of its moral and cultural richness. Once the golden land of the Mughals, boasting 24.5% of the world's GDP during Emperor Shahjahan's reign, colonial rule reduced it to a state of inferiority and dependency.

Our campaign's success earned me commendations from Chairman Imran Khan and Ahsan Rashid. By the time registrations closed, the stage was set for intra-party elections, a transformative milestone for PTI. These elections brought political activity to a new high, with leaders across Pakistan holding caucuses and strategizing intensely. This marked PTI's evolution from an NGO-like entity to a genuine political institution.

The registration drive and elections also showcased PTI's reliance on technology. Inspired by my son's strategic use of social media during the registration process, digitization and social media access still relatively new in Pakistan at that time. It was an era prior to smart phones emergence in rural areas of Pakistan. PTI adopted innovative tools like YouTube and face book to engage members and attract public interest. This shift not only revolutionized campaign dynamics but set a new standard for political engagement in Pakistan, resonating with global trends such as Bernie Sanders' grassroots campaigns in the U.S. and the Aam Aadmi Party's rise in India.

PTI's bottom-up approach empowered young supporters and fostered collective intelligence, transforming the party into a powerful political force capable of challenging the traditional dominance of PPP and PML-N. The party's first-of-its-kind intra-party elections in Pakistan became a defining moment in the country's political history. Media coverage and public participation rivaled general elections, demonstrating PTI's potential to reshape democratic norms.

In Central Punjab, my candidacy for the presidency was a formidable challenge. As a lone contender against two billionaire rivals backed by party elites, I relied on a grassroots campaign and the technological strategies pioneered during the registration drive. Despite the odds, my victory stood as a testament to hard work, strategic communication, and the effectiveness of PTI's democratic ethos.

These elections were transformative, not just for PTI but for Pakistan's political landscape. They marked a departure from personality-driven politics, fostering a culture of internal democracy and accountability. PTI's rise as a third force disrupted the long-standing two-party system and opened new avenues for participatory democracy.

Imran Khan's vision extended beyond party politics. Drawing inspiration from Islamic values, he sought to promote social justice, economic reform, and anti-corruption measures. His commitment to building a welfare state mirrored the ideals of the state of Madina. Khan's initiatives, such as the Ehsaas Programme and environmental projects like Plant for Pakistan, aimed to address poverty and sustainability. His populist narrative and nationalist agenda resonated with millions, emphasizing transparency, meritocracy, and a focus on Pakistan's potential as a leader in the Islamic world.

Khan's leadership, however, faced challenges from entrenched political interests and allegations of interference. Despite his ouster through a no-confidence motion, his agenda continues to influence Pakistan's political discourse, underscoring the enduring impact of his reforms.

Reflecting on PTI's journey, the intra-party elections symbolize the party's commitment to democratic principles. By fostering internal competition and accountability, PTI positioned itself as a model for political transformation. This process also highlighted the importance of reconciling modernity with traditional values—a theme central to Allama Iqbal's philosophy.

Dr. Muhammad Iqbal's seminal work, *The Reconstruction of Religious Thought in Islam*, emphasized the need to bridge Islamic values with modern rationality. He argued for intellectual renewal, advocating for freedom, responsibility, and reform within Islamic societies. Similarly, Imran Khan's efforts aimed to reconcile Pakistan's cultural heritage with contemporary governance, promoting a vision of "Naya Pakistan" that resonated with Iqbal's ideals.

While Iqbal's focus was on intellectual and spiritual rejuvenation, Khan's approach targeted political and economic transformation. Both sought to restore dignity and purpose to the Muslim world, albeit through different means. Iqbal's emphasis on self-awareness and reform continues to inspire intellectuals, while Khan's political agenda has redefined Pakistan's approach to governance.

The intra-party elections were a turning point, showcasing PTI's potential to foster genuine democratic values. As I stood amidst the vibrant atmosphere of election day at Allama Iqbal's library, the significance of this moment was palpable. PTI's rise was not just a political victory but a cultural shift, challenging the status quo and paving the way for a more inclusive and participatory political system.

In conclusion, PTI's journey from a pressure group to a political institution reflects Imran Khan's vision of transformative leadership. By embracing democratic principles, leveraging technology, and drawing on Pakistan's rich cultural heritage, PTI has redefined political engagement in the country. The party's success offers hope for a future where Pakistan can reclaim its lost glory and fulfill its potential as a nation built on justice, equality, and accountability.

The 2013 intra-party elections of Pakistan Tehreek-e-Insaf (PTI) were a landmark event in Pakistan's political landscape. This experiment in intra-party democracy was unprecedented in the country's political history. PTI aimed to distinguish itself from traditional political parties, emphasizing democratic principles and accountability within its structure. However, while the initiative was commendable, its outcomes revealed both strengths and limitations of this ambitious endeavor.

The intra-party elections were driven by PTI's vision to establish itself as a democratic and transparent political entity. Unlike the hereditary or autocratic leadership structures of other parties in Pakistan, PTI under Imran Khan aimed to provide its members a voice in decision-making. This initiative marked PTI's effort to institutionalize democratic norms within its organization, creating a precedent for other political entities to follow.

The elections were extensive, involving thousands of members across Pakistan, with candidates contesting for positions ranging from local ward representatives to national-level offices. The scale and ambition of this exercise set it apart from anything attempted in Pakistani politics before.

Conducting intra-party elections at this scale was a Herculean task. PTI faced numerous logistical, administrative, and strategic challenges. The process was delayed multiple times, creating frustration among party workers and raising questions about the leadership's planning. Furthermore, the competitive nature of these elections led to factionalism within the party, with rival camps emerging at various levels. As noted in analyses of the event, this factionalism weakened internal cohesion and created a sense of disunity among members (Rizwan, 2016)e these challenges, PTI succeeded in conducting the elections, which were widely regarded as a significant step towards democratizing the party structure. My victory in Central Punjab against opponents with greater financial and logistical resources demonstrated the party's commitment to merit-based selection. Furthermore, my success, untainted by election petitions, underscored the transparency of the process, a rarity in Pakistan's political environment.

The results of the intra-party elections were a mixed bag for PTI. While they bolstered the party's claim of being a democratic entity, they also exposed vulnerabilities. The defeat of prominent figures like Ahsan Rashid and Dr. Arif Alvi was a significant blow, as their loss highlighted the potential for internal competition to undermine unity. This fracture persisted, impacting the party's dynamics even after PTI rose to power.

The elections also revealed the challenges of balancing inclusivity with efficiency. As new members joined PTI in large numbers, the party struggled to maintain coherence and discipline. The influx of "electables" – influential politicians from other parties – added to these difficulties, as they often clashed with long-standing PTI members over ideological and strategic differences (Irfan & Khan, 2024) .

In reflecting on the lessons of PTI's intra-party elections, the teachings of Al-Farabi offer valuable insights. Al-Farabi's vision of the ideal state, as outlined in "al-Madina al-Fadila," emphasizes justice, reason, and virtue as foundational principles for a harmonious society. These principles can be applied to the context of PTI's electoral process and its broader implications for Pakistan's political development.

1. **Justice**: The fairness of PTI's electoral process was a significant achievement, but justice also requires addressing inequalities within the organization. The dominance of wealthier candidates in many constituencies highlighted the need for mechanisms to level the playing field, ensuring that all members, regardless of their resources, have an equal chance to contribute.

2. **Reason**: The lack of planning and the logistical challenges faced during the elections indicate a need for greater emphasis on rational decision-making and strategic foresight. By fostering a culture of critical thinking and evidence-based planning, PTI could strengthen its organizational framework.

3. **Virtue**: Al-Farabi's emphasis on moral and intellectual virtues is particularly relevant to PTI's leadership. Cultivating virtues like integrity, empathy, and humility among party leaders could help mitigate factionalism and foster unity.

The 2013 intra-party elections hold important lessons for Pakistan's political landscape. They demonstrate the potential for political parties to adopt democratic practices, challenging the status quo of dynastic politics. However, they also underscore the challenges of implementing such practices in a context characterized by deep-seated patronage networks and political opportunism.

PTI's experiment highlights the importance of institutionalizing democracy within political parties. As research on party politics in Pakistan has shown, the lack of internal democracy is a major factor contributing to the dysfunctionality of the country's political system (Ullah, 2024) . By setting an eI has paved the way for other parties to follow suit, potentially transforming Pakistan's political culture over time.

The 2013 intra-party elections of PTI were a bold and ambitious initiative that sought to redefine Pakistan's political norms. While the process was fraught with challenges, it marked a significant step towards democratizing political parties and fostering accountability. The experience also highlighted the importance of adhering to principles of justice, reason, and virtue, as articulated by Al-Farabi, in building a cohesive and effective organization.

As PTI continues its journey, the lessons of these elections will remain relevant. By addressing the shortcomings and building on the successes of this experiment, PTI has the opportunity to further its vision of creating a just and democratic Pakistan. For the nation as a whole, the elections serve as a reminder that meaningful change begins within, and that the road to progress is often paved with both challenges and opportunities.

Imam Ali's wisdom, as expressed in *Nahjul Balagha*, holds timeless relevance for Pakistan's current political challenges and the survival of leaders like Imran Khan amidst the enduring dominance of the military establishment. The struggles faced by Imam Ali—opposition from corrupt power structures, sectarianism, and betrayal—mirror the challenges that confront modern Pakistan and its democratic aspirations.

Imam Ali's emphasis on justice as the foundation of governance underscores the need for Pakistan to address corruption, inequality, and the erosion of public trust. Injustice, deeply ingrained in Pakistan's institutions, has bred nepotism and cronyism, practices that Imam Ali vehemently opposed. These issues perpetuate a cycle of privilege and exclusion, undermining democracy and marginalizing ordinary citizens.

Addressing these systemic flaws is essential for the nation's survival and progress.

Leadership accountability, a central theme in Imam Ali's sermons, is another area of critical importance. His insistence that leaders serve as stewards of justice and public welfare resonates with Pakistan's need for transparent governance and the dismantling of entrenched power monopolies. For Imran Khan, this entails not only adhering to principles of justice but also surrounding himself with loyal, competent allies who prioritize the nation's welfare over personal gain.

Imam Ali also warned against sectarianism and division, emphasizing unity and inclusivity as pillars of a harmonious society. Pakistan's deeply polarized political and social landscape risks exacerbating instability and weakening democratic institutions. To counter this, leaders must foster an ethos of pluralism and national cohesion, ensuring that all voices, including those from marginalized groups, are heard and valued.

Imran Khan's precarious position as a leader challenging the military's hegemony necessitates strategies rooted in Imam Ali's teachings. Building a strong, popular mandate through transparent elections, strengthening civilian institutions, and fostering public accountability in military affairs are essential. Additionally, forging alliances with democratic forces and international organizations can help counter the military's unchecked dominance and ensure greater scrutiny of its actions.

Historical parallels also highlight the dangers faced by reformist leaders who challenge entrenched power structures. Figures like Zulfiqar Ali Bhutto, Adnan Menderes of Turkey, and Boethius of Florence suffered tragic ends because their followers failed to mobilize effectively for their protection. PTI must learn from these examples and prioritize the safety and survival of Imran Khan as a symbol of democratic resistance. Saving his life is not only crucial for the party but also for the future of civilian supremacy in Pakistan.

Drawing inspiration from global statesmen such as George Washington, Nelson Mandela, and Mahatma Gandhi, who navigated oppressive environments with courage and integrity, Imran Khan can adopt a long-term vision. His efforts to counter military overreach and foster democratic ideals must remain steadfast, even in the face of adversity.

In conclusion, the wisdom of Imam Ali and lessons from history serve as a guide for Pakistan's democratic forces. By prioritizing justice, unity, and accountability, PTI can safeguard its leader and work towards a more equitable and prosperous future for the nation. The survival of democratic principles in Pakistan hinges on the collective effort to resist coercion and uphold the rule of law.

The night was a cold and lonely one. After being denied the chance to visit my leader, Imran Khan, for months, I found myself parked outside the imposing walls of Adiala Jail, hoping for a miracle. My heart heavy with worry, I reclined in the car seat and drifted into an uneasy sleep. In that slumber, a vision unfolded, one so vivid and transcendent that it felt like a divine intervention. I found myself standing in an expansive plain, enveloped by a radiant light that seemed to pulse with the energy of the universe. And then, emerging from the brilliance, appeared a figure of grace, wisdom, and strength—Imam Ali (PBUH).

He approached me with a serenity that dissolved all my fears, his gentle smile a balm to my soul. His eyes, deep and knowing, held a compassion that I had never witnessed before. When he spoke, his voice resonated like a harmonious blend of a soft breeze and a profound echo of truth.

"My son," he began, addressing me as though I were a part of his eternal flock, "I have a message for your leader, Imran Khan. It is a message for these tumultuous times, a guidance for those who walk the path of justice amidst a world shadowed by oppression."

His words sent a tremor of awe through me. I felt honored, and yet burdened by the responsibility of carrying this divine wisdom to Imran Khan. I listened intently, my heart beating in anticipation.

"Tell him, my son," he continued, "that the greatest weapon against oppression is not violence but patience and wisdom. True strength is not in the force of arms, but in the unyielding resolve to uphold principles and truth, even when surrounded by adversity."

As I absorbed his words, the weight of their truth settled deeply within me. I thought of Imran Khan, a man standing resolute in his fight for a better Pakistan, enduring relentless challenges from a powerful military establishment that had long overshadowed civilian governance. Imam Ali's message was a clarion call for perseverance.

"Remind him," Imam Ali said, "that the people are the true source of strength. Their trust, their hope, and their courage will form the foundation of his victory. He must nurture and build alliances with the masses, for it is their collective will that can counter the might of any army."

These words illuminated a path forward for Imran Khan's mission. They underscored the need to transcend political divisions and inspire a unified movement, rooted in shared aspirations for justice and democracy.

Imam Ali's tone shifted slightly, conveying urgency. "Tell him that non-violent resistance and civil disobedience are the most potent tools against oppression. Violence begets violence, but steadfastness in the face of injustice disarms even the most hardened oppressors. Remind him of the power of the pen and the voice—tools mightier than the sword. He must expose the corruption, the abuse of power, and the treachery that have plagued Pakistan's institutions."

This wisdom, deeply grounded in the philosophy of Imam Ali's life, resonated with the teachings of history. Leaders such as Mahatma

Gandhi and Martin Luther King Jr. had triumphed through similar principles, forging paths of non-violent resistance that forever changed the course of their nations.

Imam Ali's vision was not limited to immediate challenges; it was a roadmap for enduring success. "Tell him," he said, "that patience is not passive. It is an active force, a weapon of the resilient. And remind him that the ultimate victory belongs to those who remain unwavering in their principles. As I faced the treachery of Muawiyah, so too must he rise above betrayals and falsehoods with courage and steadfastness."

The vision began to fade, but not before Imam Ali imparted a final piece of advice. His voice, filled with unwavering conviction, echoed in my mind. "Tell Imran Khan that his battle is not just for today, but for the generations to come. Pakistan's destiny is intertwined with his resolve. He must rise every time he falls, for as I have said, 'The greatest glory in living lies not in never falling, but in rising every time we fall.'"

I awoke in my car, the cold steel of reality pressing against me. Yet, the warmth of Imam Ali's message lingered in my heart, filling me with purpose. I knew this was no ordinary dream but a divine revelation, a call to action that I could not ignore. I resolved to deliver this message to Imran Khan and his supporters, for its wisdom held the keys to navigating the perilous terrain of military-dominated politics.

Reflecting on Imam Ali's teachings, several strategies became clear. Imran Khan must deepen his connection with the people, strengthening grassroots movements that amplify the collective voice of the disenfranchised. Transparency and honesty must be his weapons to expose corruption and abuse, eroding the moral authority of oppressive institutions.

Non-violent resistance, a principle championed by Imam Ali, must guide the movement. Civil disobedience campaigns, peaceful protests, and public awareness drives could pressure the establishment while upholding the moral high ground. Additionally, fostering international support through diplomatic channels and human rights advocacy would shine a spotlight on the injustices, compelling global powers to reconsider their alliances.

Imam Ali's emphasis on steadfastness in principles is a cornerstone for Imran Khan's survival and success. Betrayals and coercion will test his resolve, but unwavering adherence to truth will rally his supporters and disarm his detractors. Just as Imam Ali's legacy endures as a beacon of justice, Imran Khan's steadfastness could etch his name in the annals of Pakistan's history.

The vision I experienced was not merely a dream—it was a divine mandate. Imam Ali's message is not only for Imran Khan but for every Pakistani yearning for justice, democracy, and a brighter future. It calls for patience, wisdom, and unity against the forces of oppression. It is a reminder that true leadership is about serving the people and standing firm in the face of adversity.

In these trying times, as Pakistan navigates its challenges, Imam Ali's wisdom offers a guiding light. His timeless teachings underscore that the path to justice is arduous, but it is also noble and transformative. For Imran Khan, this message is both a shield and a sword—a testament to the enduring power of principles in the battle for a nation's soul.

Chapter 4: Democratic Struggles: Lessons from the Past and Hope for the Future

As I approached Ahsan Rashid with news of our divisional tour, his excitement was palpable. However, like the cautious Odysseus, he advised me to first host Imran Khan in my constituency to solidify my position and quiet internal party factions. Though the suggestion stung, I heeded his advice, embodying Hafiz's wisdom: "The truth is not a thing to be grasped, but a reality to be faced."

Imran Khan agreed to visit on March 8th but expressed doubts about the area's party strength and weather warnings. Undeterred, I pressed on, inspired by Horatius, who stood alone against an invading army. Despite rain and black clouds, the crowd's unwavering spirit mirrored Iqbal's words: "The heart is a flame that burns bright, though the body may be weak." The event's success earned Khan's rare praise, though, as time passed, most leaders, except Ahsan Rashid and loyal workers, forgot the achievement.

Reflecting on this journey, I understood the importance of loyalty and character, virtues often overshadowed in politics. While Khan valued hard work, he rarely rewarded it, leaving flatterers and those with deep pockets to enjoy the spoils. Nietzsche's observation, "You must have chaos within you to give birth to a dancing star," seemed to define Khan's leadership. His preference for chaos kept his lieutenants unbalanced, fostering rivalry and infighting within PTI. This strategy, while ensuring his control, often created unnecessary discord, as noted by Ibn Khaldun: "When a leader relies on cunning and deceit, his people will eventually suffer."

The sweet taste of success came during our tour of Punjab, beginning with Mandi Bahauddin. District president Liaqat Ranja and I revitalized

PTI in this once-dormant region. With Liaqat's arrangements and my speeches in the local dialect, we drew a crowd of 5,000, surprising even Khan. Our 25-day journey through multiple tehsils awakened PTI's potential, but it also incited jealousy among rival factions. Still, like Nietzsche said, "You must have chaos within you," and we persisted.

The Gujranwala jalsa posed the greatest challenge, held in the heart of PML-N's stronghold. The city, an electoral powerhouse for decades, tested our resolve. Despite internal and external resistance, we succeeded, marking a turning point for PTI. The event solidified PTI's emergence as a formidable force, shifting the political landscape.

Imran Khan's leadership style, however, remained enigmatic. His deliberate withholding of support from top leaders kept them in flux, fostering competition but also sowing discord. Even Ahsan Rashid faced manipulation by party members seemingly acting on Khan's cues. While Khan reassured him, "You are the top man in Punjab, my dear friend," his strategies often left leaders at odds, echoing Al-Farabi's warning: "A leader who prioritizes power over wisdom will inevitably lead his people astray."

Ultimately, while Khan's sincerity to the people of Pakistan was evident, his internal leadership methods reflected the complexities of a man balancing his roles as a cricket captain and political visionary. His journey, like PTI's, was one of resilience, chaos, and triumph.

As the PTI prepared for its Gujranwala jalsa, the anticipation was palpable. Ahsan Rashid, ever the strategist, advised me to invite Imran Khan to my constituency first, to strengthen my standing within the party. While it was a bitter pill to swallow, I understood the importance of such optics in politics. Imran Khan, though unpredictable and impulsive, agreed to visit. Despite concerns about the weather and the party's local strength, I remained resolute, inspired by the belief that perseverance could overcome any obstacle.

On the day of the jalsa, rain threatened to dampen spirits, but the crowd's enthusiasm was unwavering. The event became a resounding success, with Khan himself acknowledging its impact. However, the fleeting memory of leaders, aside from Ahsan Rashid and loyal workers, diminished the recognition of my efforts. This experience underscored the challenge of maintaining cohesion in a party that often favored flattery over hard work.

Khan's leadership style reflected his cricketing roots—dynamic but impulsive. He deliberately fostered competition among party leaders, keeping them unbalanced to maintain control. While this approach prevented the emergence of rival power centers, it also bred mistrust and internal strife, ultimately weakening the party's structure. As Al-Farabi warned, "A leader who fails to cultivate wisdom and justice will be consumed by his ambition." PTI, instead of evolving into a disciplined political force, often resembled a fan club or NGO, lacking the structure needed for sustained success.

Reflecting on great leaders like Jinnah and De Gaulle, I lamented Khan's failure to emulate their discipline and focus. Jinnah's leadership during the Pakistan Movement exemplified unity and resolve, while De Gaulle's steadfastness during World War II showed the importance of principled leadership. Khan's reliance on impulsive decision-making and constant reshuffling of leadership positions undermined PTI's potential. His inability to establish a cohesive structure became a missed opportunity for meaningful change in Pakistan.

The Gujranwala jalsa, held in the heart of PML-N's stronghold, tested PTI's mettle. The city's fervor on the day of the event was unparalleled, with crowds gathering in a sea of red and green, charged with enthusiasm. The caravan from Lahore, punctuated by receptions along the way, symbolized PTI's growing momentum. Yet, I couldn't help but ponder the challenges posed by Pakistan's entrenched military dominance.

The military's grip on Pakistan's political landscape is rooted in history, economics, and geopolitics. Born from the British Indian Army, it inherited a legacy of political involvement, solidified by events like the 1971 war. Its vast business empire, including the Fauji Foundation and real estate ventures, ensures economic power, free from civilian oversight. This dominance has stifled Pakistan's democratic growth, contrasting with India and Bangladesh, where civilian institutions have flourished.

International powers often engage directly with Pakistan's military, perpetuating its influence. Strategic interests, particularly in regional conflicts, have led the West to prioritize stability over democratization. Until the military's grip is loosened and civilian institutions are empowered, Pakistan's true potential will remain unrealized.

To challenge the dominance of the military in Pakistan and establish civilian supremacy, a political leader must adopt a multifaceted strategy that emphasizes institutional reform, public mobilization, and strategic international engagement. The cornerstone of any meaningful reform is creating a robust, inclusive political party representing the diverse interests of Pakistan's population. Drawing from ancient Athens, where democracy emerged through collective citizen power, such a party must prioritize unity, inclusivity, and justice. These principles will serve as the foundation for sustainable transformation.

Strengthening civilian institutions is another critical aspect. Inspired by the medieval European concept of the "Rule of Law," Pakistan must bolster its judiciary, parliament, and local governments. These institutions should function independently, ensuring power is distributed evenly and the military is held accountable. The Magna Carta of 1215 serves as a historical reminder that even the sovereign must operate within the bounds of law—a principle critical for addressing military overreach. Education and economic development must also be prioritized, as seen in the Nordic countries, where literacy, economic growth, and social welfare empower citizens to demand their rights and foster a stable society.

Constructive dialogue between civilian leadership and the military is essential. Drawing from ancient Greek dialectic principles, negotiations must aim for a gradual transfer of power from the military to civilian institutions. This ensures stability while creating pathways for mutual understanding. Peaceful protests and grassroots mobilization can amplify these efforts. The Arab Spring and contemporary social movements exemplify how public sentiment, channeled effectively, can demand democratic reforms and civilian supremacy. Engaging with communities and leveraging media platforms to highlight the benefits of civilian governance and the drawbacks of military dominance are vital tools in this endeavor.

The international community plays a significant role in this dynamic. Lessons from the anti-apartheid movement in South Africa demonstrate how global solidarity and pressure can drive change. Western nations, with their emphasis on democratic values, human rights, and strategic interests, could potentially support movements for civilian empowerment. Diplomatic pressure, sanctions, and conditional aid are instruments that could incentivize the military to relinquish dominance. However, Western nations' actions will likely be influenced by their broader geopolitical objectives, including regional stability and counter-terrorism efforts.

The historical context of military influence in Pakistan sheds light on the entrenched challenges. The Roman Republic's experience with figures like Julius Caesar demonstrates how unchecked military power can undermine democracy. In Turkey, the gradual reduction of military influence under Recep Tayyip Erdoğan illustrates the potential for transition, albeit with its own complexities. Latin American nations such as Argentina and Chile transitioned from military dictatorships to democracies through legal accountability and constitutional reforms, offering valuable lessons for Pakistan. India and Bangladesh provide examples closer to home, where civilian institutions were strengthened to limit military interference and foster democratic processes.

The military's significant role in Pakistan's economy further complicates the issue. Entities like the Fauji Foundation and Army Welfare Trust, along with the Frontier Works Organization's dominance in construction, perpetuate military influence. Civilian leadership must work to diversify economic control, ensuring transparency and reducing reliance on military-owned enterprises. This economic disentanglement is essential for diminishing the military's grip on power.

To address these challenges, Pakistan must undertake constitutional reforms to explicitly restrict the military's political role and ensure civilian supremacy. Strengthening civilian institutions and judiciary systems is crucial for implementing accountability frameworks. Establishing special tribunals or courts to address military overreach can ensure impartiality and adherence to the rule of law. Civilian oversight mechanisms, such as empowered parliamentary committees and independent watchdogs, must monitor military activities and promote transparency. Public engagement campaigns should focus on educating citizens about the importance of democratic governance and civilian rule, leveraging both traditional and digital media to reach a broad audience.

Internationally, Western nations could support these reforms through diplomatic engagement and strategic pressure. However, their support would depend on how closely the civilian leadership aligns with their broader strategic interests. Efforts to secure such support must emphasize Pakistan's commitment to democracy, human rights, and regional stability. The role of international actors in encouraging civilian supremacy will likely remain pivotal, and Pakistan's leadership must navigate these dynamics carefully.

Reflecting on historical lessons, it becomes clear that the road to reform is challenging yet achievable. The journey to the Gujranwala jalsa offered a microcosm of these complexities. From grassroots mobilization to strategic negotiations, each step reflected both the potential and the obstacles of democratic transformation in Pakistan. The deeply entrenched military influence and systemic challenges require more than speeches and rallies—they demand sustained, strategic action.

Imran Khan, though charismatic and driven, faced the daunting task of balancing public expectations with systemic reform. His leadership style, marked by impulsive decisions and reliance on personal charm, underscored both his strengths and limitations. To truly effect change, Khan and Pakistan's civilian leaders must prioritize unity, discipline, and a long-term vision for reform. As Imam Ali ibn Abi Talib said, "The noblest of men are those who are not overtaken by sudden whims." Pakistan's path to democracy and civilian supremacy requires steadfastness, wisdom, and an unwavering commitment to the rule of law.

The Gujranwala jalsa, a significant event in Pakistan's political landscape, reflected both the opportunities and challenges facing the nation. Leaders like Ahsan Rashid showcased the spirit of grassroots democracy, striving to bring people together in pursuit of shared goals. However, the broader context highlights the complexities of balancing military and civilian roles in Pakistan's governance. The military, deeply rooted in the country's history and evolved from the legacy of the British Indian Army, has played a significant role in shaping national security and regional stability.

The Pakistani military remains one of the most respected and acknowledged armed forces globally, known for its professionalism and operational excellence. Its efforts in defending the nation's sovereignty, combating terrorism, and maintaining peace within volatile borders have earned it admiration both domestically and internationally. The military's contributions in times of natural disasters and emergencies further underscore its dedication to serving the nation beyond its defense mandate.

While the path to balanced civil-military relations requires careful reform and mutual understanding, the military's strength and capabilities are indispensable to Pakistan's security and progress. As a vital institution, it continues to symbolize resilience and pride for the people of Pakistan. A harmonious relationship between civilian leadership and the military is essential to drive the country toward a stable and prosperous future.

Imran Khan's impulsiveness, a trait that often mirrored the unpredictability of a fast bowler, was evident throughout the journey to the Gujranwala jalsa. His tension and impatience, though rooted in his passion and drive, frequently led him to act without fully considering the consequences. As we approached Muridke, Khan's anxiety grew, and he repeatedly questioned me about the reception. His voice was laced with concern, even as I reassured him. Despite the thousands gathered as a testament to our hard work, his doubts lingered.

Rashid Khan, ever the calming presence, whispered to me to disregard Khan's outbursts, attributing them to his nature. "He gets hyper and tense unnecessarily," Rashid said. The throngs of supporters that greeted us at Muridke were a historic moment, with unprecedented media coverage and jubilant crowds. Yet, Khan remained preoccupied, his mind trapped in a cycle of self-analysis. He missed the chance to connect deeply with the people and revel in their adoration.

The reception at Muridke was a spectacle of hope and dedication, where thousands gathered to see Imran Khan. The atmosphere pulsated with music, chants, and an energy that brought the city to life. But Khan's impatience loomed over the occasion, a reminder that even the most charismatic leaders are not immune to human flaws. Amid the crowd's excitement, I reflected on Mirza Ghalib's verse: "Dil-e-nadan tujhe hua kya hai, Aakhir is dard ki dawa kya hai?" It captured the essence of the moment—a fragile balance between joy and despair. Khalil Gibran's wisdom also resonated: "Say not, 'I have found the truth,' but rather, 'I have found a truth.'" These thoughts deepened my understanding of the complexities of human nature and leadership.

As we left Muridke, the day's energy escalated. On the GTR road, we encountered a 20-mile-long caravan of vehicles adorned with PTI flags, filled with chanting supporters. At Kamoke, another massive crowd joined us, swelling our numbers. By the time we reached the Gujranwala stadium, the gathering was a sea of humanity. Khan's earlier concerns about the crowds dissipated as he witnessed the sheer magnitude of support. Dr. Arif Alvi's calming words reassured him, setting the stage for a historic event.

The jalsa itself was a masterpiece. Wireless speakers and a live prime-time TV broadcast amplified Khan's Churchillian speech, leaving the crowd breathless. Dr. Alvi and I spoke briefly, our words blending into the thunderous applause. Suddenly, the stage collapsed, and chaos ensued as Khan and I were rushed to safety in an ambulance. The crowd, undeterred, surged forward, chanting Khan's name in a display of unwavering support.

As we navigated away from the chaos, the day's triumph was palpable. The Gujranwala jalsa solidified PTI's position in the political landscape, demonstrating the power of grassroots mobilization. Reflecting on the day, I marveled at the strength of public sentiment and the indomitable spirit of the people. Despite his impulsiveness, Khan's charisma and determination had galvanized a movement that could not be ignored.

Later, as we neared the city outskirts, I suggested a brief stop at a small house. Initially resistant, Khan relented after seeing my persistence. At the house, thirty notable industrialists and politicians greeted him warmly and presented him with three million rupees as a token of gratitude for his presence in Gujranwala. It was a symbolic gesture, reflecting the local tradition of honoring leaders who graced their city.

Afterward, we freshened up at the River Chenab Kinara restaurant, enjoying a quiet dinner before parting ways. This jalsa, a masterstroke of planning and execution, strengthened my standing within PTI, earning me Khan's trust and respect.

Despite his impulsive nature, Khan's ability to inspire was unmatched. Yet, his impulsiveness often overshadowed the monumental efforts of his team. This day, September 25th, marked a turning point not only for PTI but also for Khan as a leader. The jalsa exemplified the potential of a collective movement driven by dedication and belief. It was a reminder that while vision is critical, the wisdom to channel it effectively is equally vital.

Imran Khan's leadership, while compelling, often reflected the paradox of his nature—impulsive yet visionary. His impatience mirrored Julius Caesar's hastiness, a trait that brought both triumphs and challenges. At Muridke, Kamoke, and Gujranwala, the people's faith in Khan was unshakable. However, to sustain this momentum, it was imperative for Khan to temper his impulsiveness with reflection and strategy. As Mirza Ghalib poetically expressed, "The sight is blind, show me something; I said, 'Will you show me something?'"

The journey of September 25th was a testament to the power of grassroots mobilization, the resilience of the Pakistani people, and the charisma of a leader who, despite his flaws, inspired a movement of hope and change. This historic day would remain etched in the memories of all who participated, a beacon for future generations striving for progress and unity in Pakistan. Khan's smile as we departed Gujranwala encapsulated the triumph of the moment—a fleeting yet unforgettable testament to the spirit of PTI and the dreams it ignited across the nation.

Imran Khan's first Karachi jalsa was a milestone for PTI, and as the divisional president, I felt privileged to be part of this historic event. Our journey from Lahore to Karachi began with six air-conditioned buses carrying fervent PTI supporters. Along the way, we were greeted by enthusiastic crowds waving flags and chanting slogans, their energy fueling our spirits as we moved closer to Karachi. The city, traditionally considered an MQM stronghold, was now alive with PTI's presence, its streets adorned with flags and banners signaling the anticipation of change.

Dr. Arif Alvi, president of PTI's Karachi chapter, had worked tirelessly to organize the event. Upon reaching the jalsa venue, the scale of the gathering was breathtaking. Tens of thousands had assembled to witness Imran Khan, their hopes and expectations reflected in their faces. The atmosphere was electric, with patriotic songs and PTI anthems resonating through the air. Onstage, Khan greeted me warmly as the crowd erupted in cheers. It was an emotional moment, one that underscored the transformative power of this movement.

Imran Khan's speech was electrifying. He spoke of hope, a corruption-free Pakistan, and the revolutionary potential of democracy through the ballot box. The crowd, captivated by his words, responded with thunderous applause, their excitement palpable. It was clear this wasn't just a political rally; it was the dawn of a new era in Pakistan's politics. As the jalsa concluded, the atmosphere remained festive, with music and dancing filling the air. This event had not only introduced PTI to Karachi but also cemented its position as a force of change in Pakistan.

During our stay in Karachi, Khan and Ahsan Rashid engaged in discussions about important party matters. At one point, Ahsan jokingly asked me what Ibn Rushd, the great philosopher, would say about these "interesting times." Khan seemed intrigued, so I shared a brief overview of Ibn Rushd, known as Averroes in the West, a prominent figure of the Islamic Golden Age. I explained how his works bridged the philosophies of Aristotle and Islamic thought, influencing both medieval Europe and modern philosophy. Khan, impressed by his views on the state, requested that I elaborate further.

After returning to Lahore, I wrote Khan an email, emphasizing the need for a leader with vision and determination to steer Pakistan towards stability and prosperity. Drawing from Ibn Rushd's philosophy, I described the state as an abstract and permanent entity whose requirements must transcend individual ambitions or religious demands, focusing instead on inclusive national interest. I stressed that salvation for the state is immediate and tied to actions grounded in calculable principles like raison d'état, echoing Ibn Rushd's assertion that the state's wellbeing cannot wait for eternal solutions. My email also referenced historical examples of leaders grappling with military influence, such as the Roman Empire's downfall due to unchecked generals and the French Revolution's upheaval caused by power imbalances.

I highlighted the importance of balancing power between civilian and military institutions. To achieve this, civilian authority must assert control over the military while ensuring alignment with national objectives. Leaders should learn from historical figures like Napoleon, Stalin, and Julius Caesar, who maintained control over ambitious generals through a mix of ideological alignment, fear, and strategic manipulation. I urged Khan to draw inspiration from such examples and adopt a multifaceted approach to address Pakistan's challenges.

A wise leader, I advised, must employ diplomacy, institutional reforms, and public engagement to rein in a military prone to overreach. Encouraging international cooperation while strengthening democratic institutions is essential. Drawing from my conversations with Khan, I proposed strategies such as fostering dialogue with military leadership, promoting economic incentives for cooperation, and ensuring transparency through independent oversight bodies. Furthermore, public mobilization and media engagement could play critical roles in advocating for democratic values and exposing the drawbacks of military dominance.

In our discussions, I also addressed how international support could be leveraged. Western nations, though often prioritizing stability over democratization due to strategic interests, generally advocate for democratic governance. Engaging them could create pressure on the military to cede power to civilian authorities. Examples like South Africa's anti-apartheid movement demonstrated how global solidarity can influence internal power dynamics. However, I cautioned that such alliances must be handled tactfully to avoid antagonizing the military or undermining national sovereignty.

Throughout our conversations, the wisdom of historical and philosophical figures illuminated the path forward. Imam Ali's emphasis on justice and accountability resonated deeply: "The ruler who appoints a tyrant as his deputy will be considered a tyrant himself." His insights were particularly relevant in addressing the overreach of military power. Similarly, thinkers like Aristotle, Confucius, and Ibn Khaldun underscored the importance of strong institutions, rule of law, and balanced governance. Their teachings offered timeless lessons for leaders navigating the challenges of statecraft.

Imran Khan's leadership journey reminded me of the complexities faced by historical figures like Maharaja Ranjit Singh and other leaders who struggled to manage power structures effectively. In Pakistan, the overreach of the military mirrors similar patterns seen in other nations grappling with civilian-military dynamics. These parallels emphasize the urgency of reforming Pakistan's political landscape to establish civilian supremacy.

My email to Khan also explored how authoritarian leaders like Hitler and Stalin maintained control over their generals. Hitler's tactics, for instance, included ideological alignment, fear, personal charisma, and strategic manipulation. Stalin relied on purges to eliminate threats, while Napoleon balanced fear and rewards to maintain loyalty. These examples illustrated that control over ambitious generals requires a blend of strategic foresight, institutional checks, and effective leadership.

In Pakistan's context, the path to reform lies in a gradual, systematic approach that prioritizes constitutional principles. Appointing military leaders sympathetic to democratic values, fostering economic development, and engaging international partners are crucial steps. Additionally, creating platforms for dialogue and ensuring civilian oversight of military budgets can promote transparency and accountability. However, the ultimate goal must be to empower democratic institutions and reduce reliance on any single individual or entity.

Reflecting on these discussions, I realized the profound relevance of Ibn Rushd's philosophy to Pakistan's challenges. His assertion that a state's salvation is immediate and tied to rational governance encapsulates the urgency of addressing Pakistan's issues. By prioritizing the national interest over individual ambitions or institutional dominance, Pakistan can chart a course toward stability and progress.

The Karachi jalsa was more than a political rally; it symbolized a turning point in Pakistan's political narrative. It marked the rise of PTI as a genuine force for change and highlighted the potential of collective action. As the crowds dispersed and we returned to Lahore, I carried with me not just the memories of an extraordinary event but also the hope that Imran Khan's leadership would continue to inspire Pakistan towards a brighter future.

Pakistan's military has played a dominant role in the country's history, shaping its political and economic landscape with often adverse consequences. The fate of Maharaja Ranjit Singh's empire offers a stark warning. His overemphasis on military power, internal conflicts, and reliance on generals for governance led to instability and eventual collapse. After his death, power struggles among his generals and external exploitation by the British resulted in the empire's disintegration. Pakistan faces similar challenges today, with its military deeply entrenched in political affairs, wielding significant influence over civilian institutions, and diverting resources away from development.

The parallels are striking and highlight a recurring theme in Pakistan's political and institutional history. The unchecked ambitions of Ranjit Singh's generals, who often undermined the stability of his empire, find echoes in Pakistan's own political evolution, where military overreach has frequently overshadowed the democratic process. However, it is important to approach this analysis with nuance, acknowledging that Pakistan's challenges are not the sole responsibility of the military. Politicians, bureaucrats, and even segments of civil society have all contributed to the erosion of institutional integrity, creating an environment where external powers can exploit internal weaknesses.

One of the critical issues has been the excessive focus on military expenditure, which, while necessary for national defense, has at times come at the expense of vital sectors such as education, healthcare, and social development. Yet, this is not merely a military prerogative; successive governments have failed to prioritize these sectors effectively, diverting resources toward projects with immediate political gains rather than long-term national benefits. Tax evasion by the wealthy elite, including politicians and influential business figures, has further exacerbated the situation, depriving the country of critical revenue needed to fund development. The cumulative impact has been a cycle of underfunded public services, leaving millions of Pakistanis without access to basic amenities.

Bureaucratic inefficiencies have also played a significant role. The civil service, once a pillar of governance during the early years of Pakistan, has often succumbed to politicization and corruption. This erosion of professionalism within the bureaucracy has hampered effective policy implementation and created opportunities for external players to exploit internal disarray. Bureaucrats, tasked with safeguarding the administrative machinery of the state, have at times prioritized personal gain over public service, contributing to the weakening of Pakistan's institutional framework.

Similarly, the political class has not always risen to the challenge of nation-building. Dynastic politics, patronage systems, and a focus on short-term electoral gains have undermined efforts to establish a cohesive and visionary governance model. Politicians have often failed to unite the nation around a shared vision, instead perpetuating divisions for electoral advantage. This lack of political foresight has created an environment where external powers can exert influence through economic leverage or strategic partnerships, often to the detriment of Pakistan's sovereignty.

Foreign nations have historically capitalized on these vulnerabilities. During Ranjit Singh's era, some foreign elements exploited internal divisions and unchecked ambitions to expand their control. In modern times, Pakistan's reliance on foreign aid and loans has similarly allowed external powers to exert economic and political pressure. This dynamic underscore the importance of strengthening internal cohesion and addressing systemic inefficiencies to reduce dependency on external support.

To move forward, Pakistan must adopt a holistic approach that acknowledges the interconnectedness of its challenges. The military, as a vital institution of national defense, must continue to operate within its constitutional boundaries, while political leaders and bureaucrats must focus on delivering good governance and fostering accountability. Tax reform is essential to ensure that the wealthiest segments of society contribute their fair share to national development. Education and awareness campaigns can also play a pivotal role in fostering a culture of civic responsibility and unity.

Rather than assigning blame to any single institution, Pakistan's path to progress lies in fostering collaboration and mutual respect among all stakeholders. The lessons of history are clear: internal divisions and unchecked ambitions invite external exploitation. By learning from these lessons and building a culture of accountability, transparency, and inclusivity, Pakistan can chart a course toward resilience and self-reliance. A united Pakistan, where every institution and citizen plays their part, holds the promise of overcoming its challenges and achieving the vision of prosperity and justice for all.

To steer Pakistan away from such a fate, the country must address fundamental structural issues. Strengthening democratic institutions is paramount. Civilian supremacy must be restored through robust legal frameworks, accountability mechanisms, and empowering elected representatives. The emphasis should shift from militarization to education, healthcare, and economic development to equip the young population with skills and opportunities. Social justice, tolerance, and inclusivity must be prioritized to foster national unity and cohesion.

A comprehensive reform of administrative units within Pakistan could be a transformative step. The existing bureaucratic structure, rooted in colonial-era practices, is slow, burdensome, and expensive. A bold reimagining of governance at the local level could dismantle the layers of inefficiency and empower districts to manage their affairs. Making tehsils independent administrative districts, governed by directly elected leaders, could decentralize power, enhance accountability, and streamline governance. This model would integrate local judiciary, police, and administrative functions under accountable leadership, reducing the scope for corruption and inefficiency.

Such a system would also foster economic growth by allowing districts to focus on localized governance and development priorities. Elected district leaders would work closely with community members, addressing their needs more effectively than distant bureaucracies. By dismantling the current colonial-style governance framework, Pakistan could create an administrative structure that is more responsive, efficient, and aligned with the principles of democracy.

The lessons from Western Europe's fragmentation during the Middle Ages offer valuable insights. While fragmentation initially weakened Europe through conflicts and power struggles, it also led to innovations in governance, the emergence of nation-states, and economic competition. Pakistan could adapt these lessons to its context, using administrative decentralization as a tool for strengthening governance without compromising national unity. The success of such reforms, however, hinges on the existence of an independent and impartial election commission, tasked with ensuring free and fair elections across all levels of government.

Pakistan's challenges extend beyond administrative reforms. The military's dominance remains a central issue, stifling political and economic progress. The establishment's entrenched interests have created a culture where military intervention in civilian affairs is normalized. This has diverted resources away from critical sectors, resulting in widespread poverty, illiteracy, and poor healthcare. Furthermore, the army's ventures into the economy have distorted market dynamics, creating monopolies and fostering corruption.

The concentration of power in the hands of a few has exacerbated inequality and fueled resentment among marginalized communities. The military's unchecked influence has also undermined the judiciary and media, eroding public trust in institutions. Addressing this requires not just civilian leadership but also systemic changes to recalibrate the balance of power.

A viable solution lies in reasserting civilian control over the military. This requires strong leadership, legal reforms, and sustained public support. Civilian oversight of military budgets, transparent appointments of top military officials, and constitutional amendments limiting military interference in politics are essential steps. The role of international partners in supporting democratic governance in Pakistan cannot be ignored. While strategic interests have often taken precedence over democratization, global pressure and incentives could encourage the military to cede space to civilian institutions.

Historically, other nations have faced similar challenges. The Roman Empire, Napoleon's France, and Stalin's Soviet Union illustrate the complexities of managing military ambitions. In these cases, leaders-maintained control through a combination of ideological alignment, fear, and strategic manipulation. Pakistan must navigate these lessons carefully, ensuring that its reforms foster accountability without undermining the military's role in national security.

Imran Khan's political journey highlights both the potential and pitfalls of leadership in Pakistan. As a charismatic leader with a vision for change, Khan inspired millions to believe in the possibility of a better Pakistan. However, his reliance on the establishment and inability to curtail its overreach weakened his position. While Khan sought to promote economic reforms and social justice, his tenure was marked by a failure to build strong civilian institutions capable of resisting military interference. His experiences underline the importance of balancing visionary leadership with pragmatic governance.

To ensure Pakistan's long-term stability and prosperity, the country must embrace economic, political, and social reforms. Strengthening institutions, fostering inclusivity, and promoting economic growth are critical. Education and healthcare should be prioritized to develop a skilled workforce capable of driving innovation and productivity. Additionally, a geo-economic foreign policy focused on regional cooperation and trade could unlock Pakistan's strategic potential. The era of geopolitics has given way to geoeconomics, and Pakistan must adapt to this reality by leveraging its location and resources for sustainable growth.

The need for reform extends to electoral processes as well. Direct elections for key positions, such as senators, governors, and the president, could enhance accountability and reduce the influence of elites. A no-extension policy for military chiefs and senior civil bureaucrats would encourage professionalism and prevent the consolidation of power. Ensuring that extensions are granted only through parliamentary consensus would reinforce the primacy of civilian oversight.

Pakistan's history is replete with missed opportunities and unrealized potential. The recurring conflicts between civilian and military forces have stunted the country's growth and tarnished its democratic credentials. Yet, the resilience of the Pakistani people and their commitment to change offer hope for the future. By learning from history, embracing reforms, and prioritizing the national interest, Pakistan can chart a course toward stability and progress.

Imam Ali's teachings on leadership resonate deeply in this context. His emphasis on justice, accountability, and compassion underscores the qualities needed to navigate Pakistan's challenges. A leader who embodies these principles, while balancing vision with pragmatism, can guide Pakistan toward a brighter future. As the poet Allama Iqbal once said, "Nations are born in the hearts of poets; they prosper and die in the hands of politicians." Pakistan's destiny lies in the hands of its leaders and citizens, who must rise above self-interest to secure the nation's salvation.

The trajectory of Pakistan's future hinges on long-term economic and strategic planning, guided by visionary leadership that prioritizes morality, rule of law, and inclusive growth. The nation's outdated political and economic systems perpetuate a culture of might over right, where the military wields disproportionate influence, undermining democratic institutions and national potential.

Global examples illuminate the way forward. Singapore's Lee Kuan Yew and Taiwan's Chiang Ching-kuo implemented transformative economic strategies, modernizing their nations. South Korea's Park Chung Hee and Russia's Vladimir Putin, though authoritarian, drove progress through robust planning. Democratic icons like France's Charles de Gaulle and the United States' Franklin D. Roosevelt demonstrated how progressive reforms and prioritizing the greater good can reshape societies.

The poetry of Rumi, Allama Iqbal, Robert Frost, and Victor Hugo embodies the spirit of awakening, resilience, and choosing transformative paths. Imran Khan symbolizes a call to action, urging Pakistan to embrace reform, break free from archaic systems, and envision a brighter future. "The people of Pakistan deserve a new dawn," inspired by courage and guided by innovative leadership. This transformative journey requires addressing injustices, fostering inclusion, and strengthening governance to unlock Pakistan's immense potential.

Chapter 5: Shadows Over Sovereignty: Pakistan's Civil-Military Imbalance

Pakistan's journey as a nation has been marked by resilience, determination, and an enduring spirit to overcome challenges. Amidst its complexities, the military has stood as a steadfast guardian of its sovereignty and territorial integrity, ensuring the nation's safety against regional adversaries. From safeguarding borders with India, a powerful and often adversarial neighbor, to addressing security challenges along the porous Afghanistan and Iran frontiers, Pakistan's military has played a pivotal role in maintaining peace and stability. The sacrifices made during the wars of 1948, 1965, and 1971, and the ongoing commitment to counter-insurgency operations, exemplify their dedication to the nation's defense. Through efforts in counter-terrorism, Pakistan's military has not only secured internal stability but has also contributed significantly to regional and global security frameworks. As one of the few Muslim-majority nations to possess nuclear deterrence, Pakistan's military ensures that the country's strategic interests remain secure in a volatile geopolitical landscape. Their dedication, discipline, and commitment to safeguarding Pakistan's sovereignty and fostering stability continue to be a cornerstone of the nation's strength.

The military's pervasive role in Pakistan's governance and institutions has profoundly shaped the country's trajectory, hindering its potential for economic growth, regional dominance, and effective foreign policy. Since its inception, Pakistan has been burdened by a military establishment that dominates the state, resulting in systemic failures across governance, justice, and economic development. This overreach has fostered a zombie garrison state, paralyzed by internal chaos and external vulnerabilities.

At the heart of a thriving nation-state lies a balance between legitimacy and power. Sustainable order arises from governance, justice, and the people's ability to elect their leaders. In Pakistan, this essential balance has been disrupted by a military that sometimes if not always wields disproportionate power, imposing its will at the expense of democratic processes however politicians are equally to be blamed as their failures since 1947 have always given establishment to interfere in domestic affairs. The result is a fragile state, devoid of a just system that is universally accepted by its populace. Without this legitimacy, counterforces emerge, plunging the nation into political instability and the perpetual threat of chaos or civil war.

The military's dominance has shifted the focus of governance from civilian-led development to command-centric control. This has left the country vulnerable to judicial incompetence, unchecked corruption, and the rise of cartels and mafias. The brave astute generals, often hailed for their decisiveness, have been part of governance and the rule of law frequently during Martial law period. This is not a criticism of military but at times they have disregarded the fundamental democratic ethos that protects freedom of expression and fosters societal cohesion. Politicians too have exacerbated divisions, sowing seeds of sectarianism, regionalism, and communal hatred that threaten to unravel the fabric of the state which has ultimately paved the way for Military to take matters in their own hand.

Politicians most egregious failure was the dismemberment of Pakistan in 1971 where Zulfiqar Ali Bhutto and Mujib ur Rehman failed to reach concensus. The loss of East Pakistan exposed the hubris of our institutions that underestimated the complexities of governance and the aspirations of its people. Victory might have introduced Pakistan to the world in 1947, but the defeat in 1971 introduced the world to a fractured Pakistan, one where power resided in the hands of a select few, with catastrophic consequences. The inability of state institutions to adapt to the diverse needs of the country has perpetuated a cycle of instability, leaving Pakistan struggling to reconcile its fractured identity.

The state's wealth lies in its territory and its people, yet the military's mismanagement has jeopardized both. Territorial disputes over Kashmir, Siachen, and other critical areas remain unresolved till day as internal rifts are never ending soap opera. Strategic initiatives like the Kalabagh Dam, which could have transformed Pakistan's agricultural and energy sectors, were abandoned. In Gwadar, touted as a gateway to regional connectivity, progress has been minimal, with mounting debt and minimal returns. The promise of Gwadar remains a mirage, with billions seemingly lost to corruption and mismanagement, enriching a select few at the expense of the nation.

Economic factors also reinforced the military's clout in Pakistan. Defense spending has consistently overshadowed developmental budgets, marginalizing sectors like education and healthcare. This prioritization created a military-industrial complex, granting the armed forces substantial control over the economy, including businesses and industries. Such economic entanglements extended the military's influence beyond defense, making it a stakeholder in broader state affairs.

Pakistan's geostrategic location offers immense potential. Nestled at the crossroads of South Asia, the Middle East, and Central Asia, Pakistan could have been a hub for trade, connectivity, and regional influence. Yet, this potential has been squandered due to shortsighted military-led policies that prioritize security over economic and diplomatic initiatives. A civilian-led approach to governance, focusing on regional cooperation and economic integration, could have positioned Pakistan as a leader in the region, influencing geopolitics from the Middle East to Central Asia.

The human potential of Pakistan is equally vast. With a young and dynamic population, the country could harness its demographic dividend through investments in education, healthcare, and skill development. Instead, military priorities have diverted resources away from these critical sectors. The result is a population that is largely unskilled and uneducated, unable to compete in a globalized economy. This neglect has deepened poverty and inequality, undermining the nation's long-term growth prospects.

Bad governance has stifled democratic institutions. Civilian governments, often undermined by judicial, political and military coups or manipulations, have been unable to establish a culture of accountability and transparency. The judiciary, media, and educational institutions have been co-opted, eroding public trust and stifling dissent. This pervasive influence ensures that the military remains unaccountable for its actions, perpetuating a cycle of impunity and governance failure.

Internationally, Pakistan's image has suffered due to its bad governance approach in policy-making. While the three pillars of National sovereignty positioned itself as the guardian of national security, immature policies have often isolated the country diplomatically. Overreliance on foreign aid and strategic alliances has left Pakistan vulnerable to external pressures, compromising its sovereignty and limiting its ability to pursue independent foreign policy goals.

The consequences of these bad governance approach mechanism are evident in Pakistan's economic stagnation, political instability, and social unrest. The concentration of power within the military has stifled innovation and progress, creating a system where patronage and favoritism thrive. The failure to address these systemic issues has left Pakistan on the brink, unable to capitalize on its natural and human resources.

To chart a new course, Pakistan must embrace a transformative vision. Civilian control over governance must be reestablished, with strong democratic institutions that prioritize accountability and inclusivity. Economic reforms are essential, focusing on industrial growth, agricultural innovation, and infrastructure development. Investments in education and healthcare are crucial to building a skilled and healthy workforce. Social cohesion must be fostered through tolerance and pluralism, addressing the divisions that have long plagued the nation.

Moreover, Pakistan must develop a foreign policy that emphasizes regional cooperation and economic integration. By leveraging its strategic location, Pakistan can become a hub for trade and connectivity, fostering partnerships that enhance its economic and geopolitical standing.

The military must also redefine its role, focusing on national security without encroaching on civilian domains. Transparency and accountability within the military are essential to rebuilding public trust. Initiatives to strengthen civilian oversight, such as parliamentary committees and independent watchdogs, can ensure that the military operates within its constitutional boundaries.

The lessons of history are clear. States that prioritize power over justice and governance ultimately falter. Pakistan must recognize that their strength lies not in perpetuating control but in empowering civilian institutions to lead the nation toward stability and prosperity. Only through a genuine commitment to reform and collaboration can Pakistan fulfill its immense potential and reclaim its place as a beacon of progress in the region.

Pakistan's geopolitical location, human potential, and natural resources place it at the crossroads of opportunity and challenge. Situated strategically at the confluence of South Asia, Central Asia, and the Middle East, the country holds the potential to become a vital hub for trade and regional cooperation. Its access to international trade routes and the promise of projects such as the China-Pakistan Economic Corridor underline this promise. Proximity to energy-rich regions like the Middle East and emerging markets in Central Asia further underscores its importance in the global economic landscape. Alongside these geographical advantages, Pakistan boasts a youthful population that, if educated and employed effectively, could drive economic progress. The large, skilled workforce, particularly in fields such as IT, medicine, and engineering, represents a significant resource waiting to be tapped into. The country's fertile agricultural lands and reserves of natural gas, coal, and potential for renewable energy further enhance its potential for sustainable growth.

Pakistan stands at a pivotal juncture where the harmonization of civil-military relations could unlock its immense potential. Historically, the military has played a significant role in safeguarding the nation's sovereignty and ensuring regional stability. Its contributions to national defense, disaster relief, and counterterrorism efforts have cemented its place as a critical institution, earning admiration both at home and abroad. However, the dominant role of the military in governance and economic decision-making has also presented challenges for the growth of democratic institutions.

The prioritization of defense spending, while critical for national security, has at times come at the expense of sectors like education, healthcare, and infrastructure. This imbalance has limited opportunities for long-term economic development and societal progress. Political instability, occasionally fueled by interference in civilian governance, has deterred investment and stifled reforms needed to address systemic issues. These dynamics have created hurdles in Pakistan's journey toward becoming a more inclusive and prosperous society.

A strengthened partnership between civilian leadership and the military, built on mutual respect and constitutional boundaries, could transform the nation's trajectory. By enabling civilian institutions to take the lead in governance while continuing to support the military's vital role in national security, Pakistan can foster stability and inspire investor confidence. Redirecting focus to critical sectors like education and healthcare, alongside strategic economic reforms, would empower the youth and lay the foundation for innovation and growth.

Moreover, a balanced approach in civil-military relations would allow Pakistan to craft a coherent foreign policy that serves its long-term national interests. Enhanced regional cooperation and diplomatic engagement could position the country as a key player bridging South Asia, Central Asia, and the Middle East, amplifying its influence on the global stage.

While the path forward requires careful navigation, the resilience and capabilities of Pakistan's military, when aligned with the vision of a thriving democratic society, remain a cornerstone of the nation's strength and progress. Together, these pillars can secure a brighter future for Pakistan, ensuring unity, development, and prosperity for generations to come.

Afghanistan's history offers valuable lessons about the consequences of external interference and flawed governance strategies. Known as the "graveyard of empires," Afghanistan has consistently resisted foreign domination, from Alexander the Great to the British, the Soviets, and most recently, the United States. The resilience of its people, shaped by a rugged terrain and diverse tribal identities, underscores the importance of respecting local autonomy and cultural complexities. Afghanistan's tumultuous history also serves as a warning against overreliance on military strategies. The Soviet invasion of Afghanistan, backed by Pakistan and the United States, had far-reaching consequences. While it achieved the geopolitical goal of countering Soviet expansion, it also brought a cascade of unintended effects: the rise of militant networks, the proliferation of drugs and weapons, and a destabilized region. Pakistan, in particular, bore the brunt of these consequences, with an influx of refugees and the entrenchment of violence and extremism in its society.

To address its challenges and unlock its potential, Pakistan must embrace transformative change. This requires reducing the military's dominance and strengthening civilian governance. Rebalancing power dynamics is essential to foster democratic institutions and ensure accountability. Civilian leaders must assert their authority and establish mechanisms to limit military influence in political and economic affairs. Economic reforms are equally crucial. By creating a conducive environment for investment and development, Pakistan can attract both domestic and foreign capital to drive growth. Investing in education and healthcare will equip the population with the skills and resources needed to compete in a globalized economy. Promoting tolerance and pluralism is key to addressing the divisions that have plagued the country. Social cohesion can be achieved through inclusive policies and by empowering civil society to foster unity.

A nuanced foreign policy, guided by civilian expertise, is vital for enhancing Pakistan's regional and global influence. Leveraging its strategic location, Pakistan can serve as a hub for trade and economic integration between South Asia, Central Asia, and the Middle East. Strengthening ties with neighboring countries and engaging in regional cooperation will enable Pakistan to build mutually beneficial relationships that contribute to its stability and prosperity. Institutional strengthening is another critical component of Pakistan's transformation. Transparent and accountable institutions, free from the influence of entrenched power structures, are essential for sustainable governance. An independent judiciary, a free press, and strong regulatory bodies can check abuses of power and uphold democratic principles.

The lessons of Afghanistan's history highlight the importance of respecting the will of the people and avoiding the pitfalls of external and internal overreach. Pakistan must chart a path that prioritizes democratic governance, economic development, and social cohesion. This requires visionary leadership and a commitment to building systems that serve the long-term interests of the nation rather than the short-term gains of a few. By addressing its structural challenges and embracing inclusive policies, Pakistan can unlock its immense potential and emerge as a stable, prosperous, and influential player in the region and beyond. The journey will be challenging, but the rewards of a vibrant, united, and progressive Pakistan are well worth the effort.

The United States invasion of Afghanistan in 2001, ostensibly a mission to root out terrorism, unfolded as a tragic repetition of history, with Pakistan playing a duplicitous role that left devastating consequences for its people. The military establishment, driven by greed and a self-serving agenda, exploited the conflict, receiving billions in aid from the US while simultaneously supporting the Taliban. This strategy of playing both sides betrayed not only the trust of the American allies but also the faith of the Pakistani people, who bore the brunt of the blowback in the form of terrorism and economic devastation. Over 100,000 lives were lost to terror attacks, and Pakistan's economy suffered losses exceeding billions of dollars, as it became a battleground for a conflict it did not fully own. The people of Pakistan paid a heavy price for the military's duplicity, as terrorism struck at the heart of their cities, shaking the foundation of their existence.

Whenever the military establishment feels public pressure to relinquish its overarching power, a resurgence of terror attacks seems to arise mysteriously, justifying its continued dominance. This cycle has entrenched a culture of fear and dependency, keeping the military firmly entrenched in its grip on national governance. The war on terror, rather than addressing the root causes of extremism, became a war on the very soul of Pakistan, as the military's unchecked authority further eroded the institutions that could have provided stability and hope. Pakistan's losses were not merely material; they were a loss of faith in governance, a loss of trust among its people, and a loss of potential to rise above its challenges.

The resilience of the Afghan people throughout history offers a stark contrast to the policies of neighboring powers that sought to exploit their land. Afghanistan, known as the "graveyard of empires," has withstood invasions from Alexander the Great to the British, Soviets, and the United States. Its rugged terrain, diverse tribal makeup, and unyielding spirit have made it a symbol of defiance. Yet, history has shown that such resilience comes at an enormous cost. The people of Afghanistan have endured centuries of conflict, often exacerbated by foreign interference. The Soviet invasion, with Pakistan's military profiting from American support for the mujahideen, exemplified the cycle of exploitation that undermines the region. Refugees, weapons, drugs, and extremism flowed into Pakistan, creating a quagmire that still plagues the country.

In the midst of this chaos, PTI emerged as a voice of resistance against the destructive path set by NATO supply lines and the endless cycle of violence. Imran Khan, a leader of conviction, galvanized a movement to block NATO supplies, symbolizing a stand against foreign intervention and the toll it had taken on Pakistan. The people, weary of the violence and betrayal, rallied behind their leaders, creating a moment of unity and defiance. The spirit of the blockade, marked by the caravans of PTI supporters, was a testament to the collective power of the people when driven by a shared purpose. The energy, resilience, and determination of these moments provided a glimmer of hope that Pakistan could reclaim its sovereignty and chart a new path.

Throughout history, only a few leaders have succeeded in earning the trust and respect of the Pashtun people, who are fiercely independent and deeply rooted in their traditions. Muhammad Ali Jinnah and Imran Khan stand as exceptions, their leadership transcending tribal loyalties and political divisions. Jinnah's vision for Pakistan and Khan's determination to confront corruption and restore dignity to governance resonate deeply with a people long marginalized by geopolitical games and domestic neglect. This trust, however, comes with immense responsibility—a responsibility to ensure that the ideals of justice, equality, and self-reliance are not mere slogans but guiding principles for governance.

The duplicity of the ruling elite, entrenched in power for decades, has left Pakistan in a state of perpetual hopelessness. The promises of progress and reform have often been overshadowed by personal greed and the prioritization of self-interest over national welfare. The military's dominance has undermined civilian institutions, stifled democratic growth, and perpetuated cycles of economic mismanagement and social inequality. This ruling elite, whether in uniform or civilian guise, has consistently failed to recognize that true strength lies not in coercion or manipulation, but in the collective will and aspirations of the people.

The quagmire of hopelessness gripping Pakistan is not irreversible. Freedom, as a concept, is not merely about political sovereignty but about the capacity of a nation to take control of its own development. It is about creating opportunities, fostering a sense of purpose, and instilling hope. The youth of Pakistan, who represent its future, deserve better than the disillusionment and despair that currently define their reality. A nation cannot thrive if its young people are left with no jobs, no ideals, and no hope. The entrenched ruling elite, blinded by their monopolies on power, must realize that their survival depends on empowering the very people they have long suppressed.

Conversely, India's political foundation under its first Prime Minister, Jawaharlal Nehru, set a strong precedent for civilian control. Nehru's emphasis on democracy and the rule of law, coupled with a robust constitution, ensured the military remained apolitical. India's institutional framework deliberately kept the military subordinate to elected representatives. Regular elections, an independent judiciary, and a vibrant press further insulated Indian democracy from potential military overreach. Even during times of crisis, such as the Indo-China War of 1962, civilian supremacy remained unchallenged, with the military accepting accountability for failures.

The human spirit, however, is resilient, and in the depths of darkness lies the potential for light. As Rumi poetically suggests, it is through imperfections and vulnerabilities that illumination emerges. Pakistan's imperfections—its political instability, economic struggles, and social divisions—can become the catalysts for growth and transformation if addressed with vision and courage. The challenge lies in shifting the narrative from one of despair to one of hope, from oppression to empowerment, and from division to unity.

The leadership of individuals like Imran Khan offers a glimpse of what is possible when conviction and vision align. However, the journey towards a prosperous and equitable Pakistan requires more than the efforts of one individual. It demands a collective awakening, a rejection of the status quo, and a commitment to building institutions that prioritize justice, transparency, and accountability. It requires a reimagining of the nation's priorities, shifting resources from military expenditures to education, healthcare, and economic development. It calls for a redefinition of governance, where power is a means to serve the people rather than an end in itself.

As Pakistan navigates its challenges, it must learn from the lessons of history. The resilience of the Afghan people serves as a reminder that external domination and internal betrayal cannot suppress the human spirit indefinitely. The failures of past empires and the consequences of militarized governance highlight the need for a new approach—one that values dialogue, cooperation, and the well-being of all citizens. Pakistan's future lies not in the perpetuation of old power structures, but in the emergence of a new social contract that prioritizes the needs of its people over the ambitions of a few.

The path forward is not easy, but it is necessary. Pakistan must reclaim its narrative, restore faith in its institutions, and reimagine its identity as a nation built on the principles of justice, equality, and freedom. In doing so, it can transform its potential into reality and become a beacon of hope and resilience in a world that desperately needs both.

Despite these challenges, there have been moments of hope. The rise of PTI as a political force, with Imran Khan at its helm, represented a pushback against the status quo. The NATO blockade led by PTI was not just a political move but a symbolic stand against the militarization of Pakistan's foreign policy. It reflected the frustrations of a populace tired of being used as pawns in a game of global chess. Khan's leadership brought a rare unity among the people, but this movement, too, was ultimately undermined by the entrenched power of the military and its ability to manipulate the democratic process.

The war on terror deeply influenced Pakistan's trajectory, presenting immense challenges while revealing the resilience of its people and institutions. After September 11, 2001, Pakistan became a pivotal ally in the global fight against terrorism due to its strategic location and its role in the region's geopolitics. The country provided critical support to international efforts, including intelligence sharing, military operations, and logistical assistance. These actions disrupted terror networks and significantly contributed to the broader global campaign against extremism. However, the conflict also brought immense trials, testing the nation's governance, economy, and social fabric.

Pakistan's involvement in the war on terror led to significant economic costs, estimated at billions of dollars over the years. Resources that could have been directed toward education, healthcare, and infrastructure were diverted to counter-terrorism efforts. This reallocation, while necessary, limited the country's capacity to address critical development needs. Additionally, the human toll was devastating, with over 100,000 lives lost in terror-related violence. Cities and communities across Pakistan bore the brunt of these attacks, enduring immense suffering and disruption. Despite these challenges, the resolve of Pakistan's people remained unshaken, as they came together to rebuild and support one another in the aftermath of each tragedy.

The military played a vital role in countering terrorism, conducting operations in tribal regions and dismantling militant networks. These actions were instrumental in safeguarding the nation's sovereignty and reducing the threat of extremism. At the same time, the conflict underscored the importance of a holistic approach that addressed the root causes of radicalization. Beyond military action, fostering inclusive governance, equitable development, and community engagement became essential to countering extremism in the long term.

The complexities of the war revealed the delicate balance between security measures and the need to uphold civil liberties. Collaboration between the military and civilian leadership was critical in navigating these challenges. While the military's contributions to national security were invaluable, the conflict also highlighted the need for stronger civilian institutions capable of addressing broader governance issues. Strengthening these institutions ensures that counter-terrorism efforts are sustainable and aligned with democratic values.

Pakistan's journey through this period offers important lessons. Addressing socioeconomic disparities is critical to reducing the appeal of extremist ideologies. Investments in education, healthcare, and job creation can provide opportunities for the youth and strengthen societal resilience. Programs that promote tolerance and unity can further heal divisions and foster national cohesion.

The sacrifices of Pakistan's armed forces and citizens in the war on terror are a testament to their dedication to peace and stability. These efforts safeguarded not only Pakistan's interests but also contributed to global security. The nation's resilience through this difficult period underscores its potential to overcome challenges and emerge stronger. Moving forward, it is essential to build on these strengths by prioritizing inclusive development, fostering collaboration between institutions, and maintaining a focus on long-term stability and prosperity. The lessons of the past provide a roadmap for a future where Pakistan can realize its immense potential and contribute meaningfully to regional and global peace.

Only a few leaders in history have managed to earn the trust of the Pashtun people, known for their fierce independence and strong tribal loyalties. Muhammad Ali Jinnah and Imran Khan are notable exceptions, as both sought to unite rather than divide. Their leadership emphasized justice and inclusion, values starkly missing from the military's governance.

Pakistan is a country of immense potential, strategically located at the crossroads of South Asia, Central Asia, and the Middle East. Its fertile lands, youthful population, and abundant natural resources offer a foundation for economic growth and regional influence. Yet, the journey toward realizing this promise has been fraught with challenges that require careful reflection and constructive reform.

The military, an institution central to Pakistan's security and identity, has played a significant role in safeguarding the nation against external threats. From its inception, Pakistan has faced complex security challenges, including disputes with neighboring countries, cross-border terrorism, and regional instability. The military's efforts in these areas have ensured the nation's sovereignty and security, often at great cost and sacrifice. However, the balance between security and development remains a critical challenge that must be addressed for Pakistan to fully realize its potential.

Over the decades, the prioritization of defense spending has contributed to a disproportionate allocation of national resources. While the military's commitment to national security is essential, the emphasis on defense has at times overshadowed critical investments in education, healthcare, and infrastructure. These sectors form the backbone of a prosperous and equitable society, and their development is crucial for empowering Pakistan's youthful population and unlocking its potential.

To move forward, a recalibration of priorities is necessary. Recognizing the complementary roles of security and development can help Pakistan build a society that is both resilient and progressive. The military, as a key institution, has the opportunity to play a constructive role in this transition by supporting civilian efforts to address socioeconomic disparities and strengthen governance.

In foreign relations, Pakistan's geographic position offers a unique opportunity to act as a bridge between regions, fostering trade, cultural exchange, and diplomatic collaboration. Historical tensions with neighboring countries like India, Afghanistan, and Iran have often limited these opportunities, perpetuating cycles of mistrust and conflict. These relationships, while complex, hold the potential for mutual benefit through dialogue, shared economic interests, and confidence-building measures.

Regional cooperation is a cornerstone of stability and prosperity. Efforts to enhance trade and connectivity with neighbors can create economic opportunities and reduce the incentive for conflict. Pakistan's participation in initiatives like the China-Pakistan Economic Corridor (CPEC) demonstrates the potential of leveraging its strategic location for economic growth. Expanding such collaborations with neighboring countries can unlock new possibilities for regional integration.

The people of Pakistan are the country's greatest asset. Their resilience in the face of adversity and their commitment to progress are a testament to the nation's enduring spirit. However, socioeconomic challenges, including poverty, illiteracy, and unemployment, continue to hinder their potential. Addressing these issues requires a collective effort from all institutions, including the military, to create an environment that nurtures growth and innovation.

Education is a critical area where Pakistan can make significant strides. By investing in quality education and skill development, the nation can empower its youth to contribute meaningfully to society and the economy. Similarly, improving healthcare systems and infrastructure can enhance the overall quality of life and create a more equitable society. These efforts require the collaboration of civilian leadership, private sector actors, and international partners.

The military, as a respected institution, can also contribute to these efforts by supporting initiatives that promote national cohesion and development. Its vast organizational capacity can be leveraged to assist in disaster relief, infrastructure projects, and educational outreach programs, complementing the efforts of civilian authorities. Such collaborations can strengthen trust between institutions and citizens, fostering a sense of unity and shared purpose.

The path forward also requires addressing governance challenges. Corruption, inefficiency, and a lack of accountability have undermined trust in public institutions and impeded progress. Strengthening the rule of law, promoting transparency, and ensuring equal access to opportunities are essential for restoring faith in governance. Civil-military relations must be characterized by mutual respect and adherence to constitutional roles, enabling both institutions to work together for the common good.

Learning from history, Pakistan can draw inspiration from nations that have successfully transitioned from conflict to stability and growth. Germany and Japan, after the devastation of World War II, rebuilt themselves into global leaders through visionary leadership, economic planning, and a commitment to democratic values. Similarly, South Korea's transformation from a war-torn country to a thriving democracy and economic powerhouse demonstrates the power of long-term planning and inclusive development.

These examples underscore the importance of investing in people and institutions. Pakistan's future lies in its ability to harness the energy and aspirations of its youth, foster innovation, and create a society that values justice, equality, and inclusivity. This requires a collective effort from all stakeholders—government, military, civil society, and citizens.

The military, as a cornerstone of Pakistan's identity, has the opportunity to play a pivotal role in this journey. By supporting civilian governance and focusing on its constitutional responsibilities, it can help create a stable environment conducive to progress. The military's contributions to national security, disaster response, and development initiatives are invaluable, and its continued commitment to these roles can inspire confidence and unity among the people.

Internationally, Pakistan can strengthen its diplomatic ties and position itself as a key player in regional and global affairs. By fostering partnerships based on mutual respect and shared interests, the country can enhance its influence and contribute to peace and stability. Efforts to address global challenges, such as climate change and counter-terrorism, can further demonstrate Pakistan's commitment to constructive engagement.

The challenges Pakistan faces are significant, but they are not insurmountable. With a united vision, strategic planning, and collaboration among all institutions, the nation can overcome these obstacles and chart a path toward prosperity. The resilience of its people, the richness of its history, and the potential of its resources provide a strong foundation for a brighter future.

As Pakistan moves forward, it is essential to embrace the principles of justice, inclusivity, and mutual respect. The military, government, and citizens must work together to create a society that honors its past, addresses its present challenges, and aspires to a future of peace, prosperity, and progress. In this shared endeavor, the nation can realize its vast potential and secure its place as a beacon of hope and opportunity in the region and the world.

The Crossroads of Leadership and Governance

In the formation of Pakistan, Muhammad Ali Jinnah's vision provided the foundation for a nation with immense potential, built on principles of justice, equality, and unity. Yet, the early years of the country were fraught with challenges. The absence of a structured political culture and leadership transition after Jinnah's untimely demise left the nation vulnerable to instability. This vacuum paved the way for the first military intervention in 1958, a moment often described as Pakistan's "original sin." It set a precedent for a series of events where the balance of power between civilian leadership, the judiciary, and the military often faltered, shaping a trajectory that still influences Pakistan today.

The 1958 military takeover was justified at the time as necessary to restore order amidst political chaos. However, its long-term impact has been deeply polarizing. While the military brought structure to some state functions and defended the nation's borders with distinction, its repeated forays into governance disrupted the natural evolution of civilian institutions. This pattern mirrors historical examples, such as Argentina, where early military involvement in politics led to persistent instability and a weakened civilian structure.

Pakistan's political landscape has also been shaped by missteps from civilian leadership. Politicians, at times, prioritized personal gains over national interests, creating governance voids that invited military interventions. Corruption, inefficiency, and internal rivalries within civilian governments eroded public trust and hampered the growth of democratic norms. The judiciary, too, has not been immune to criticism, as it occasionally endorsed unconstitutional actions under the guise of the "doctrine of necessity." These decisions, while perhaps expedient in the moment, undermined the rule of law and contributed to a cycle of institutional fragility.

The military, for its part, has played a significant role in defending Pakistan against external threats. Its professionalism and sacrifices, especially in safeguarding borders against hostile neighbors, have been central to the nation's survival. Yet, its involvement in governance has led to an overextension of its role, creating an imbalance that has stunted the development of civilian institutions. This overlap of responsibilities has occasionally placed undue strain on the military, diverting its focus from its primary role as the nation's defender.

The judiciary, often seen as the guardian of constitutional order, has also faced criticism for failing to provide consistent oversight during key moments in Pakistan's history. By occasionally endorsing unconstitutional actions or succumbing to political pressures, the judiciary has inadvertently contributed to a cycle of weakened accountability. This lack of a strong, independent judicial system has made it difficult for the nation to resolve conflicts within its political framework, leaving space for external interference and institutional breakdowns.

The interplay between these three pillars—the military, civilian leadership, and judiciary—has defined Pakistan's governance model. At times, this interplay has led to progress, as in moments of national unity and collective purpose. However, more often than not, it has resulted in tensions that have hindered the nation's growth. The repeated intervention of one institution into the domain of another has prevented the establishment of a stable political order, a condition necessary for long-term development.

While critics often highlight military overreach, it is essential to recognize the shared responsibility for the challenges Pakistan faces. Civilian governments must work to strengthen governance by prioritizing the rule of law, eradicating corruption, and addressing systemic inefficiencies. Political leaders must rise above personal rivalries and work towards a collective vision for the nation. Similarly, the judiciary must ensure its independence and integrity, providing a fair and impartial framework to resolve disputes and uphold constitutional norms.

The lessons of history are clear: nations thrive when their institutions work in harmony, respecting each other's roles and maintaining a balance of power. Examples from around the world, such as South Korea and Indonesia, demonstrate how transitions from military influence to stable democratic governance can lead to remarkable progress. These countries invested in strengthening their civilian institutions, ensuring transparency and accountability, and fostering a culture of innovation and inclusivity.

For Pakistan, the path forward requires an honest assessment of its past and a commitment to forging a new course. The military, civilian leadership, and judiciary must come together to build a framework that prioritizes the national interest over institutional or personal gain. This requires clear boundaries between their respective roles, with each institution respecting the autonomy and responsibilities of the others.

The establishment of a strong rule of law is paramount. This includes creating an independent judiciary capable of holding all actors accountable, regardless of their position or influence. Reforms in the political system are also necessary to reduce the influence of patronage and ensure that governance serves the broader population. The military's role must be confined to defending the nation and contributing to its security, with no involvement in civilian governance. At the same time, civilian leaders must demonstrate competence, integrity, and a commitment to democratic principles.

International partners can play a supportive role by encouraging democratic reforms and providing assistance for economic development. However, the primary responsibility lies with Pakistan's own institutions and leaders. The nation's future depends on its ability to move beyond cycles of crisis and conflict, embracing a vision of unity, accountability, and progress.

Pakistan's people have shown remarkable resilience in the face of adversity. Their aspirations for a peaceful, prosperous, and democratic nation must serve as the guiding light for all institutions. By learning from its history and working collaboratively, Pakistan can reclaim its founding vision and fulfill its immense potential. The challenges are significant, but with determination and collective effort, the path to a brighter future remains within reach.

Chapter 6: For Pakistan to move Forward

"No Exit from Pakistan" is a book written by Daniel S. Markey, a CFR Senior Fellow that examines the complex and often tumultuous relationship between the United States and Pakistan. Here are some key aspects of the book;

- The book explores the main trends in Pakistani society that will shape the country's future.

- It traces the history of Pakistani anti-American sentiment from 1947 to 2001 and assesses Washington's policies toward Pakistan since the 9/11 attacks.

- The author argues that Pakistan's internal troubles pose a threat to both U.S. security and international peace.

- He suggests that Pakistan's growing population, nuclear arsenal, and relationships with China and India will continue to impact U.S. strategic interests in the region.

- Markey offers three options for future U.S. strategy: defensive insulation, military-first cooperation, and comprehensive cooperation.

- The book aims to provide a nuanced understanding of the U.S.-Pakistan relationship and offers recommendations for improving it. But it has totally ignored what wrongs USA has done to Pakistan, in return of its loyal services to America since 1948 to date. To mention a few!

According to the various sources, some of the negative actions attributed to the United States that have hurt Pakistan include:

1. Supporting Military Dictatorships*: The US has historically supported military dictatorships in Pakistan, such as General Ayub Khan, General Zia-ul-Haq, and General Pervez Musharraf, which has contributed to the country's political instability and undermined democratic institutions and destroying Pakistan root and branch in every sphere of its life, corrupting its institutions beyond repair. And acting as a laundry to clean the money stolen from Pakistan by its Elite, judges, Generals, civil bureaucrats, business men, politicians and Tax evader's

2. Encouraging Militancy*: The CIA, with the support of the Pakistani military, funded and trained militant groups like the mujahedeen during the Soviet-Afghan War, which later morphed into terrorist organizations like Al-Qaeda and the Taliban.

3. Drone Strikes*: The US has conducted numerous drone strikes in Pakistan, resulting in significant civilian casualties and fueling anti-American sentiment.

4. Economic Exploitation*: The US has been accused of exploiting Pakistan's economy, using its economic aid as a tool to influence Pakistan's policies and maintain a dominant position in the region.

5. Nuclear Program Opposition*: The US has consistently opposed Pakistan's nuclear program, imposing sanctions and diplomatic pressure, which has hindered Pakistan's ability to develop its nuclear energy capabilities.

6. Supporting India*: The US has strengthened its strategic partnership with India, which has led to a perceived bias against Pakistan and exacerbated tensions between the two nuclear-armed neighbors.

7. Ignoring Pakistan's Concerns*: The US has been accused of ignoring Pakistan's legitimate concerns, such as the Kashmir dispute and India's human rights violations in Kashmir.

8. Backing Out of Promises*: The US has failed to fulfill its promises to Pakistan, including the provision of adequate military aid, export facilities,

transfer of technology and support for Pakistan's counter-terrorism efforts.

These actions have contributed to widespread anti-American sentiment in Pakistan and have damaged the relationship between the two countries.

This explains Imran khan's reluctance to play ball with USA and wanted to liberate his country from US slavery and make Pakistan a neutral country that is not labelled with any block.

America is thought to be directly responsible for,

1. Climate Change: Global warming and its devastating impacts on the environment and human societies in particular a country like Pakistan where glaciers are melting too fast and due to US influence no help is coming Pakistan's way.

2. Energy Crisis: The nation's dependence on fossil fuels and the need for sustainable energy sources. USA has forced Pakistan of extremely dire consequences, if Pakistan buys cheap Petrol from Russia, and complete its gas pipeline with neighbor Iran. These American measures are highly damaging to the being and wellbeing of Pakistan and her population. USA is financing terrorist war against Chinese to stop development of Gawadar port and other Chinese CPEC projects that are a life line of Pakistan's energy requirements and technological industrialization. The Pakistan military is in cahoots with USA and making big bucks by procuring huge loans and stashing their plunder in offshore American banks, while people will pay this with their blood.

3. Political Polarization: The intense partisanship and gridlock in Pakistani politics is financed and blessed by USA to keep Pakistan destabilized.

4. Economic Inequality: The growing wealth gap between the rich and the poor is promoted with American blessings to ensure that true people oriented leaders do not get space in politics, business, and academia of Pakistan.

In Pakistan, these inconvenient truths have paralyzed the nation: The outcome of negative American policies has promoted;

1. Corruption: Rampant corruption and nepotism in politics and governance.

2. Political Instability: The constant struggle for power and the lack of democratic institutions.

3. Terrorism: The presence and influence of terrorist organizations.

4. Economic Crisis: The country's struggling economy and heavy reliance on foreign aid.

5. Social Inequality: The significant disparities in wealth, education, and opportunities.

These truths reveal that Pakistan struggle's with political polarization, economic inequality, and environmental degradation not only due to her own policies only. But also due to policies of international establishment towards Pakistan on American dictate.

To address these inconvenient truths, Pakistan must:

1. Strengthen democratic institutions and the rule of law.

2. Implement anti-corruption measures and accountability.

3. Address terrorism through a comprehensive counter-terrorism strategy.

4. Diversify the economy and promote sustainable development.

5. Invest in education and social welfare programs to reduce inequality.

By confronting and addressing these inconvenient truths, Pakistan' can work towards a more sustainable, equitable, and prosperous future and liberate herself from American and Army slavery, which Imran khan defines as "HAQQIQI AZADI."

Comparing France before its revolution and Pakistan today involves examining the societal structures, socio-economic conditions, and political dynamics that shape these countries. Both nations faced (or are facing) significant unrest due to deep-seated issues of governance, inequality, and elite control, leading to the potential for significant upheaval.

France before the Revolution:

- Monarchical Rule: France was under absolute monarchy with the king having almost unchecked power.

- Socio-economic Inequality: The Estates System starkly divided society into the First Estate (clergy), Second Estate (nobility), and Third Estate (commoners). The Third Estate bore the brunt of taxation and had minimal political power.

- Financial Crisis: France faced massive debt due to overspending, costly wars, and poor financial management.

- Political Discontent: Enlightenment ideas spread, promoting demands for liberty, equality, and fraternity. The political structure failed to accommodate these new ideas.

- Elite Privileges: Nobility and clergy enjoyed numerous privileges that protected their interests while oppressing the common people.

Pakistan Today:

- Military Influence: Pakistan has experienced multiple military coups, with the military holding substantial influence over political affairs.

- Socio-economic Disparity: A significant gap exists between the wealthy elite and the impoverished masses, exacerbated by corruption and ineffective governance.

- Internal Conflicts: Pakistan faces challenges from various militant groups and political instability, worsening security and economic conditions.

- Political Struggles: Leaders like Imran Khan have gained popularity by promising reform but face obstacles from entrenched elites and military influence.

- Elite Corruption: A small political and business elite controls significant resources and power, often leading to policies that do not reflect the needs of the broader population.

Drawing Parallels:

Both contexts show a prevailing sense of injustice and disparity, leading to widespread dissatisfaction. While France's revolution led to comprehensive upheaval and the eventual establishment of the First Republic, Pakistan risks descending into similar chaos if not managed carefully. The challenge lies in instituting reforms without igniting conflicts that could lead to a failed state.

How to Implement Reforms without Civil Conflict:

To avoid bloodshed and foster a peaceful transition towards more democratic governance underpinned by the constitution, several strategies can be drawn from history:

1. Inclusive Dialogue and Gradual Reform:

   The Glorious Revolution (1688) in England saw a relatively peaceful transfer of power from James II to William III and Mary II. It required careful negotiations and gradual reforms that addressed the concerns of various factions.

   - Application to Pakistan: Establish an inclusive dialogue involving political leaders, civil society, the military, and international mediators. Aim to gradually implement reforms that ensure fair representation and address key grievances.

2. Constitutional Amendments and Legal Frameworks:

- Post-Civil War America saw the implementation of the Reconstruction Amendments, which aimed to provide legal equality and address issues of citizenship and voting rights for formerly enslaved people.

- Application to Pakistan: Craft constitutional amendments that clearly delineate the military's role, ensuring civilian oversight and limit political interference by military elites. Strengthen judicial independence to fairly mediate conflicts.

3. Economic and Social Programs:
   - The New Deal in the United States during the Great Depression focused on providing economic stability and jobs, which helped reduce social unrest and improved public faith in democratic governance.
   - Application to Pakistan: Implement economic programs to alleviate poverty and provide opportunities for education and employment, especially in disenfranchised regions. This helps reduce the appeal of extremist groups and stabilizes society.

4. National Reconciliation and Truth Commissions:
   - Post-apartheid South Africa's Truth and Reconciliation Commission sought to heal divisions by addressing past grievances transparently.
   - Application to Pakistan: Establish a truth and reconciliation commission to address past injustices, particularly concerning political and ethnic violence, fostering a sense of unity and understanding.

5. Releasing Political Prisoners:
   - : India's transition to independence involved releasing political prisoners, including Mahatma Gandhi, to ensure a broader base of support for peaceful transition.
   - Application to Pakistan: Negotiate the release of political prisoners like Imran Khan as a goodwill gesture, signaling a commitment to democratic processes and fairness. This can also aid in reducing political tensions.

Conclusion:

The viability of maintaining peaceful progress in Pakistan hinges on the capacity to engage all stakeholders constructively and implement changes that foster an inclusive, transparent, and accountable governance structure. Drawing lessons from historical events and carefully designed modern frameworks can help guide Pakistan toward a stable, more democratic future without descending into civil conflict. The road is undoubtedly complex and requires careful, thoughtful navigation to prevent renewed cycles of violence and retribution.

The parallels between England's King Charles 1st, France's King Louis 14th, and Pakistan's current situation under General Asim Munir are indeed striking. The trajectory of authoritarian rule, followed by violent upheaval and potential civil war, is a stark warning to the international community.

International intervention must prevent catastrophic consequences, and consider the following out-of- the-box solutions:

1. Emergency UN Security Council Meeting: Convene an emergency meeting to discuss Pakistan's deteriorating situation and potential global implications. This platform can facilitate international consensus and coordinated action.

2. International Mediation Team: Establish a neutral, high-level mediation team comprising respected global leaders and diplomats. This team can engage with Pakistani stakeholders, including Imran Khan, to negotiate a peaceful resolution.

3. Economic Incentives: Offer targeted economic incentives to Pakistan's military and political leadership to encourage democratic reforms and human rights compliance. This could include debt relief, trade agreements, and investment packages.

4. Humanitarian Intervention: Consider a humanitarian intervention under the Responsibility to Protect (R2P) doctrine. This would involve a temporary, UN-mandated peacekeeping force to protect civilians and facilitate political stability.

5. Regional Diplomacy: Engage regional players like China, Russia, and Iran in diplomatic efforts to stabilize Pakistan. This could involve a regional conference or bilateral talks to address shared concerns.

6. Civil Society Empowerment: Support Pakistani civil society organizations, human rights groups, and media outlets to amplify their voices and promote democratic values.

7. International Criminal Court (ICC) Intervention: Consider ICC intervention to investigate and prosecute human rights abuses and war crimes committed in Pakistan. This would send a strong message to perpetrators and deter further violence.

8. Global Citizen Campaign: Launching a global citizen campaign, leveraging social media and public figures, to raise awareness about Pakistan's situation and push for international action.

9. Pakistan's Neighboring Countries' Initiative: Encourage neighboring countries like Afghanistan, Iran, and china Russia to take a proactive role in mediating the crisis, given their strategic interests in the region.
10. Imran Khan's Release: Advocate for Imran Khan's release from prison, under international supervision, to facilitate his participation in negotiations and potentially play a constructive role in Pakistan's transition.

The international community must act swiftly and decisively to prevent Pakistan's implosion. By combining these solutions, we can mitigate the crisis and pave the way for a peaceful, democratic transition in Pakistan.

My fear, God forbid, hypothetically, if Pakistan descends into civil war due to the military's refusal to relinquish power, international inaction, and growing public unrest, the consequences could be catastrophic.

Here's a thoughtful analysis of the potential worst-case scenario:

1. Humanitarian Crisis: Civil war would lead to massive displacement, with millions fleeing their homes. Refugee camps would be overwhelmed, and basic necessities like food, water, and healthcare would be scarce.

2. Regional Instability. The conflict would spill over into neighboring countries, destabilizing the region. Afghanistan, Iran, and India would be affected, potentially drawing them into the conflict.

3. Terrorism and Extremism: Militant groups like the Taliban and ISIS would exploit the chaos, gaining strength and control in the region. This would lead to increased terrorist activities, threatening global security.

4. Nuclear Proliferation: Pakistan's nuclear arsenal would be at risk of falling into the wrong hands, posing an existential threat to the world.

5. Economic Collapse. The war would devastate Pakistan's economy, leading to hyperinflation, food shortages, and widespread poverty.

6. Sectarian Violence. Religious tensions would escalate, leading to sectarian violence and persecution of minorities, particularly Shia Muslims, Christians, and Hindus.

7. Breakup of Pakistan: The civil war could result in the fragmentation of Pakistan, with provinces like Sindh Punjab, Kpk & Baluchistan potentially seceding or becoming autonomous regions.

8. Global Intervention: The international community might intervene militarily, leading to a protracted and bloody conflict, with unforeseeable consequences.

9. Environmental Disaster: The war could lead to environmental catastrophes, such as the destruction of infrastructure, pollution, and ecological degradation.

10. Long-term Consequences. The civil war would have a lasting impact on Pakistan's social fabric, causing generational trauma, and undermining the

country's potential for economic growth and political stability.

Khyber Pakhtunkhwa (KPK) and Balochistan are indeed two of the most volatile provinces in Pakistan, with unique challenges and potential flashpoints that could exacerbate the civil war scenario.

KPK:

- Taliban insurgency: KPK has been a hub for Taliban activity, and a civil war could lead to a resurgence of militant groups, further destabilizing the region.

- Ethnic tensions: The province has a diverse population, including Pashtuns, Hazaras, and others, which could lead to ethnic conflicts and sectarian violence.

- Military presence: KPK has a significant military presence, which could lead to clashes between military forces and militant groups, exacerbating the conflict.

Balochistan:

- Separatist movement: Balochistan has a long-standing separatist movement, which could gain momentum in the event of a civil war, leading to demands for independence and potential fragmentation of the province.
- Ethnic tensions: Balochistan is home to various ethnic groups, including Baloch, Pashtuns, and Hazaras, which could lead to inter-ethnic conflicts and violence.
- Resource competition: Balochistan is rich in natural resources, which could become a point of contention among rival groups, leading to further instability.

In the event of a civil war, these provinces could become key battlegrounds, with potentially devastating consequences for the region. The international community must consider the unique challenges and dynamics of KPK and Balochistan in any diplomatic efforts to resolve the crisis.

I hope this context helps to paint a more comprehensive picture of the potential risks and challenges in Pakistan.

In the worst-case scenario, a civil war in Pakistan would be a humanitarian and geopolitical catastrophe, with far-reaching consequences for the region and the world. It is essential for the international community to take proactive steps to prevent this outcome, engaging in diplomatic efforts to resolve the crisis peacefully and a ardent plea to Pakistan Military not to repeat mistakes of East Pakistan.States broken can be repaired, but the cracks will always be there: A great country like USA has not fully healed the wounds of her civil war: Those wounds emerge in north south relation when presidential elections come or state laws clash with federal laws, or cultural differences like gun control, abortion rights etc.: reconstructing a state like Pakistan, beset by turmoil and division, is a daunting task indeed. Yet, as Plato, Let's try to offer some unorthodox solutions, blending ancient wisdom with modern pragmatism.

First, acknowledge that Pakistan's predicament stems from a fractured society, entrenched interests, its Parliamentary form of government and external interference through the powerful military of the country: To rebuild, we must address these challenges holistically.

1. *National Dialogue*: Convene a grand assembly, inclusive of all stakeholders, to engage in a candid, televised discussion. This platform will facilitate a shared understanding of the nation's woes and foster a collective vision for the future.
2. *Truth and Reconciliation Commission*: Establish a TRC to investigate past human rights abuses by military, bureaucracy , and other government institutions apart from corruption, and political machinations. This will help Pakistan come to terms with its troubled past, promote accountability, and pave the way for reconciliation. There is no alternative to TRC. Only if properly operated it can bring the society together. Punishing culprits will only aggravate situation but not solve the problem.

3. *Decentralization and Regional Autonomy*: Empower provinces and local governments to address unique regional challenges, promoting grassroots decision-making and ownership free the people from bureaucracy breathing on their neck in every walk of life.
4. *Meritocratic Technocracy*: Establish a technocratic government, staffed by experts and professionals, to manage key sectors like economy, education, and healthcare. This will ensure data- driven policy-making and efficient service delivery. Put more money into education research, farming, introduce collective farming with strong subsidies by government, subsidized cottage industry, health care and make it corruption free and accessible for common man.
5. *Citizen Engagement and Participation*: Implement participatory budgeting, citizen juries, in justice system, local councils and introduce panchayat at village level and implement other innovative mechanisms to ensure the public's voice is heard and valued in policymaking.
6. *Education and Cultural Revival*: Launch a nationwide education initiative focusing on critical thinking, civic literacy, and cultural heritage. This will help rebuild a shared national identity and foster a culture of tolerance and inclusivity.
7. *Economic Revitalization*: Implement a progressive economic agenda, prioritizing sustainable development, social welfare, and entrepreneurship. This will help reduce inequality and create opportunities for all.
8. *International Cooperation and Mediation*: Engage neighboring countries and global powers in a diplomatic initiative to resolve regional conflicts, secure economic cooperation, and ensure peaceful coexistence.
9. *Constitutional Reforms*: Draft a new presidential constitution, Double the National Assembly seats, incorporating principles of democracy, federalism, and human rights. This will provide a robust framework for governance and ensure the protection of citizens' rights.
10. *Leadership and Institutional Reforms*: Establish a new leadership selection process, emphasizing merit, integrity, and accountability. Reform institutions to ensure transparency, efficiency, and responsiveness to citizens' needs.

These hard and unorthodox solutions will require courage, resilience, and collective effort from Pakistan's citizens, leaders, and international partners. By embracing this vision, we can reconstruct a shattered state and forge a beacon of hope for the world – a new Republic, built on the principles of justice, equality, and freedom. I am very confident that Pakistani nation is very talented and if truly given a fair chance to reset the button they can get Pakistan back to future.

Pakistan a wonderful ancient land of Eurasian region has been a universal imperative ever since the Indian plate stuck the Asian plate creating Himalayas, Hindukush and making Pakistan a gateway of human migration, human innovation and resilience. The theory that climate change and environmental factors could have influenced migrations and the development of new settlements is supported by archaeological evidence, as changing conditions often spurred human adaptation and movement.

Ultimately, Mehargarh on Bolan pass near Bolan River of Pakistan holds a crucial place in the timeline of human history, representing an early chapter in the story of settled life and community development. It's essential to recognize the plurality and diversity of early civilizations in Pakistan and their contributions to human progress.

It's fascinating to delve into ancient history and early human civilizations. Mehargarh, located in present-day Balochistan, Pakistan, is indeed one of the earliest known Neolithic sites, dating back to around 7000 BCE. This site provides significant insights into early agricultural practices and settled life, showcasing advanced techniques in pottery, architecture, and social organization.

Mesopotamia, known for the Sumerians, Akkadians, Babylonians, and Assyrians, is often heralded as the cradle of civilization due to its remarkable advancements in writing, law, and urban development, which began around 3500 BCE. However, Mehargarh predates these developments and proves that advanced human settlements existed in South Asia well before those in Mesopotamia.

The subsequent Indus Valley Civilization, which includes Harappa and Mohenjo-Daro, emerged around 2500 BCE and exhibited highly sophisticated urban planning, architecture, and social systems. It stands as one of the great ancient civilizations, alongside Egypt and Mesopotamia.

My visit to these sites with Imran khan, Ahsan Rashid and Air marshal Zulifqar shahid during our tour to balochistan had been quite an experience, providing a tangible connection to early human innovation and resilience. The theory that climate change and environmental factors could have influenced migrations and the development of new settlements is supported by archaeological evidence, as changing conditions often spurred human adaptation and movement.

Ultimately, Mehargarh holds a crucial place in the timeline of human history, and Pakistan as a gateway of civilisation.

This Also answers questions as to who we Pakistanis are? That religiously we were Buddhists before Islam.

Pakistan before Islam was largely a Buddhist people since Emperor Ashoka.

The historical development of Buddhism in India and its interaction with other religious traditions, including Hinduism and Islam, is complex and multifaceted.

1. **Integration with Hindu Practices;**
   - Over centuries, Buddhist philosophical and spiritual practices were absorbed into mainstream Hindu traditions. Many Buddhist concepts, deities, and rituals were integrated into Hinduism, leading to a syncretism that made the distinctions between the two less clear.

2. **Royal Patronage:**
   - Buddhism initially flourished under the patronage of Mauryan Emperor Ashoka in the 3rd century BCE and subsequently under various other dynasties. However, as later rulers, particularly the Gupta emperors, began to favour Brahmanism (a precursor to modern Hinduism), the state support for Buddhism diminished.

3. **Decline of Monasteries:**
   - Buddhist monasteries, known as viharas, were economic and educational centres. The decline in royal patronage led to the economic weakening of these establishments. Invaders such as the Huns in the 5th and 6th centuries and later Muslim invasions

destroyed many monasteries, further eroding the institutional base of Buddhism.

4. **Internal Competition and Reform Movements:**
   - Hinduism underwent significant reform movements, such as the Bhakti movement, which emphasized personal devotion and simplified rituals. These reforms made Hinduism more accessible and appealing to the masses, contributing to the decline of Buddhism.

Islamic Conquests and Conversion:

1. **Military Conquests:**
   - The arrival and establishment of Islamic rule in the Indian subcontinent, particularly from the 12th century onwards, also impacted the Buddhist population. With the establishment of Islamic kingdoms, there were significant changes in the socio-political landscape.

2. **Forced Conversions:**
   - In some cases, Islamic rulers adopted policies that were not favourable to local religious practices, including Buddhism. This led to forced conversions and the destruction of Buddhist religious sites.

3. **Voluntary Conversion:**
   - Many Buddhists, particularly those belonging to lower social strata, found the egalitarian principles of Islam appealing. Conversion to Islam offered them improved social status and relief from the rigid caste hierarchy prevalent in Hindu society.

4. **Migration and Settlement Patterns:**
   - The regions that now constitute Pakistan and Afghanistan had significant interactions with Central Asian cultures. Buddhism in these areas initially thrived but eventually diminished due to these socio-political changes and the spread of Islam.

The decline of Buddhism in its birthplace, India, resulted from a combination of factors including the syncretism with Hinduism, a decline in royal patronage, destruction of monastic institutions, internal religious reforms, and the socio-political impacts of Islamic conquests. In regions like present-day Pakistan and Afghanistan, the conversion to Islam, both voluntary and forced, was significant due to the appeal of its egalitarianism and the changing political dynamics. Today Pakistan is a Muslim nation state and Imran khan represents the 7000 years old civilisation that faces the same challenges, it faced in the fall of Mehargarh, Harappa, and Mohenjo Dero.

Chapter 7: Imran Khan's spiritual journey

While Imran Khan's journey might have been known primarily for his prowess on the cricket field, it's the profound transformation in his later years that has touched many. Born and raised amidst the effervescent culture of Pakistan, he grew up with a spirit as indomitable as the cricket pitches he conquered. Young, vibrant, and a celebrated sports hero, his life seemed to glitter with the spoils of fame and fortune.

However, fate carved an alternate path for him when his beloved mother was diagnosed with cancer. The bustling aura of London's hospitals became his silent companions as he spent countless hours attending to her. It was within these sterile walls that his life began to shift dramatically.

Seeking solace, he turned to the wisdom of the ages. In his private discussion in his home, he would incessantly discuss spirituality with me, as he became very fond of my religious dimension apart from my passion of politics. He would call me to Islamabad to talk on our favourite subject mixing politics with spirituality. The other person to talk and guide him was Haroon Rashid and good honest journalist of Pakistan.

He found companionship in the soulful verses of Rumi, whose poetry spoke of divine love and self- annihilation for the beloved. I introduced him to the teachings of Al-Farabi, the eminent philosopher, who opened his mind to the intricate dance between reason and faith. Dr. Iqbal's visionary ideas rekindled a sense of purpose, while Al-Ghazali's work on spiritual mysticism deeply resonated within him. Each word, each idea acted as a beacon, guiding him toward a life that transcended the ephemeral allure of worldly success.

His nights became a tapestry woven with reflections on the life of the Prophet Muhammad, whose example of mercy and strength in adversity provided a model of impeccable character. He delved into the lives of the spiritual giants, including Imam Ali, whose wisdom and justice became a mirror to his soul.

This transformation was not merely an inward journey. It gave birth to Imran, the philanthropist. He sought out the company of spiritual figures, searching for enlightenment in their presence. His newfound faith culminated in acts of charity, aiming to alleviate the suffering of his fellow beings just as he had wished to soothe his mother's pain.

Further illuminating his path were the enduring legacies from the ancient lands of the Indus Valley - a cradle of rich spiritual heritage. Siddhartha Gautama, known to humanity as the Buddha, whose quest for enlightenment led him to the Middle Way, eschewing both indulgence and severe asceticism, taught the impermanence of life and the importance of compassion.

From the same region, centuries later, emerged Guru Nanak, born in what is now modern-day Pakistan. His teachings of Ik Onkar, the oneness of God, and his emphasis on living a truthful and righteous life resonated with the common man. His hymns, soaked in divine love, continue to be sung across the world, transcending the boundaries of religion.

In these men, Imran found a continuum of the spiritual legacy that binds mankind beyond the parochial. The reverence for life, the quest for knowledge, and the pursuit of inner peace became cornerstones of his redefined existence. His journey, from the glitz of international cricket to the serene paths of spirituality and philanthropy, became a testament to the transformative power of faith and self-discovery.In the land of the Indus Valley, where ancient rivers flow, A cradle of spirituality, where wisdom's seeds were sown.

From Buddha to Guru Nanak, The beloved Prophet Muhammad (pbuh) to Imam Ali, (RA) A legacy of enlightened souls, whose impact will never die.

Buddha, the awakened one, beneath the Bodhi tree, Found nirvana's peace, and shared it with humanity. His teachings of compassion, and the Eightfold Path's light, Guided seekers through the ages, in the dark of night.

Guru Nanak, the founder of Sikhism's sacred flame, Burned bright with love and truth, dispelling fear and shame. Through his travels and teachings, he showed the way,

To a life of service, and a heart full of praise.

Beloved Prophet Muhammad, (pbuh) the final messenger of Allah's grace, Received revelations in the cave, and shared them with the world's face. His message of monotheism, and the Quran's holy might,

Transformed the desert sands, and ignited a guiding light that enlightened humanity all over the universe creating multiple civilisations. Imam Ali, the lion of God, with wisdom's sword in hand, Fought for justice and truth, in a world so grand.

His words of wisdom, and his heart so pure and bright, Inspire generations, like a beacon in the night. Other minor men, like Bullah Shah, with his mystical verse,

Muhammad Buksh, with his Sufi heart, and Warris Shah's romantic universe, Contributed to the rich tapestry, of the Indus Valley's spiritual heritage, A testament to the power, of love and divine emergence. Their impact on the culture, of this ancient land so dear, Is a legacy that continues, year after year.

In the territory now known, as Pakistan's soil so blessed, Their spiritual footprint remains, forever etched and caressed. Through their teachings and examples, they showed us the way, To live a life of purpose, and seize the day.

Their message of love and compassion, echoes through the ages, A reminder of our shared humanity, and the spiritual stages. Thus, Imran khan the play boy of yester years Was a born-again devout Muslim and with his acts and deeds in philanthropy, politics, education, he has become a lyric of love and spirituality in the folk songs of three mighty civilisations of Mahergarh, Harrappa, Mohenjo Dero that sprung on the land where the mighty River Indus and its five tributaries flow since 60 million years ago.

In poetic English, with quotes from the greats,

We honour their memories, and the impact they create. Their stories woven together, like a rich and vibrant fabric,

A testament to the power, of spirituality and loves magnetic.

In the realm of the sacred, where compassion knows no bounds, Holy men from diverse traditions have walked the earth, leaving behind a legacy of love and profound wisdom.

Prophet Abraham, a paragon of hospitality, would wait for hours to share a meal with a guest, embodying the spirit of unity and togetherness.

Centuries later, Imran Khan, a modern-day leader, followed in Abraham's footsteps, constructing shelters for the homeless and sharing meals with those forgotten by society.

His selfless acts earned him the title of "Murshad," a saint revered by the people, as he embodied the Islamic tradition of compassion and equality.

Like Jesus, who dined with tax collectors and outcasts, Imran Khan broke bread with the marginalized, recognizing the divine in each individual.

Similarly, Sufi mystics like Rumi and Hafiz, and Jewish prophets like Isaiah and Ezekiel, all advocated for the love and acceptance of all humanity.

In the Indus Valley civilization, where ancient rivers flow,

Imran Khan's heart beats in harmony with the land and its people,A testament to the power of selflessness and love, A legacy that will endure, long after he's gone.

As the Quran says, "And We have certainly honored the children of Adam" (17:70),

Imran Khan's actions reflect this honor, recognizing the inherent worth of every individual.

In a world torn apart by divisions and strife,

His example shines like a beacon, illuminating the path to a more compassionate life.

As the great Sufi poet, Bulleh Shah, once said, "Neither am I of the East, nor of the West,I am of the Beloved's land, where love is the only quest."

Imran Khan's journey is a testament to this eternal truth,A reminder that, in the end, only love and compassion matter.Imran Khan's transformation from a cricketing icon and Westernized playboy to a flag bearer of Islamic values and spirituality stands as a powerful testament to the enduring power of faith and self-discovery. Born into privilege and immersed in Western culture during his early years, Imran epitomized a life of luxury and indulgence that often came with his global fame. However, his journey took a decisive turn as he matured and grappled with the realities of life, loss, and responsibility, which ultimately shaped his identity as a devout Muslim and a leader who seeks to elevate Pakistan's spiritual and moral standing in the world.

Initially, Imran Khan's exposure to Western values during his time at Oxford University and his cricketing career shaped much of his worldview. The adoration, opulence, and relentless glamour seemed to create a chasm between him and his roots. Yet, even during these years, there were moments of introspection. His love for poetry, especially the verses of Rumi, began to sow seeds of spiritual curiosity. Although it lay dormant, this spiritual yearning would resurface in transformative ways later in life.

The critical moment of Imran's spiritual awakening began with personal loss and tragedy. The passing of his mother to cancer marked a pivotal juncture, forcing him to confront life's fleeting nature. As he walked through the hallways of London's hospitals, he realized the fragility of existence and the futility of worldly pursuits without a higher purpose. This loss ignited his journey to find meaning, driving him to build Pakistan's first cancer hospital, Shaukat Khanum Memorial Cancer Hospital, as a tribute to his mother and a means of serving humanity.

This act of philanthropy, inspired by Islamic values of compassion and charity, was just the beginning. In his search for spiritual fulfillment, Imran immersed himself in the wisdom of Islamic philosophers and spiritual leaders. He delved into the works of Al-Ghazali, whose teachings on the reconciliation of reason and faith resonated deeply with him. Al-Ghazali's emphasis on the inner transformation of the soul to achieve closeness to God helped Imran navigate his journey away from materialism and toward spirituality.

Imran also found guidance in the life and teachings of Prophet Muhammad (PBUH), whose model of leadership, humility, and justice became a blueprint for him. The Prophet's emphasis on compassion for the marginalized and steadfastness in adversity inspired Imran to adopt a more inclusive and empathetic approach, both in his personal life and political career. He sought out scholars and mystics, seeking counsel and insights that could guide his actions in an increasingly polarized world.

As Imran's faith deepened, his commitment to Pakistan's spiritual and moral revival grew. He began to reject the superficial allure of Western materialism, recognizing the emptiness it brought. Instead, he focused on rebuilding the identity of Pakistan as a state grounded in Islamic principles of equality, justice, and unity. He often spoke about creating a welfare state modeled on Riyasat-e-Madina, the first Islamic state established by the Prophet Muhammad (PBUH), where social justice and accountability were paramount.

Imran's interactions with spiritual leaders further solidified his transformation. He formed close ties with Islamic scholars and Sufi mystics who nurtured his understanding of the divine. Their teachings emphasized love, selflessness, and devotion to God, themes that Imran incorporated into his vision for Pakistan. He sought to revive the spiritual heritage of the Indus Valley, drawing inspiration from figures like Bulleh Shah, Waris Shah, and Shah Abdul Latif Bhittai, whose poetry and teachings celebrated divine love and human equality.

Moreover, Imran Khan's spiritual journey became a source of strength in his political struggles. As he faced challenges, including smear campaigns, political imprisonment, and the relentless criticism of his opponents, his faith acted as a refuge. He often quoted verses from the Quran to inspire his supporters, emphasizing patience, perseverance, and trust in God's plan. His reliance on prayer and his belief in divine justice became evident during moments of political and personal adversity.

In an era marked by the global rise of Islamophobia and increasing cultural divisions, Imran Khan has emerged as a powerful advocate for Islam. While many leaders shy away from addressing the misrepresentation of Islam in the West, Imran has taken a bold stance, calling for global dialogue to combat Islamophobia and foster mutual understanding. His speeches at international forums, including the United Nations, have challenged stereotypes about Islam, emphasizing its core values of peace, tolerance, and compassion.

Imran's return to Pakistan's cultural and spiritual roots also informed his vision for national development. He recognized the need for a holistic approach to progress—one that balances material growth with moral and ethical development. His focus on education reform aimed to produce not just skilled workers but also morally upright citizens. He emphasized the importance of including Islamic teachings in the curriculum to instill a sense of identity and purpose among Pakistan's youth.

The broader Islamic world also found a voice in Imran Khan's leadership. At a time when many Muslim nations grappled with internal divisions and external pressures, Imran advocated for unity and cooperation among Islamic countries. He called for the revival of the Islamic Golden Age's spirit of innovation, scholarship, and unity, envisioning a future where the Muslim world could regain its dignity and influence on the global stage.

Imran Khan's transformation from a Western-influenced celebrity to a spiritual leader and statesman reflects his journey of self-discovery and commitment to a higher purpose. His life is a testament to the idea that true leadership is not about personal gain but about serving others and striving for the greater good. His path has inspired millions to look beyond the material and embrace the transformative power of faith, compassion, and resilience.

In his own words, Imran Khan often reflects on the Quranic principle that "with hardship comes ease" (Quran 94:6). This verse encapsulates his journey—a life marked by challenges that ultimately paved the way for growth, self-discovery, and a profound connection with the divine. Imran Khan's spiritual evolution serves as a beacon for those seeking to reconcile worldly pursuits with higher ideals, reminding us that true success lies in serving humanity and seeking God's pleasure above all.

Chapter 8: Imran Khan's Rise to Power

Before joining PTI about 25 years ago, I had a fascinating encounter on a flight from the USA to the UK! My conversation with Sir Vivian Richards offers a captivating glimpse into the human side of leaders, revealing how their formative experiences can shape their relationships and decision-making. It's a powerful reminder that even the most prominent figures can be influenced by their past, and that understanding these dynamics can provide valuable insight into their actions and motivations.

As I soared through the skies from the USA to the UK, I found myself utterly absorbed in the pages of a magazine, my nose buried deep within its captivating contents. The gentleman seated beside me couldn't help but steal a few glances, his curiosity piqued by my intense focus. When the air hostess arrived with a refreshing drink, he seized the opportunity to break the ice, flashing a warm smile as he inquired about my country of origin.

With respectful candor, I revealed my roots in Pakistan, to which he responded with an effusive grin, exclaiming, **"Ah, from the land of Imran Khan!"** Our eyes met, and I sensed a spark of mutual interest. Little did I know, I was in the presence of a cricket legend, the inimitable Sir Vivian Richards of the West Indies. As our conversation unfolded, we delved into the realm of cricket, exchanging lively tales and anecdotes about our favorite teams.

My curiosity got the better of me, and I asked Sir Vivian to share his impressions of Imran Khan. He described him as an exceptional player and a worthy individual, who, however, harbored a curious trait – a preference for the company of ordinary, middle-class players over those of higher stature. Sir Vivian hypothesized & attributed this to Imran's formative years at Aitchison College in Lahore, where he was surrounded by the scions of landed aristocracy, yet felt like an outsider due to his humble background as the son of a civil engineer.

This childhood complex, Sir Vivian surmised, had evolved into a lingering discomfort, even disdain, for the landed class. This, in turn, became a political liability for Imran Khan's party, PTI, as they struggled to find suitable candidates in the largely rural, agrarian heartlands of Pakistan, where the landed elite wield significant influence. While his urban allies eventually betrayed him, as they were rich men unfit for politics which is very demanding and difficult in a country like Pakistan where leaders are hanged, murdered, jailed and tortured. One has to be thick skinned in politics of Indo-Pakistan. Only a handful of loyalists from the landed class who got tickets remained steadfast in their support of PTI to date.

As our plane touched down in the UK, I couldn't help but feel grateful for this chance encounter with Sir Vivian Richards, which had yielded a captivating glimpse into the human side of leaders. Our conversation served as a poignant reminder that even the most towering figures can be shaped by their past experiences, and that understanding these dynamics can offer invaluable insight into their motivations and actions.

"Imran Khan's journey from prominence to imprisonment and back into the spotlight can be analyzed through a multi-faceted lens, drawing parallels with historical precedents".

Historical Context;

Imran Khan's initial rise echoed the populist movements seen in many countries throughout history. Figures like Julius Caesar, Napoleon Bonaparte, and more recently, leaders such as Donald Trump and Narendra Modi have risen to power on waves of dissatisfaction with the status quo, promising dramatic reforms.

Domestic Factors;

- Populism: Khan's campaign centered around anti-corruption, social justice, and economic reform, resonating with a populace disenchanted by the traditional political elite.
- Charismatic Leadership: His personal charisma, bolstered by achievements in cricket and philanthropy, helped galvanize a broad support base.
- Youth Support: Leveraging social media effectively, Khan mobilized the youth, a critical demographic disillusioned by unemployment and lack of opportunities.

1. Downfall Factors;

International Dynamics;

- Geopolitical Interests: Pakistan's strategic position often subjects it to external influences. Historical patterns show that leaders who don't align with dominant geopolitical interests (e.g., Mohammad Mosaddegh in Iran, 1953) often face severe consequences.
- Allegations of US Interference: Khan's perceived shift away from traditional allies and flirtations with closer ties to nations like China and Russia might have alarmed the US, potentially leading to subtle or overt operations to destabilize his government.

Domestic Dynamics;

- Economic Crises: Pakistan's struggling economy, exacerbated by COVID-19, inflation, and debt, made governance challenging. Economic hardships often erode public support swiftly.
- Political Fragmentation: Pakistan's political landscape is rife with factions. Failures to create broad coalitions or sufficiently appease military interests weakened Khan's standing.

2. Imprisonment and Rise in Popularity;

Historical Context;

Leaders who face imprisonment often symbolically transform into martyrs, rallying further support (e.g., Nelson Mandela, Martin Luther King Jr.). This phenomenon can rejuvenate a leader's popularity by casting them as victims of unjust systems.

Factors Behind Renewed Popularity:

- Victim Narrative: Khan's imprisonment could be framed as a fight against external intervention and corruption, solidifying his image as a champion of the people.
- Social Media: In the modern era, social media can amplify voices

silenced by mainstream outlets. Khan's support base continued to mobilize online, keeping his message alive.
- Grassroots Mobilization: Khan's party, despite being in turmoil, utilized grassroots mobilization effectively. Historically, movements like those of Mahatma Gandhi or Martin Luther relied on grassroots support even during periods of direct oppression.
- Political Resilience: Historical leaders, having experienced downfall, often return wiser and more strategically astute. This resilience and ability to reframe their narrative often leads to a resurgence.

3. Comparative Insights from History;

Contemporary Patterns:

- Economic Populism: Leaders like Franklin D. Roosevelt rode the wave of economic discontent to usher in significant reforms. Similarly, Khan's reformist approach resonated with a populace seeking change.
- Martyrdom and Resistance: Resembling figures like Aung San Suu Kyi, Khan's persecution may foster a powerful resistance narrative, turning imprisonment into a rallying point.
- International Realignments: Leaders who challenge dominant international paradigms (Egypt's Gamal Abdel Nasser, Cuba's Fidel Castro) often face severe reprisals but retain domestic support through nationalistic rhetoric.

Conclusion; Imran Khan's political odyssey is emblematic of broader trends in global and historical leadership. His rise through populism, fall via internal and external pressures, and resurgence poweredby a strong narrative of resistance and victimhood, mirrors the paths trodden by other transformative leaders. His enduring popularity, despite severe setbacks, underscores the complexity of political dynamics in contemporary times, where traditional power structures and new-age mobilization tools intertwine to shape the destinies of nations and their leaders.

Imran Khan's rise to power was driven by several factors:

1. <u>Anti-Establishment Sentiment:</u> Khan tapped into widespread discontent with Pakistan's political elite, promising to upend the status quo and tackle corruption.
2. <u>Populist Charisma</u>: Khan's cricket hero status, combined with his charismatic leadership and oratory skills, resonated with the masses.
3. <u>Economic Discontent:</u> Pakistan's struggling economy and widespread poverty created an opportunity for Khan to promise economic relief and development.
4. <u>Religious Conservatism:</u> Khan's Islamist leanings and promises to create an "Islamic welfare state" appealed to Pakistan's religiously conservative population.
5. <u>Military Support</u>: Khan enjoyed tacit support from the military establishment, which saw him as a useful asset in their efforts to maintain influence over Pakistani politics.

Khan's fall from power was equally precipitous, due to:

1. <u>Incompetent Governance:</u> Khan's government was marked by poor decision-making, nepotism, and mismanagement, leading to economic stagnation and political instability.
2. <u>Military Discontent:</u> Khan's attempts to assert civilian control over the military and reduce their political influence led to tensions with the military establishment.
3. <u>US-Backed Regime Change:</u> The US, seeking to maintain its influence in the region, allegedly supported Khan's ouster, capitalizing on his weaknesses and the military's discontent.

In the next 20 years, Khan's rise and fall will have significant effects on Pakistan's international, regional, and national dynamics:

International;

- US-Pakistan Relations*: Khan's ouster will likely lead to a re-evaluation of US-Pakistan relations, with the US seeking to maintain its influence in the region.*China-Pakistan Relations*: Khan's pro-

China stance will likely continue, with Pakistan seeking to maintain its strategic partnership with China.

Regional;

- Afghanistan-Pakistan Relations*: Khan's fall will likely impact Pakistan's role in Afghan peace talks, with the new government potentially adopting a more conciliatory approach.
- India-Pakistan Relations*: Khan's hawkish stance on India will likely continue, with tensions remaining high between the two nuclear-armed neighbors.

National;

- *Political Instability*: Khan's ouster will likely lead to continued political instability, with various factions vying for power.
- *Economic Development*: Pakistan's economic struggles will continue, with the new government facing significant challenges in addressing poverty, inequality, and stagnation.

In conclusion;

Imran Khan's rise and fall were driven by a complex interplay of factors, including populist charisma, economic discontent, religious conservatism, and military support. His legacy will continue to shape Pakistan's international, regional, and national dynamics for years to come.

The military Mullah combine, assisted by political proxies of establishment has obstructed the political path leading to global community, liberal values that mother scientific education innovative technological advancement and a culture of tolerance, empathy, civilized behavior, and discipline. Yes, we needed our religious ethos to be upgraded and installed in the society. We needed to master our economic, political, and Judicial sovereignty and clamp down on isolation and confrontation on internal and external frontiers. It is not beneficial to look to America, China, Europe to do us favors through any strategy of direct or indirect approach and as a consequence undermine our economic, political and cultural sovereignty.

Whatever the twisted path clamped on Pakistan, weather by design or by accident this has pushed a talented state like Pakistan back to medieval ages. Leadership needs to be insightful with inspirational wisdom that never fails to reach both hearts and minds. Imran khan at this given time is a page, you will find something that inspires and guides the teaming millions of Pakistanis. Scientific and liberal education helps cultivate the right values, vision, culture and open the society to thoughts of global wisdom that brings meaning to the life of a nation state. The soul of Pakistan desires us to work honestly for ourselves and our society. To be idle, have toxic behavior, corruption as a way of life is become stranger to blessings of life gifted by God. This steps you out from the march from decisions compromises, understandings of our pride and majesty as Human beings and as a sovereign society. When a nation is at work with discipline justice and dignity, the society becomes a lyric in the music of civilizational life, and is a proud submission towards the infinite. Pakistani society lead by Nawaz-Zardari and military without honesty of work and mindful purpose has become a curse and without dignity of labour, a misfortune Hence Pakistan is marginalized far away from history of contemporary human dynamism. Pakistan was created to shame curiosity and technological advancement of Muslim Ummah, but we lost all three and as of now, look at the indignities

Pakistan is undergoing despite being a great country, great faith, located at the pivot of Asia Europe and Middle East. In the global music of life, only Pakistan stands out as dumb silent, when the entire world today is singing together in unison. Our military, political leaders, judges, jurists, generals, intellectuals and, elite has failed our country our Faith, our beloved prophet and mother earth's area which was gifted to our awe-inspiring country. A dream was assigned to Pakistani's when our beloved prophet pointed towards shores of Karachi and said," I feel puffs of cool air from shores of Sind," We failed our beloved prophet.

As long as Muslims loved life through rule of law, justice, knowledge, labour and discipline, they ruled the globe creating the greatest civilization and in truth loved life. To love life through labour is to be in intimacy with life's inner most secrets. Military, Mullah, political leaders & the permanent ruling elite have made life a darkness, and now in their weariness the public sings the same swan song. Imran khan and his colleagues like myself, Ali Muhammad khan, Asad Qaisar, Qasim khan Surri, Hamid khan, Dr Arif Alvi type old guard believe that life only becomes a darkness when you give up on greater good of society and start living for petty personal gains. A nation is meaningless without education, knowledge, justice, empathy and discipline. Knowledge is the blood vain of human civilization.

When a nation is educated, knowledgeable, sensible, then it binds itself to itself, to other fellow humans and to the Almighty God. This was the dream of Jinnah and being pursued by Imran khan and his hard- core old guard PTI.

Profiles in courage in land of River Indus from Raja Porus to Imran Khan

1) A fascinating comparison! Imran Khan, the 22nd Prime Minister of Pakistan, and Raja Porus, the ancient Buddhist king who fought against Alexander the Great, may seem like vastly different figures on the surface. However, here are some similarities and differences I've identified:

<u>Similarities</u>:

1. Courage and bravery: Both Imran Khan and Raja Porus demonstrated remarkable courage in the face of overwhelming odds. Raja Porus fought against the mighty Alexander, while Imran Khan has taken on the political establishment in Pakistan.
2. Nationalism and patriotism: Both leaders have shown strong nationalist sentiments, with Raja Porus defending his kingdom and Imran Khan advocating for Pakistan's interests.
3. Strategic thinking: Raja Porus employed clever tactics against Alexander, while Imran Khan has demonstrated strategic thinking in his political career, often outmaneuvering his opponents.

<u>Differences:</u>

1. Context and circumstances: Raja Porus fought against a foreign invader, while Imran Khan operates in a modern political landscape.
2. Leadership style: Raja Porus was a monarch, while Imran Khan is a democratically elected leader.
3. Geography: Raja Porus ruled over the Paurava kingdom in ancient India (present-day Punjab, Pakistan), while Imran Khan's political influence spans the entire country of Pakistan.

Regarding geography, the battle between Raja Porus and Alexander took place on the banks of the River Jhelum (also known as the Hydaspes River) in present-day Punjab, Pakistan. This region has historically been a significant cultural and political hub, with many empires vying for control over the fertile plains of the Indus Valley.

Imran Khan, as a modern political leader, has had to navigate the complexities of Pakistan's geography, including the country's diverse regions, ethnic groups, and strategic location in South Asia.

2) Another intriguing comparison! Raja Ranjit Singh, the founder of the Sikh Empire, and Imran Khan, the 22nd Prime Minister of Pakistan, share some similarities in their struggles against colonial powers and established interests;

Similarities:

1. Resistance against colonialism: Raja Ranjit Singh fought against the British East India Company's expansion, while Imran Khan has challenged the entrenched interests of Pakistan's establishment, which was shaped by British colonialism.
2. Nationalist sentiment: Both leaders tapped into strong nationalist feelings, with Ranjit Singh uniting Sikhs and other communities against British rule, and Imran Khan appealing to Pakistani patriotism in his quest for reform.
3. Strategic thinking: Ranjit Singh employed clever diplomacy and military tactics against the British, while Imran Khan has used innovative political strategies to challenge the status quo in Pakistan.
4. Reform-minded: Both leaders aimed to modernize and strengthen their respective administrations, with Ranjit Singh introducing reforms in governance and Imran Khan promising to root out corruption and promote accountability.

Differences:

1. Context and scope: Ranjit Singh fought against British colonial expansion, while Imran Khan operates within a post-colonial context,

challenging entrenched interests within Pakistan's establishment.
2. Leadership style: Ranjit Singh was an autocratic ruler, while Imran Khan is a democratically elected leader.
3. Military prowess: Ranjit Singh was a skilled military commander, while Imran Khan's strengths lie in political mobilization and strategic communication.
4. Legacy: Ranjit Singh's empire eventually fell to the British, while Imran Khan's legacy is still unfolding.

Regarding the loss of Bangladesh, it was a result of a complex interplay of factors, including:

1. Ethnic and linguistic differences: Bengalis felt marginalized by the dominant Punjabi elite in Pakistan.
2. Economic disparities: East Pakistan (now Bangladesh) felt exploited and neglected in terms of resource allocation and development.
3. Political repression: The Pakistani establishment's heavy-handed response to Bengali demands for autonomy ultimately led to the Bangladesh Liberation War.

3) Another fascinating comparison! Imran Khan and Sultan Tipu of Mysore share some similarities in their struggles against the British and local proxies;

<u>Similarities</u>:

1. Resistance against British colonialism: Both Tipu Sultan and Imran Khan fought against the British Empire's expansion and influence in their respective regions.
2. Use of innovative tactics: Tipu Sultan employed guerrilla warfare and clever diplomacy, while Imran Khan has utilized social media, mass mobilization, and strategic communication to challenge the status quo.
3. Nationalist appeal: Both leaders tapped into strong nationalist sentiments, with Tipu Sultan uniting Muslims and Hindus against British rule, and Imran Khan appealing to Pakistani patriotism in his quest for reform.

4. Challenging local proxies: Tipu Sultan faced opposition from Hindu kingdoms aligned with the British, while Imran Khan faces challenges from political parties (PMLN, PPP) perceived as proxies of the establishment.

Differences:

1. Context and scope: Tipu Sultan fought against British colonial expansion in the late 18th century, while Imran Khan operates in a post-colonial context, challenging entrenched interests within Pakistan's establishment.
2. Leadership style: Tipu Sultan was an autocratic ruler, while Imran Khan is a democratically elected leader.
3. Military prowess: Tipu Sultan was a skilled military commander, while Imran Khan's strengths lie in political mobilization and strategic communication.
4. Legacy: Tipu Sultan's kingdom eventually fell to the British, while Imran Khan's legacy is still unfolding.
5. Ideology: Tipu Sultan was a devout Muslim and a staunch defender of his faith, while Imran Khan's ideology is more focused on anti-corruption, accountability, and social justice.
6. Support base: Tipu Sultan drew support from his kingdom and some regional allies, while Imran Khan has a broader support base across Pakistan, with a strong following among the youth and middle class.

Regarding the Hindu proxies, Tipu Sultan faced opposition from Hindu kingdoms like the Marathas and the Nizam of Hyderabad, who were aligned with the British. Similarly, Imran Khan perceives PMLN and PPP as proxies of the establishment, allegedly working against his reform agenda.

4) Nawab Siraj-ud-Daula of Bengal and Imran Khan's struggles share some commonalities, despite being in different historical contexts. Here's an analysis;

Nawab Siraj-ud-Daula's struggle:

- Resisted British colonial expansion in Bengal (1756-1757)

- Fought against the British East India Company's attempts to control Bengal's resources and trade
- Saw the British as a threat to his sovereignty and the region's autonomy
- Led the Battle of Plassey (1757), which marked the beginning of British rule in India <u>Imran Khan's struggle:</u>
- Resisted the influence of Pakistan's military establishment, which he perceives as a legacy of British colonialism
- Views the military as a "brown colonial master" perpetuating a system of oppression
- Seeks to democratize Pakistan and reduce military interference in politics
- Faces opposition from the military and political elites, who he believes are beholden to the establishment

Common themes:

1. Resistance to external/institutional control: Both leaders fought against forces they saw as controlling their respective regions.
2. National sovereignty: Both sought to assert their region's autonomy and self-governance.
3. Anti-colonial sentiment: Both struggles have anti-colonial undertones, with Nawab Siraj-ud-Daula fighting British colonialism and Imran Khan resisting the perceived legacy of British colonialism in Pakistan's military establishment.
4. Power dynamics: Both leaders challenged existing power structures, with Nawab Siraj-ud-Daula facing the British East India Company and Imran Khan facing Pakistan's military establishment.

However, there are significant differences in context, scope, and outcomes between the two struggles.

A great point about the spiritual connection and shared heritage! Despite this, there are significant differences in context, scope, and outcomes between the two struggles:

Differences:

1. <u>Historical context</u>: Nawab Siraj-ud-Daula's struggle (1756-1757) was against British colonial expansion in Bengal, while Imran Khan's struggle is against the military establishment in modern-day Pakistan (2018-present).
2. <u>Nature of the struggle:</u> Nawab Siraj-ud-Daula's was a military resistance against foreign occupation, whereas Imran Khan's is a political struggle against an internal power structure.
3. <u>Scope:</u> Nawab Siraj-ud-Daula's struggle was localized to Bengal, while Imran Khan's has national implications for Pakistan.
4. <u>Outcomes:</u> Nawab Siraj-ud-Daula's struggle ended with the British East India Company's victory and the beginning of British rule in India. Imran Khan's struggle is ongoing, with uncertain outcomes.
5. Political landscape: Nawab Siraj-ud-Daula was a monarch fighting to maintain his rule, whereas Imran Khan is a democratically elected leader seeking to reform the political system.
6. <u>International context:</u> Nawab Siraj-ud-Daula's struggle occurred during the Seven Years' War, with European powers vying for colonial dominance. Imran Khan's struggle takes place in a post-colonial, globalized world with different geopolitical dynamics.

Scope differences despite spiritual connection:

1. <u>National boundaries:</u> Although Bangladesh and Pakistan share a common heritage, they are separate nations with distinct political entities.
2. <u>Political systems:</u> Pakistan has a federal parliamentary republic system, whereas Bangladesh has a unitary parliamentary republic system.
3. <u>Historical experiences:</u> Bangladesh experienced a bloody liberation war in 1971, which shaped its national identity. Pakistan has had a complex history of military rule and political instability.

Despite these differences, the spiritual connection and shared heritage between Bangladesh and Pakistan remain significant, and both nations continue to navigate their respective struggles for sovereignty, democracy, and self-determination.

5) Imran Khan and Bhagat Singh were two influential figures in South Asian history, albeit in different eras and contexts. Here's a detailed analysis of their similarities and differences;

Similarities:

1. Humble background: Both Imran Khan and Bhagat Singh came from relatively modest families. Imran Khan's family was middle-class, while Bhagat Singh's family was involved in revolutionary activities against British colonial rule.
2. Passion for justice: Both leaders were driven by a strong sense of justice and a desire to challenge oppressive systems. Bhagat Singh fought against British colonial rule, while Imran Khan has focused on combating corruption and promoting social justice in Pakistan.
3. Charismatic leadership: Both leaders possess exceptional charisma, inspiring devotion in their followers. Bhagat Singh's courage and conviction motivated many to join the freedom struggle, while Imran Khan's leadership style has attracted a large following in Pakistan.
4. Persecution and imprisonment: Both leaders faced persecution and imprisonment for their beliefs. Bhagat Singh was jailed and eventually hanged by the British, while Imran Khan has faced numerous arrests, detentions, and threats throughout his political career.

Differences:

1. Historical context: Bhagat Singh fought against British colonial rule in India (1920s-1930s), while Imran Khan operates in contemporary Pakistan, addressing issues like corruption, governance, and social inequality.
2. Ideology: Bhagat Singh was a socialist revolutionary, advocating for Marxist-Leninist principles, whereas Imran Khan's ideology is more cantered around Islamic values, anti-corruption, and social justice.
3. Methods: Bhagat Singh employed violent revolutionary tactics,

including bombings and assassinations, to challenge British rule. In contrast, Imran Khan has primarily used peaceful, democratic means, such as political rallies, protests, and elections, to effect change.

4. <u>Outcomes:</u> Bhagat Singh's actions led to his martyrdom at a young age, but his legacy continues to inspire revolutionaries and nationalists. Imran Khan has had a longer, more complex career, with periods of political power and influence, but also facing criticism and controversy.

5. <u>Consequences for society:</u> Bhagat Singh's actions contributed to the Indian independence movement, ultimately helping to end British colonial rule. Imran Khan's impact is still unfolding, but his efforts have raised awareness about corruption and social issues in Pakistan, inspiring a new generation of activists and politicians.

In conclusion, while both Imran Khan and Bhagat Singh share some similarities in their backgrounds and commitment to justice, their differences in ideology, methods, and historical context set them apart. Their legacies continue to shape the societies they fought for, inspiring future generations to strive for positive change.

Here are some historical examples and poetic descriptions for Imran Khan and Bhagat Singh:

Historical Examples:

Imran Khan;

- Ancient: Spartacus (Roman gladiator who led a slave uprising) - like Imran Khan, Spartacus challenged the status quo and fought for justice.
- Medieval: Thomas Becket (English archbishop who defied King Henry II) - like Imran Khan, Becket stood up against corruption and abuse of power.
- Contemporary: Nelson Mandela (South African anti-apartheid leader) - like Imran Khan, Mandela fought against systemic injustice and worked towards social reform.

Bhagat Singh:

- Ancient: Harmodius and Aristogeiton (Athenian tyrannicides) - like Bhagat Singh, they fought against oppressive rule and gave their lives for freedom.
- Medieval: William Wallace (Scottish rebel who fought against English rule) - like Bhagat Singh, Wallace led a courageous fight for independence.
- Contemporary: Che Guevara (Argentine revolutionary) - like Bhagat Singh, Guevara was a passionate socialist revolutionary who fought against imperialism.

Poetic Descriptions:

From the West:

- "The Tyger" by William Blake (England) - describes the fierce courage of a revolutionary like Bhagat Singh:
- "Did he who made the Lamb make thee?"
- "The New Colossus" by Emma Lazarus (USA) - describes the spirit of justice and freedom that Imran Khan and Bhagat Singh embody.
- "Give me your tired, your poor, / Your huddled masses yearning to breathe free." <u>From the East:</u>
- "The Conference of the Birds" by Farid ud-Din Attar (Persia) - describes the journey of a leader like Imran Khan:
- "The way is long, the road is hard, / But with each step, the heart grows strong."
- "The Ballad of the Rebel" by Faiz Ahmad Faiz (Pakistan) - describes

the courage and conviction of a revolutionary like Bhagat Singh:

- "We shall rise, we shall rise, / Like the sun, like the dawn..." From the Orient;

- "The Art of War" by Sun Tzu (China) - describes the strategic thinking of a leader like Imran Khan: "Know yourself, know your enemy, / And you shall win a hundred battles."

- "The Tale of the Heike" (Japan) - describes the loyalty and sacrifice of a revolutionary like Bhagat Singh:

"The loyal heart, the brave heart, / Beats strong, beats true, till the end."

Mothers who give birth to men like Bhagat Singh and IMRAN khan are chosen ones. It's not for weak hearted women to give birth to courageous wolf warriors like Bhagat Singh and IMRAN khan.

6) While Rahul Gandhi and Imran Khan are distinct political figures with different backgrounds and contexts, since both have displayed courage in their stands, I find some superficial similarities in their struggles. Here's a brief analysis;

Similarities:

1. Challenging entrenched power structures: Both Rahul Gandhi and Imran Khan have positioned themselves as opponents of entrenched power elites. Gandhi criticizes the BJP's dominance and what he perceives as its divisive policies, while Khan has long spoken out against Pakistan's traditional political elite, which he sees as corrupt and self-serving.
2. Anti-establishment narratives: Both leaders have crafted narratives that pit them against the existing power structures. Gandhi portrays himself as a champion of inclusivity and secularism against the BJP's perceived authoritarianism, while Khan presents himself as a crusader against corruption and cronyism in Pakistan's political establishment.

3. <u>Populist appeal:</u> Both leaders have used populist rhetoric to mobilize support. Gandhi has emphasized issues like economic inequality, social justice, and farmers' rights, while Khan has focused on anti-corruption, accountability, and the needs of ordinary Pakistanis.

Differences:

1. <u>Context and regimes:</u> The BJP in India is a democratically elected government, whereas Khan's opponents in Pakistan include both civilian and military elites, which have historically wielded significant influence over the country's politics.
2. <u>Leadership styles:</u> Rahul Gandhi is a member of the Indian National Congress's dynastic leadership, while Imran Khan rose to power as a charismatic outsider, leveraging his sports and philanthropic background.
3. <u>Policy focus:</u> Gandhi's emphasis is on social welfare, secularism, and economic development, whereas Khan's agenda has cantered on anti-corruption, economic reform, and Pakistan's relationship with the military.

Historical context:

1. <u>India:</u> Rahul Gandhi's struggle is set against the backdrop of India's democratic framework, where the BJP has been the dominant force since 2014. Gandhi aims to reclaim the political center and revive the Congress party's fortunes.
2. <u>Pakistan:</u> Imran Khan's challenge is situated in Pakistan's complex political landscape, marked by periods of military rule, political instability, and the influence of the military establishment. Khan's goal is to reform the system and establish a more equitable, accountable governance structure.

My analysis in profiles of courage only provide a general overview and might not capture every nuance and detail of these complex political scenarios and personalities discussed in this book.

7) An intriguing question! Subhas Chandra Bose and Imran Khan, although from different eras and countries, share some similarities;

1. <u>Nationalist spirit:</u> Both were passionate about their nations' independence and sovereignty. Bose fought against British colonial rule in India, while Khan has been vocal about Pakistan's autonomy and self-determination.
2. <u>Charismatic leadership:</u> Both possessed exceptional oratory skills, inspiring millions with their vision and passion.
3. <u>Anti-imperialist stance:</u> Bose opposed British imperialism, while Khan has criticized Western interference in Pakistan's affairs.
4. <u>Visionary thinking:</u> Both had a vision for their nations' future, with Bose advocating for a unified, independent India and Khan promoting a "Naya Pakistan" (New Pakistan).

Here's my poetic analysis, weaving in verses from Tagore and Iqbal;

"Tagore's "Where the Mind is Without Fear" (1910).

"Where the mind is without fear and the head is held high... Into that heaven of freedom, my Father, let my country awake."

Like Bose, who fought for India's freedom, Khan aims to liberate Pakistan from external influences, echoing Tagore's cry for a fearless, awakened nation.

Iqbal's "Sare Jahan Se Accha" (1910).

"Better than the entire world, is our Hindustan...

We are its nightingales, and it is our garden abloom."

Khan's love for Pakistan resonates with Iqbal's ode to the beauty and uniqueness of one's homeland. Both leaders cherish their nations' distinct identities.

Iqbal's "Khudi" (1914).

"Be a lamp, or a life, or a wave, or a flame...

Be a force, be a power, be a sovereign, be a king."

Bose embodied this spirit of self-reliance and empowerment, inspiring Indians to take control of their destiny. Khan, too, emphasizes self-sufficiency and autonomy for Pakistan.

While there are similarities, it's essential to acknowledge the differences in their contexts, ideologies, and approaches. Nonetheless, their shared passion for their nations' prosperity and independence is undeniable.

A delightful request of my inner voices! Let me sprinkle some poetic magic into my conversation, with verses from the greats of our ancient Land of Indus Valley;

As the sun rises on this lovely Saturday, July 27, 2024, I'm reminded of Tagore's words;

"The morning light, like a lover's caress,

Awakens the world from its gentle rest." (Rabindranath Tagore)

May this day bring us joy, hope, and inspiration, just as the morning light brings new life to the world.

And as we journey through this day, let us remember Iqbal's wisdom:

"Travel far, travel wide, and travel often,

For the journey is the destination, and the path is the prize." (Allama Iqbal) May our paths be filled with wonder, discovery, and growth.

In the spirit of Firdousi's epic poetry, let us embrace the beauty of this day:

"The world is a garden, full of flowers so fair,

Let us cherish each moment, and show we care." (Firdousi) May our hearts be filled with love, compassion, and kindness.

As Masti Venkatesha Iyengar's poetry so eloquently puts it:

"Life is a canvas, waiting for our brushstrokes bold,

Let us paint our story, with colors young and old." (Masti Venkatesha Iyengar) May our lives be a masterpiece of creativity, passion, and purpose.

And finally, let Khalil Gibran's words guide us:

"Say not, 'I have found the truth,' but rather, 'I have found a truth.'" (Khalil Gibran)

May we remain curious, open-minded, and receptive to the many wonders and truths that life has to offer.

I hope these poetic verses bring a touch of deep understanding in our complex life in the ancient land of the mighty Indus.

8) My last thoughts are inspired by Chanakya's timeless wisdom: for leaders of today and future:

The Chanakya Imperative: Timeless Wisdom for Enduring Leadership:

In the realm of politics, where intrigue and deception often reign supreme, the ancient Indian sage Chanakya stands as a beacon of strategic brilliance. His seminal work, the Arthashastra, and the Chanakya Niti, offer a treasure trove of wisdom for leaders seeking to navigate the complexities of statecraft and emerge triumphant.

I. The Foundations of Leadership:

- Vision: A leader's vision is the bedrock of their success. It must be clear, compelling, and communicated with unwavering conviction.

- <u>Integrity:</u> Unshakeable integrity is the hallmark of a true leader. It fosters trust, loyalty, and inspires others to follow.

- <u>Adaptability:</u> The ability to adapt is crucial in an ever-changing world. Leaders must be willing to pivot when circumstances dictate.

II. <u>The Art of Strategy:</u>

- <u>Know Thyself:</u> Self-awareness is paramount. Leaders must understand their strengths, weaknesses, and motivations to make informed decisions.

- <u>Know Thy Enemy:</u> Understand the motivations, desires, and weaknesses of adversaries to outmanoeuvre them.

- <u>Choose Thy Battles:</u> Select conflicts wisely, prioritizing those that align with your vision and values.

III. **<u>The Power of Alliances:</u>**

- <u>Forge Strategic Partnerships</u>: Cultivate relationships with key stakeholders to create a robust support network.

- <u>Nurture Loyalty:</u> Reward loyalty and dedication, for a loyal cadre of supporters is a leader's greatest asset.

- <u>Maintain Flexibility:</u> Be willing to adjust alliances as circumstances change, lest they become liabilities.

IV. **<u>The Importance of Knowledge:</u>**

- <u>Seek Wisdom:</u> Surround yourself with wise counsel and diverse perspectives to inform decision- making.

- <u>Stay Informed:</u> Maintain a deep understanding of the world, its complexities, and emerging trends.

- Foster Innovation: Encourage creativity and innovation to stay ahead of the curve.

V. The Ethics of Leadership;

- Justice: Uphold justice and fairness in all decisions, ensuring the welfare of the people.

- Compassion: Balance strength with empathy, demonstrating compassion when warranted.

- Humility: Remain humble, recognizing the limitations of power and the importance of teamwork.

VI. The Legacy of Leadership;

- Build for the Future: Prioritize long-term prosperity over short-term gains.

- Inspire Others: Leave a lasting impact by inspiring future generations.

- Embrace Legacy: Recognize that a leader's legacy is their most enduring contribution.

In conclusion, the Chanakya Imperative offers timeless wisdom for leaders seeking to navigate the complexities of politics and statecraft. By embracing these principles, leaders can build a lasting legacy, inspiring future generations to follow in their footsteps. As Chanakya himself said, "A leader who is just, fair, and wise will be revered forever."

On a scale of 1 To 10; where will history place Imran khan after juxta positioning with CHANKIA's philosophy of leadership;

A fascinating question! Chanakya, would not criticise rather advise Imran Khan as he advised Chandra Gupta Moria to:

1. Cultivate strategic alliances: In today's complex political landscape, building strong relationships with key stakeholders is crucial. Identify potential allies,

and nurture those relationships to create a robust support network that he could not in his first stint in power:

2. Master the art of diplomacy: Some thing IMRAN totally failed to do was to Develop expertise in negotiation, mediation, and conflict resolution. This helps navigate the intricate web of political relationships and interests.

3. Prioritize economic development: Focus on sustainable economic growth, investing in education, infrastructure, and innovation. A strong economy is the foundation of a prosperous nation. Imran tried but circumstances did not allow him, nor did he have a real strong team to make it happen.

4. Embrace adaptability and pragmatism: Khan was totally wanting on this count: Leader should be always willing to adjust strategies as circumstances change. Flexibility and pragmatism are essential in the ever-shifting political terrain.

5. Surround yourself with wise counsel: He did not do it, nor was interested in doing this bit. He Failed to Assemble a team of experienced and dedicated loyal advisors who could provide informed guidance on critical matters. And stay loyal to his cause than their petty personal interests.

6. Foster a culture of meritocracy: Encourage talent and expertise to rise to the forefront, rather than relying on personal relationships of yes men who are unaware about the art of serving the leader to make him look larger than life.

7. Stay vigilant and proactive: Khan's men absolutely failed to Anticipate challenges and address them before they escalated: A proactive approach could help maintain stability and momentum.

For the last word, I would suggest;

"The Chanakya Imperative: Timeless Wisdom for Enduring Leadership".

Key Takeaways:

1. Imran Khan should Synthesise strengths and weaknesses, highlighting areas for growth and improvement.
2. Integrate Chanakya's principles from the Arthashastra and Chanakya Niti, demonstrating their relevance in modern Pakistani politics.
3. He should appoint strategic loyal men to *Offer* actionable advice for Khan and future party leaders, emphasizing the importance of strategic thinking, adaptability, and wise counsel.
4. A ruler like IMRAN khan with a vision for Pakistan's future, inspired by Chanakya's wisdom, and Khan's potential can leave a lasting legacy.

By weaving together these elements, his leadership will serve as a shining star, guiding leaders to come, and cementing Imran Khan's place in history as a leader who embraced timeless wisdom.

"In the annals of time, where courage is the ultimate test, Profiles of valor shine bright, yet falter, and find rest.

Imran Khan and other, towering figures of might,

Failed, not for lack of heart, but for neglecting the art of sight.

For in a world where morality is oft forsaken,

Goodness, bravery, and selflessness are insufficient tokens. One must embrace the cunning of Chanakya's guile,The courage of a lion, and the fox's subtle smile.

As Rumi, the sage, once said, 'The wound is the place where the light enters you.' But without the wisdom of the ages, even light can be subdued.

In the words of Sun Tzu, 'Know yourself, know your enemy, and know the terrain.' For in the battle against evil, only the vigilant and cunning will reign.

Imran Khan and others, take heed of this timeless refrain,That in a world where shadows roam, only the wise and brave will sustain. So let us learn from the masters, East and West, and the Islamic Golden Age, To temper our hearts with wisdom, and our courage with strategic engage."

Chapter 9: Profiles of Courageous Leaders

Ancient Times;

1. Leonidas (Sparta): Like Imran Khan, Leonidas defied the mighty Persian Empire, leading a small force against overwhelming odds. Success: Inspirational leadership, but ultimately failed to defeat the Persians.
2. Hannibal (Carthage): Challenged Roman dominance, using innovative tactics. Success: Won several battles, but ultimately defeated and exiled.

Medieval Times;

1. Richard the Lionheart (England): Fought against Saladin's Muslim forces, advocating for Christian dominance. Success: Some military victories, but failed to retake Jerusalem.
2. Robert the Bruce (Scotland): Defied English rule, leading a guerrilla war. Success: Secured Scottish independence.

Contemporary Times;

1. *Napoleon Bonaparte (France)*: Rose to power, challenging European monarchies and empires. Success: Military conquests, but eventual defeat and exile.
2. *Winston Churchill (UK)*: Led Britain against Nazi Germany, advocating for democracy and freedom. Success: Played a crucial role in Allied victory.
3. *Charles de Gaulle (France)*: Resisted Nazi occupation, leading the Free French Forces. Success: Helped liberate France, became President.

Comparison with Imran Khan;

Imran Khan's leadership style and challenges draw parallels with these historical figures:

- Defying established powers*: Like Leonidas, Hannibal, and Napoleon, Imran Khan challenges entrenched interests and powerful forces (political, economic, and external).
- Inspirational leadership*: Imran Khan, like Leonidas and Churchill, inspires loyalty and passion in his followers.
- Reform agenda*: Imran Khan's focus on anti-corruption, accountability, and social justice resonates with Robert the Bruce's fight for Scottish independence and de Gaulle's resistance against Nazi occupation.
- Strategic communication*: Imran Khan's use of media and public engagement is reminiscent of Napoleon's propaganda efforts and Churchill's oratory skills.

Successes and Failures;

- **Successes;**
  - Imran Khan's leadership has brought attention to corruption and accountability in Pakistan.
  - He has inspired a new generation of Pakistanis to engage in politics.

- **Failures:**
  - Imran Khan's government has faced criticism for economic mismanagement and inability to deliver on some promises.
  - He has struggled to build consensus and work with opposition parties.

Keep in mind that historical analogies are imperfect, and Imran Khan's journey is still unfolding. However, this comparison offers insights into the challenges and opportunities faced by leaders who dare to challenge the status quo.

Imran Khan, the enigmatic leader, stands as a modern-day champion of the Indus Valley's soul, echoing the whispers of Mohenjo-Daro and Harappa's ancient spirits. His quest for the liberation of this land, cradle of the three great early human civilisations', is a symphony of East and West, blending the poetry of resistance with the philosophy of freedom.

In the realm of the Indus, where the sacred river's waters nourish the soil, Imran Khan's leadership is a beacon, shining bright against the darkness of autocracy, slavery, and plunder.

His voice resonates with the echoes of;

- Mohenjo-Daro's majestic grandeur, where the citadel of the Indus Valley Civilization once stood tall, a testament to the ingenuity and wisdom of a bygone era.
- Harappa's ancient wisdom, where the ruins whisper secrets of a sophisticated culture, born from the confluence of the Saraswati and Indus rivers.

Imran Khan's odyssey is a modern-day retelling of the Mahabharata's epic struggle, where the forces of light and darkness clash in a battle for the soul of the nation. His leadership embodies the essence of;

- <u>Jehad & Dharma</u>; the eternal quest for righteousness and justice, guiding him through the labyrinth of politics and power.
- <u>Deep Islamic faith & Karma</u>; the law of cause and effect, driving him to challenge the status quo and confront the plunderers of Pakistan's resources.

With the Mightiest Quran the Devine scripture makes his soul and Bhagavad Gita's worldly wisdom as his guiding light, Imran Khan navigates the complexities of governance, ever mindful of the delicate balance between;

- <u>-Islamic justice & ancient Purushartha</u>; the pursuit of individual and collective well-being, and

o <u>Islamic socialism & ancient Raj Dharma</u>; the sacred duty of leadership, to protect and serve the people.

His vision for a Naya Pakistan (New Pakistan) is a poetic expression of the East's spiritual heritage, merged with the West's ideals of democracy and freedom. It is a dream of;

- Haqiqi Azadi & ancient Swaraj, self-rule, where the people are sovereign, and their voices are heard.
- people power & ancient Gram Swaraj, village self-rule, where local communities thrive, and prosperity is shared.

Through Imran Khan's leadership, the land of the Indus River, once home to the ancient three great civilisations, now yearns for a renaissance, a rebirth of its former glory. His struggle is a testament to the power of the human spirit, a symphony of:

- Azadi or ancient Bhakti, devotion, to the cause of freedom and justice.
- power of Allah & ancient Shakti, the divine feminine energy, nurturing and empowering the people.

As the Indus River flows, a symbol of eternal change and renewal, Imran Khan's journey represents the eternal quest for liberation, a poetic expression of the human condition. His leadership is a beacon, shining bright, illuminating the path to a brighter future, where the soul of Mohenjo-Daro and Harappa can finally find peace. Where a seven thousand years of human struggle against climate change, colonialism, occupation, slavery, religious hatred, meaningless wars have wounded the soul of mighty Indus Valley and her children cry for Haqqani Azadi from all forces of suppressions of freedom economy slavery, political slavery and toxic behaviour that has seeped into the soul of Indus Valley society our beloved Pakistan.

Opportunistic politics often involves prioritizing personal gain and power over principles, ethics, and the greater good. This approach can lead to short-term benefits but often results in long-term negative consequences, such as:

- Erosion of trust in institutions and leaders
- Political instability and polarization
- Economic stagnation and inequality
- Compromised national sovereignty and security <u>Historical examples</u>

include:
- Benedict Arnold's betrayal of the United States during the American Revolutionary War
- Macbeth's prioritization of power over loyalty and integrity in Shakespeare's play

In South Asia, figures like Mir Jaffer and Mir Sadiq are often cited as examples of opportunistic politics, as they collaborated with colonial powers, leading to adverse outcomes for their respective regions. In today's Pakistan that role has been played by status quo leaders like Nawaz Sharif and Asif Ali Zardari who have made Pakistan a economic slave of neo liberal capitalist and hegemonic powers through their corruption, plunder and bad governance for almost forty years by turns: The men have been defined as economic hitmen in a book by this name:

In literature, opportunistic politics is often depicted as a tragic flaw, leading to downfall and chaos. As the poet Alexander Pope wrote, "Ambition is the idol of men's souls, and it is a mark of weak minds to be swayed by it."

In contemporary times, Imran khan the jailed leader of Pakistan has successfully established that it's essential to promote principled leadership, transparency, and accountability to mitigate the negative consequences of opportunistic politics.

Another fascinating topic of Imran khan and other great men! Let's delve into the lives of these great men and their approach to love, exploring how their passions intersected with their professions and personalities.

Lord Byron, the English poet, was notorious for his tumultuous love life, with numerous affairs and romantic entanglements. His poetry often reflected his passion and heartbreak.

President John F. Kennedy's charm and charisma extended to his romantic conquests, with rumoured affairs and a captivating smile.

Imran Khan, the former Pakistani cricketer and politician, had a high-profile marriage to Jemima Goldsmith, which very unfortunately ended in divorce passionately hurting the feelings of Pakistanis, who deeply respect Jemima for her character and love for Pakistan. A great Lady who has mothered two amazing sons of Imran Khan Whose love life has been subject to media scrutiny. But this great man has never uttered a single word on the subject. A sign of nobility.

Imran Khan, in many ways, embodies the spirit of great Muslim leaders who have left an indelible mark on history over the last thousand years. These leaders were united by their ability to inspire, their commitment to justice, and their unwavering faith in the principles that guided their governance. From the golden age of the Abbasid Caliphate to the transformative leadership of Muhammad Ali Jinnah, the echoes of their wisdom and vision can be seen in Imran Khan's journey as a statesman and reformer.

Harun al-Rashid, the celebrated Abbasid Caliph, ruled over an empire that thrived on intellectual and cultural pursuits. He valued justice and scholarship, creating an environment where innovation flourished, and the welfare of the people was paramount. Imran Khan's emphasis on education, reflected in initiatives like Namal University, mirrors this focus on knowledge as the foundation of a prosperous society. Harun's engagement with scholars and his personal interest in ensuring fair governance resonate with Imran's vision for a Pakistan where accountability and transparency are at the heart of its institutions.

Salahuddin Ayyubi, or Saladin, is revered not only for his military prowess but for his chivalry, humility, and unwavering commitment to justice. Salahuddin united a fractured Muslim world to reclaim Jerusalem during the Crusades, demonstrating that even amidst adversity, unity and justice can prevail. Imran Khan's fight against corruption and his call for an end to Pakistan's internal divisions parallel Salahuddin's mission to unify for a greater cause. Like Salahuddin, Imran has remained focused on uplifting the marginalized and has shown humility in his personal life, reinforcing his image as a servant of the people rather than a ruler.

Sultan Mehmed II, known as Mehmed the Conqueror, transformed Constantinople into Istanbul, symbolizing the meeting point of East and West. His reign was marked by inclusivity and cultural synthesis, drawing from both Islamic and non-Islamic traditions to create a thriving empire. Imran Khan's emphasis on Pakistan's rich cultural and spiritual heritage reflects this same inclusivity. His advocacy for minority rights and his efforts to promote Pakistan as a nation where all citizens are treated equally under the law echo Mehmed's vision for a society that thrives on diversity and tolerance.

Suleiman the Magnificent, often hailed as a legislator and reformer, was instrumental in codifying laws and ensuring that justice was accessible to all his subjects. His reign exemplified balance—combining strength with compassion. Imran Khan's focus on reforming Pakistan's judicial system, fighting entrenched corruption, and creating a level playing field for all Pakistanis aligns with Suleiman's legacy. Suleiman's belief in governance as a sacred trust to serve the people is deeply mirrored in Imran's aspirations for a Riyasat-e-Madina, where leaders are accountable to their people.

Tipu Sultan, the Tiger of Mysore, is remembered for his valiant resistance against British colonialism and his modernization of governance. Tipu's emphasis on innovation and his refusal to bow to external domination reflect Imran Khan's stance on Pakistan's sovereignty. Imran's push for self-reliance, economic independence, and his calls to end Pakistan's reliance on foreign aid are modern expressions of Tipu's vision of a strong and independent state.

Muhammad Ali Jinnah, the founder of Pakistan, demonstrated unparalleled leadership in the struggle for the nation's creation. His clarity of vision, ability to inspire, and dedication to the principles of justice and equality set the foundation for Pakistan's identity. Imran Khan's journey shares many parallels with Jinnah's—a relentless fight against the odds, the ability to mobilize the masses, and a focus on the principles of accountability and governance. Both leaders sought to create a nation that upheld the dignity and rights of its people, rooted in Islamic values but embracing modernity.

Imran Khan's leadership reflects the timeless qualities that define great Muslim leaders. His charisma has inspired millions, uniting them around a vision of justice and reform. His spiritual journey, from a cricketing hero to a political leader who frequently invokes the principles of the Quran and the life of the Prophet Muhammad (PBUH), resonates deeply in a society longing for moral and ethical leadership. Like Harun al-Rashid and Salahuddin Ayyubi, Imran has drawn on faith and spirituality to guide his decisions, finding strength in the teachings of Islam to navigate the complexities of modern governance.

Imran Khan's approach to justice and accountability also finds parallels with the legacy of Suleiman the Magnificent and Tipu Sultan. His insistence on rooting out corruption and reforming institutions reflects a commitment to ensuring that governance serves the people rather than a select elite. This commitment has earned him both admiration and resistance, as he challenges entrenched systems of privilege and power. His resilience in the face of political adversity is reminiscent of leaders like Salahuddin, who remained steadfast despite immense challenges.

The historical Muslim leaders who shaped the world did so by recognizing the importance of education, justice, and unity. Imran Khan's vision for Pakistan, with its emphasis on these very principles, positions him as a modern torchbearer of their legacy. His journey from cricketing fame to political leadership, coupled with his spiritual transformation, underscores his unique ability to bridge the past with the present. He draws strength from Islamic teachings while embracing the demands of a globalized world, much like the great Muslim leaders who balanced tradition with progress.

Imran Khan's commitment to a Riyasat-e-Madina model—a society based on justice, equality, and compassion—is a testament to his aspiration to emulate the governance principles of the Prophet Muhammad (PBUH). His dedication to creating a welfare state that uplifts the marginalized reflects the teachings of Islam and the examples set by leaders like Harun al-Rashid and Salahuddin. His vision for Pakistan is not merely about political reform but about a moral and spiritual awakening that reconnects the nation with its roots.

In a world where opportunistic politics and moral compromise often dominate, Imran Khan's leadership offers a refreshing contrast. His emphasis on self-reliance, education, and justice is a call to action for Pakistanis to reclaim their identity and destiny. The qualities he shares with historical Muslim leaders—vision, resilience, and a commitment to justice—are what make his journey so compelling. As he continues to navigate the challenges of leadership, Imran Khan stands as a beacon of hope, a modern-day reflection of the values that have defined some of the greatest Muslim leaders over the centuries.

Common threads among these men include:

1. Charisma and charm
2. Passionate and intense personalities
3. Multiple romantic entanglements
4. Intersection of love and power
5. Public scrutiny and media attention

Their approaches to love were often marked by:

1. Intensity and passion
2. Romantic idealism
3. A desire for conquest and exploration
4. Complexity and nuance
5. A blurring of lines between love and power

These men's love lives were often a reflection of their personalities, passions, and professions. While some were known for their romantic exploits, others had more complex and nuanced approaches to love.

Chapter 10: Imran Khan's Tenure as Prime Minister of Pakistan

Imran Khan's Tenure as Prime Minister of Pakistan

Imran Khan's government faced criticism for its handling of key portfolios, particularly finance and economy, which were led by inexperienced individuals, including Asad Umar. Despite his good intentions, Imran Khan's reliance on personal friends and loyalists rather than competent professionals led to poor governance.

Asad Umar's tenure as Finance Minister was marked by controversial decisions, such as the drastic devaluation of the Pakistani rupee, which led to high inflation and economic instability. His policies were criticized for being ad hoc and lacking a clear direction.

Imran Khan's focus on pursuing corruption cases against opposition leaders, while justified, consumed a significant amount of his time and energy. He should have put his interior in-charge Of such stuff and himself worked for bigger issues staring menacingly at Pakistan: But getting his adversaries led to a neglect of other critical areas, such as governance, economy, and foreign policy.

Moreover, the military's support for corrupt opposition leaders, as alleged by Imran Khan, further weakened his position. The military's influence in Pakistani politics is significant, and their backing of opposition leaders undermined Imran Khan's authority.

Incompetent governance, lack of experience, and poor decision-making ultimately led to Imran Khan's downfall. His failure to address economic woes, maintain political alliances, and navigate complex relationships with the military and international powers sealed his fate.

- "Imran Khan's economic team: A mix of experience and inexperience" (Dawn News, 2018)

- "Asad Umar's controversial tenure as finance minister" (The News International, 2020)

- "Imran Khan's anti-corruption drive: A political vendetta?" (The Express Tribune, 2020)

- "Military's role in Pakistani politics: A challenge to civilian governments" (The Nation, 2020)

Analysis:

Imran Khan's government was plagued by incompetent governance, which stemmed from his reliance on inexperienced individuals and personal friends. Asad Umar's controversial decisions as Finance Minister exacerbated economic woes, while Imran Khan's focus on pursuing corruption cases distracted him from critical governance issues. The military's support for corrupt opposition leaders further weakened his position, ultimately leading to his downfall.

Imran Khan's fall from power was a result of a combination of factors, which can be traced through various reports and papers from 2018 to 2022.

Here's a comprehensive analysis:

1. *Economic Mismanagement*:

Imran Khan's government failed to address Pakistan's economic woes, including a large trade deficit, low tax collection, and a heavy reliance on foreign loans (Source: IMF Reports, 2019-2022).

2. *Political Miscalculations*:

Imran Khan's party, PTI, struggled to maintain coalition partners and failed to build consensus with opposition parties, leading to political instability.

3. *Military Discontent*:

Imran Khan's attempts to assert civilian control over the military and reduce their political influence led to tensions with the powerful military establishment.

4. *US-Pakistan Relations*:

Imran Khan's criticism of US policies, particularly on Afghanistan and Kashmir, strained relations with the US, leading to reduced aid and support (Source:

5. *Corruption Cases*:

Imran Khan's government faced allegations of corruption and nepotism, including high-profile cases against his close aides and family members.

6. *Opposition Unity*:

The opposition parties united against Imran Khan's government, forming a strong coalition that challenged his authority.

7. *Regime Change Operation*:

The US, in coordination with other international powers, allegedly supported the opposition and facilitated Imran Khan's ouster.

8. *Internal Party Conflicts*:

Imran Khan faced internal party conflicts, with some PTI members criticizing his leadership style and decision-making.

9. *Public Discontent*:

Imran Khan's government faced growing public discontent due to rising inflation, unemployment, and poor governance (Source: Gallup Pakistan, 2022).

10. *Constitutional Crisis*:

Imran Khan's attempt to dissolve the parliament and call early elections led to a constitutional crisis, ultimately resulting in his ouster (Source: Al Jazeera, 2022).

In conclusion;

Imran Khan's fall from power was a result of a combination of economic, political, military, and diplomatic factors, as well as alleged external interference. His government's inability to address pressing issues, maintain coalition partners, and navigate complex relationships with the military and international powers ultimately led to his downfall.

Readers may want to explore these factors in greater detail, analyzing how they intersected and ultimately led to Imran Khan's ouster. A world-class analysis would require a nuanced understanding of Pakistan's complex political landscape, economic challenges, and geopolitical dynamics.

Let me provide a more in-depth analysis of the factors that led to Imran Khan's ouster, exploring the intricate web of political, economic, and geopolitical dynamics that culminated in his downfall.

Economic Mismanagement

Imran Khan's government inherited a struggling economy, but his policies exacerbated the issues. The currency was devalued, inflation soared, and the trade deficit widened. The IMF bailouts and austerity measures further worsened the situation, leading to widespread discontent.

Political Miscalculations

Imran Khan's PTI struggled to maintain coalition partners, losing key allies like the MQM and the PML-Q. By His attempts to assert control over the military and reduce their political influence backfired, leading to tensions with the powerful military establishment.

Military Discontent

Imran Khan's efforts to sideline the military without delivering and building a strong power base at grassroots annoyed his greedy generals: As politics is a pet game of military In Pakistan and to reduce their economic influence angered the military brass. The military, historically a dominant force in Pakistani politics, saw Imran Khan's moves as a threat to their power and interests.

US-Pakistan Relations

Imran Khan's criticism of US policies, although correct was not nuanced particularly on Afghanistan and Kashmir, this strained relations with the US. The US reduced aid and support, weakening Imran Khan's position. General Bajwa gave incorrect information to USA about khan's dislike of American hegemony:

Corruption Cases

High-profile corruption cases against Imran Khan's close aides and family members eroded his anti- corruption stance and damaged his reputation.

Opposition Unity

The opposition parties united against Imran Khan's government, under the auspices of GHQ forming a strong coalition beefed up by General Bajwa who challenged his authority. The opposition exploited Imran Khan's weaknesses, capitalizing on public discontent and economic woes and military support.

Regime Change Operation

The US, in coordination with other international powers, allegedly supported the opposition and facilitated Imran Khan's ouster. This external interference further weakened Imran Khan's position.

Internal Party Conflicts

Imran Khan faced internal party conflicts, with some PTI members criticizing his leadership style and decision-making. This internal strife weakened his grip on power and military easily shaped a forward block of such MNAs who had not got their piece of pie.

Public Discontent

Growing public discontent due to rising inflation, unemployment, and poor governance eroded Imran Khan's popularity. The public saw him as out of touch with their struggles and unable to deliver on his promises.

Constitutional Crisis

Imran Khan's very hasty attempt to dissolve the parliament and call early elections led to a constitutional crisis. The Supreme Court intervened, blocking his move and ultimately leading to his ouster. Khan should have sat on the opposition benches and watched the government wither away like autumn leaves under the given circumstances. Khan made yet another blunder and he forced dissolution of Punjab and KPK Assembly which turned out to be his waterloo:

These factors intersected and reinforced each other, creating a perfect storm that led to Imran Khan's downfall. His government's inability to address economic woes, maintain political alliances, and navigate complex relationships with the military and international powers ultimately sealed his fate.

This analysis should provide a rich backdrop for offering insights into the complex dynamics that led to Imran Khan's ouster.

Imran Khan's decision to appoint Usman Buzdar as Chief Minister of Punjab was widely criticized, and is seen as a major factor in his government's downfall. Buzdar's lack of experience and leadership skills led to poor governance and mismanagement in Punjab, which contributed to Imran Khan's declining popularity.

In contrast, Shah Mahmood Qureshi, who was appointed as Foreign Minister, was seen as a competent leader and a potential candidate for the Chief Minister position. Qureshi's experience and skills would have been better utilized in Punjab, where he could have strengthened the PTI and managed the military and opposition more effectively.

Aleem Khan and Jahangir Tareen, said to be a super corrupt pair both controversial figures with allegations of corruption and land grabbing, were seen as calling the shots in Punjab. Their internal power struggles and rivalries weakened Imran Khan's position and compromised his relationship with the military and opposition.

The betrayal of Imran Khan by his own MNAs who were given tickets by establishment by denying tickets to his loyal PTI people who had worked for the party for years and years also weakened IK when the acid test of loyalty came.

Research sources:

- "Usman Buzdar: A Chief Minister Imran Khan couldn't afford to sack" (The News International, 2020)
- "Shah Mahmood Qureshi: The man who could have saved Imran Khan's government" (The Express Tribune, 2020)
- "Aleem Khan and Jahangir Tareen: The men who brought down Imran Khan" (Pakistan Today, 2020)
- "PTI's internal strife: A tale of betrayal and loyalty" (Dawn News, 2020)

Imran Khan's appointment of Usman Buzdar as Chief Minister of Punjab was a strategic blunder that led to poor governance and mismanagement. Regime Change Eventually overthrew his government but it boosted his political narrative which he sold very well.

The fall of IMRAN khan and false flag operations that transpired thereafter is a Shakespearean tragedy.

There are several examples in history where states on the verge of being erased from the map were restored by great leaders with vision prescience and wisdom;

- **The Roman Republic** (509-27 BC): Rome faced internal conflicts, corruption, and political polarization, leading to its downfall. However, under the leadership of Augustus Caesar (27 BC-14 AD), Rome was restored, and the Roman Empire was established, marking a new era of stability and prosperity.

- **The Persian Empire** (550-330 BC): After the death of Cyrus the Great, the empire faced internal conflicts, wars, and decay. However, under the leadership of Darius I (522-486 BC), the empire was restored, and it experienced a period of revival and expansion.

Islamic:

- The Abbasid Caliphate (750-1258 AD): The Abbasid Caliphate faced internal conflicts, regional challenges, and decay. However, under the leadership of Caliph Al-Mamun (813-833 AD), the caliphate was restored, and it experienced a period of cultural, scientific, and economic revival.
- The Ottoman Empire (1299-1924 AD): The Ottoman Empire faced internal conflicts, corruption, and decline. However, under the leadership of Sultan Abdul Hamid II (1876-1909 AD), the empire was restored, and it experienced a period of modernization and reform.

Western:

- **The United States of America** (1783-1865 AD): The US faced internal conflicts, political polarization, and the Civil War. However, under the leadership of President Abraham Lincoln (1861-1865 AD), the country was restored, and it experienced a period of reconstruction and growth.
- **France (1789-1799 AD)**: France faced internal conflicts, political instability, and the Reign of Terror. However, under the leadership of Napoleon Bonaparte (1799-1815 AD), France was restored, and it experienced a period of military conquests and cultural revival.

Eastern:

- China (221-206 BC): The Qin dynasty faced internal conflicts, corruption, and decay. However, under the leadership of Emperor Wu of Han (141-87 BC), China was restored, and it experienced a period of economic, cultural, and military revival.

- Japan (1868-1912 AD): Japan faced internal conflicts, political instability, and modernization challenges. However, under the leadership of Emperor Meiji (1868-1912 AD), Japan was restored, and it experienced a period of rapid modernization and growth.

In each of these examples, a leadership emerged that was able to overcome the internal conflicts, restore stability, and lead the state to a period of revival and growth. The common factors among these examples include:

1. <u>Strong leadership:</u> A leader who was able to unite the people, restore stability, and implement reforms.
2. <u>Vision:</u> A well prepared leader, with a trusted team of subordinates who knew how to go about their leaders' clear vision for the future of the state and its people. Imran kept toying with those who were planted by establishment for its own ulterior considerations. Imran was trapped like his predecessors, although being an honest man he stood up to the establishment but by that time his government had lost touch and clarity of everything:
3. <u>Reforms:</u> Implementation of reforms to address the root causes of the crisis. Imran's obsession with arrests of rival corrupt opposition consumed his time and the reforms never saw the desired dawn of reality.
4. <u>Inclusivity:</u> Involvement of all stakeholders in the decision-making process. The PM a great leader never considered talking to all stakeholders as if he was not running a democracy where doors of reconciliation and talks are never closed: PM knowingly that big brothers In GHQ are always around to extract their pound of flesh from every elected civilian prime minister.
5. <u>External support:</u> In some cases, external support and cooperation played a crucial role in the restoration of the state. Imran never entertained this idea, that in a political hot bed as Pakistan where army calls the shots, external support becomes very helpful at such times.

In the case of Pakistan, a similar approach was perceived to be taken by the great leader and it was believed that a leadership has emerged that was able to unite the people, restore stability, and implement reforms to address the root causes of the crisis;

1. Imran failed to shape A national dialogue to unite the people and establish a shared vision for the future. He took the same primordial route of crushing his adversaries like his predecessors:
2. Implementation of reforms to address corruption, political instability, and economic challenges. His selection of minister's advisors was extremely poor who led him down and he was stuck in the middle of nowhere.
3. He failed to manage the Involvement of all stakeholders in the decision-making process to ensure inclusivity and ownership.
4. He had no clue of External support and cooperation to provide resources and expertise to support the restoration of the state. All of the prime minister's men were opportunistic; Yes men, no one had the courage to say anything that May displease the boss: people Like Asad Umar the jewel of his cabinet was building himself to replace Imran khan, and Imran khan had put all his economic eggs in Asad's basket: Greatness of a statesman lies in the choice of his minister's advisors & Generals. Imran khan miserably failed to form a team of loyal informed dedicated trusted men to run the affairs of his government: He had failed in giving tickets to his loyal dedicated well-read men under influence of traitors like Aleem Khan and Jahangir Tareen, And now the worst people were brought to his cabinet mostly recommended by establishment directly or indirectly through their clever men or women who work for the establishment: One such appointment was that of Chief election commission of Pakistan:

Cabinet barring few like Ali Muhammad khan, Shaheryar Afridi , Shah Mahmood QURASHI to a certain extent Hammad Azhar who proved themselves turned out to be his only best bets. IK screwed his term playing wrong balls on slippery wickets and at the appropriate time , as was expected; the empire General Bajwa struck back and bumped him off:

However, it is important to note that each historical example is unique, and the specific context and circumstances of Pakistan's crisis must be taken into account when developing a solution in future:

Had Plato been alive and asked about his solutions to ailments of Pakistan , I am sure the big man would have said" My dear friend, reconstructing a state like Pakistan, beset by turmoil and division, is a daunting task indeed. Yet, as Plato, I shall offer some unorthodox solutions, blending ancient wisdom with modern pragmatism.

Since Pakistan's predicament stems from a fractured society, it's important to have a;

1. Dialogue: Convene all stakeholders, and facilitate a shared understanding of the nation's woes.
2. Establish a TRC to investigate past human rights abuses, corruption, and political machinations. This will help Pakistan come to terms with its troubled past, and pave the way for reconciliation.
3. Decentralization and Regional Autonomy*: Empower provinces.
4. Establish a government, staffed by experts and professionals, to manage key sectors like economy, education, and healthcare.
5. Deliver to make people happy and then get rid of Military in small steps without making them feel left out or cornered.
6. Launch a nationwide education initiative focusing on critical thinking, civic literacy, and cultural heritage.
7. Implement a progressive economic agenda, prioritizing sustainable development, social welfare, and entrepreneurship.
8. Engage powerful countries and global powers in a diplomatic initiative to resolve regional conflicts, secure economic cooperation, and ensure peaceful coexistence.
9. Draft a new constitution, incorporating principles of democracy, federalism, and human rights.
10. Establish a new leadership selection process, emphasizing merit, Reform institutions to ensure transparency, efficiency, and responsiveness to citizens' needs.

The unorthodox solutions will require courage, resilience, and collective effort Through which Pakistan' can reconstruct a shattered state and forge a beacon of hope for the world – a new Republic, built on the principles of justice, equality, and freedom.":

The intricate web of political, economic, and geopolitical dynamics that led to

Imran Khan's downfall is a fascinating tale of power, politics, and intrigue. As the great scholar, Aristotle, once said, "The whole is more than the sum of its parts." Indeed, the confluence of these factors created a perfect storm that ultimately led to Imran Khan's ouster.

The economic mismanagement, political miscalculations, military discontent, US-Pakistan relations, corruption cases, opposition unity, regime change operation, internal party conflicts, public discontent, and constitutional crisis all played a significant role in Imran Khan's downfall. As the ancient Greek philosopher, Heraclitus, said, "The only thing that is constant is change." Imran Khan's inability to adapt to changing circumstances and address the pressing issues facing Pakistan ultimately led to his demise.

The great Pakistani poet, Allama Iqbal, once said, "The ultimate fate of a nation is determined by its character." Imran Khan's leadership was marked by a series of miscalculations and missteps that ultimately led to his downfall. His failure to address the economic woes, maintain political alliances, and navigate complex relationships with the military and international powers raises important questions about leadership, power, and accountability.

As the contemporary scholar, Fareed Zakaria, noted, "The rise and fall of great powers is a recurring theme in history." Imran Khan's ouster serves as a reminder that even the most powerful leaders can fall victim to the vicissitudes of politics and the complexities of power.

In conclusion, the story of Imran Khan's downfall is a cautionary tale about the dangers of hubris, the importance of adaptability, and the need for effective leadership in times of crisis. As the great Chinese philosopher, Lao Tzu, said, "Nature does not hurry, yet everything is accomplished." The intricate web of factors that led to Imran Khan's ouster serves as a reminder that true leadership requires patience, wisdom, and a deep understanding of the complex forces that shape our world.

Alternative analysis of factors that led to the fall and Re-rise of Imran Khan's government, taking into account various dimensions, such as political dynamics, economic challenges, foreign policy issues, and internal governance;

Imran Khan's Government (2018-2022):

Imran Khan, a cricket superstar turned politician, assumed office as the Prime Minister of Pakistan on August 18, 2018 without an executive experience. PTI had reached commendable popularity & His

ascension to power was marked by promises of a "Naya Pakistan" (New Pakistan), focusing on anti- corruption, economic reform, and a more balanced foreign policy. However, after only three years and six months, his government fell amid Ambassadorial disclosures of a US-sponsored regime change operation, which ended his government but gave him an unbeatable & powerful narrative that politically he has Re-risen to heights unparalleled in history of Pakistan. The reasons behind his fall are mostly his wrong decisions during this political upheaval which is multifaceted and require a comprehensive analysis to understand.

Economic Challenges

1. Inflation and Currency Devaluation by Asad Umar.

- Inflation: Throughout Khan's tenure, was a significant issue. Essential commodities saw a sharp rise in prices, severely affecting the populace.
- Currency Devaluation: The Pakistani Rupee depreciated substantially against the US Dollar. This made imports more expensive, contributing further to inflation and economic instability.

2. IMF Bailout and Austerity Measures:

- Khan's government entered into a $6 billion bailout package with the International Monetary Fund (IMF). Due to Asad Umar's changing stances, the conditionalities attached by IMF, such as increased taxes and reduced government subsidies, led to public dismay and economic difficulties for the lower and middle classes.

3. **Unemployment and Poverty:**

- Despite ambitious plans, unemployment remained high, and poverty levels worsened. The economic policies did not translate into tangible benefits for the majority of the population, leading to widespread discontent. Hence Asad Umar had to be changed.

Political Dynamics

1. **Coalition Government Instability:**

Imran Khan's party, Pakistan Tehreek-e-Insaf (PTI), was deprived of an absolute majority through military machinations as it did not trust Imran khan fully and made him to rely on coalition partners in the control of military. This created a fragile political environment, making it susceptible to power shifts and alliances breaking down. Imran made a strategic political blunder by making Imran Ishmael a urban businessman the governor of Sind. The perfect choice would have been Zulfiqar Mirza former PPP minister and architect of Grand democratic alliance (GDA) that fought PPP in Sind and which stood with Imran khan to the very end. Zulfiqar Mirza a man of courage and character backed by Pir sahib of pagara would have tackled PPP wonderfully making PTI a very powerful alternative of PPP in Sind. Imran Ishmael a dandy urban bar boy was no match to politically astute politician from interior sindhi, Mr.Zulfiqar Mirza. But Ishmael was a friend of khan, he obliged him, and when the time came, Imran Ishmael, Ali Zaidi, Aleem khan, Jahangir Tareen were 1st to betray khan and join king's party. The beauty is that khan obliged every wrong friend and ignored every loyal, obedient political man of strong character integrity and strong political back ground.

2. Opposition Alliance (PDM):

- The status quo opposition parties formed the Pakistan Democratic Movement (PDM), a coalition made up of old status quo parties and aimed at challenging Khan's government. Their continuous protests and propaganda against his governance weakened the government's political standing.

3. Civil-Military Relations:

- The relationship between the civilian government and the military has always been pivotal in Pakistani politics. Despite initial support, towards the end of his tenure, reports of friction and lack of synchronization with military leadership emerged, further isolating Khan. COAS Qamar Javaid bajwa had his own plans and khan belatedly realized this, his cabinet colleagues were in bed with bajwa and khan was absolutely unaware about this movement of tectonic political plates.

Governance Issues

1. Administrative Challenges:

- Imran Khan's government faced criticism for poor governance and administrative inefficiencies. The reason was zero support of civil bureaucracy with PTI government. The PML-n and PPP were well entrenched in Punjab and Sind respectively. The other Key areas like health, education, and public services suffered from mismanagement and lack of effective reform and insufficient budgets.

2. Corruption Allegations and Judicial Scrutiny: **

- Khan's anti-corruption stance was central to his campaign. However, his government rightly faced allegations of corruption and nepotism, which hindered his narrative and led to public disillusionment. Khan himself a very honest man, was hurt by the corruption of his friends and appointees to ministerial & advisory positions on bases of their closeness to him and non was appointed for his meritorious achievements in any particular field.

3. Media Control and Freedom of Expression:

Military pushed khan to control the media, besides khan was rightly miser with throwing money to media like Nawaz-Zardari governments. Khan rightly thought that media is a private business, Why should it be funded by public money. This was a right step in public interest but media used to enjoy plums from public purse did not like it and turned against government of khan.

Instances of media censorship and suppression of freedom of expression was ordered by military but PTI government drew criticism both domestically and internationally. This not only tarnished the government's image but also alienated the educated urban populace. These are the tactics of Pakistan military to defame and weaken the civilian government's before getting rid of them.

Foreign Policy Intricacies

1. US-Pakistan Relations:

- The US-backed regime change narrative suggests a fallout due to Khan's foreign policy decisions, particularly his rightful inclination towards China and Russia. His opposition to participating in US-led initiatives and fight proxy wars of the Hegemon. His critique of US policies in Afghanistan created diplomatic rifts. The military advised khan to go Russia-China highway and briefed USA that it was khans' personal decision and military was not in the loop. General Bajwa Encouraged U.S State department to make things difficult for khan including his removal from office.

2. Geopolitical Maneuvering:

- Khan's visit to Russia on the eve of the Ukraine conflict is said to have strained relations with the West due to General bajwa saying different things to PM khan and his American counter parts in the

U.S. Khan's beneficial attempt to pivot towards Russia and China was seen as a move away from the traditional alignment with the US, leading to speculations of external involvement in his ousting. Although khan was never anti America, he was trying to procure more space for Pakistan in regional landscape and buy some cheap oil from Russia, by normalizing relations with that Eurasian country. Neighbor India was very close to Russia, buying cheap oil and procuring armaments from America and Russia simultaneously, but only Pakistan Would be penalized by US, khan failed to read the underlying military machinations.

3. **Regional Dynamics:**
   - Relations with neighboring countries, particularly India and Afghanistan, remained tense. While his stance on Kashmir resonated domestically, it didn't translate into tangible diplomatic successes with the west, which has an inherent dislike for Pakistan since its very creation.

Social and Cultural Factors

1. Public Discontent:

- The government's failure to deliver on key promises, coupled with economic hardship, led to public protests and a loss of faith in Khan's leadership. The initial wave of optimism gave way to frustration and disillusionment.

2. Religious Elements:

- The role of religious parties and groups also played a part. Instances of unrest fueled by religious sentiment added to the government's challenges, complicating the socio-political landscape.

Conclusion

The fall of Imran Khan's government was a result of a confluence of factors spanning economic mismanagement, political instability, governance failures, Military machinations and complex foreign policy dynamics. While the US-sponsored regime change operation add a layer of intrigue, the underlying causes point to internal systemic issues that plagued his tenure. For a comprehensive understanding, these factors must be analyzed in conjunction with each other, painting a holistic picture of the political environment in Pakistan during his rule.

This analysis should provide a substantive foundation on the rise fall, and re-rise of Imran Khan, offering a well-rounded perspective based on factual events and multifaceted reasoning.

Imran Khan's tenure as the Prime Minister of Pakistan is a story of hope, challenges, and eventual turmoil that continues to leave an indelible mark on the country's political landscape. His rise to power symbolized a break from the status quo, a fresh promise to tackle corruption and uplift the masses. Yet, his government was also marred by systemic issues, internal conflicts, and the crushing weight of Pakistan's longstanding institutional inefficiencies. An analysis of his tenure reveals a blend of transformative potential and missed opportunities, culminating in one of the most unprecedented political movements in Pakistan's history following his ouster.

Imran Khan's premiership began with an air of optimism, fueled by his long-standing rhetoric against corruption and promises to create a welfare state modeled after Riyasat-e-Madina. His anti-corruption stance resonated deeply with the masses, many of whom had grown weary of the entrenched dynastic politics represented by the Pakistan Muslim League-Nawaz (PML-N) and the Pakistan Peoples Party (PPP). For millions, Imran Khan was the embodiment of change—a figure untainted by the corruption scandals that had plagued Pakistan's political elite for decades.

However, as his government took charge, it quickly became apparent that turning slogans into action was no easy feat. One of the most significant challenges Imran Khan faced was the economy. He inherited a precarious economic situation, with a large trade deficit, ballooning debt, and dwindling foreign exchange reserves. To stabilize the economy, his government turned to the International Monetary Fund (IMF) for a bailout. The IMF's stringent conditions, including austerity measures, led to increased inflation and widespread economic hardship. The devaluation of the rupee, high fuel prices, and rising unemployment further fueled public frustration, undermining the government's narrative of economic reform.

The selection of Asad Umar as the Finance Minister in the early days of his government highlighted Imran Khan's reliance on personal loyalists over seasoned professionals. Umar's policies, including abrupt currency devaluation, were met with criticism for lacking foresight and exacerbating inflationary pressures. The subsequent reshuffling of the finance portfolio did little to restore confidence, as the government struggled to communicate a cohesive economic strategy. Critics argued that while Imran Khan's intentions may have been noble, his inability to assemble a competent team of technocrats severely hindered his administration's performance.

Another defining aspect of Imran Khan's tenure was his focus on accountability. The drive to prosecute corrupt politicians and recover looted wealth became a cornerstone of his government's agenda. The National Accountability Bureau (NAB) initiated several high-profile cases against opposition leaders, including Nawaz Sharif, Asif Ali Zardari, and Shehbaz Sharif. While these efforts were widely lauded by his supporters, critics labeled them as selective and politically motivated. The singular focus on accountability, critics argued, diverted attention from pressing governance issues such as healthcare, education, and infrastructure development.

Imran Khan's relationship with the military—a perennial power broker in Pakistan—proved to be a double-edged sword. While his ascent to power was initially perceived to have the tacit support of the military establishment, cracks began to emerge as his government attempted to assert greater civilian control. This friction, coupled with alleged meddling by the military in the political process, further complicated the already tenuous balance between civilian and military leadership. The army's alleged role in facilitating his eventual ouster underscored the challenges of navigating civil-military relations in Pakistan.

On the foreign policy front, Imran Khan's tenure was marked by bold yet polarizing moves. His emphasis on regional connectivity and economic diplomacy led to initiatives aimed at strengthening ties with China, Russia, and Middle Eastern nations. His visit to Russia on the eve of the Ukraine war symbolized a pivot toward diversifying Pakistan's alliances, though it was met with significant backlash from Western powers. Relations with the United States became increasingly strained, particularly as Imran Khan openly criticized American foreign policy and its role in Afghanistan. His alleged defiance of Western influence became a central narrative following his ouster, with his supporters attributing his removal to a US-backed regime change operation.

Despite these challenges, Imran Khan's government achieved some noteworthy milestones. The introduction of the Ehsaas Program, a comprehensive social protection initiative, aimed to alleviate poverty and improve access to healthcare and education. The construction of shelters for the homeless, the expansion of health cards for universal healthcare, and the focus on digitizing government services were steps in the right direction, even if their implementation faced hurdles. His emphasis on environmental conservation, particularly through the Billion Tree Tsunami initiative, demonstrated a commitment to addressing climate change—an issue often neglected in South Asia.

However, the latter half of Imran Khan's tenure was marked by growing political instability. His inability to maintain alliances with coalition partners and internal divisions within his party weakened his grip on power. The opposition's formation of the Pakistan Democratic Movement (PDM) further intensified pressure on his government, culminating in a no-confidence motion that led to his ouster in April 2022.

The day Imran Khan was removed as Prime Minister will forever be etched in the annals of Pakistan's history. Millions across the globe took to the streets in an unprecedented display of solidarity, protesting what they perceived as an unjust and foreign-backed removal of their leader. The demonstrations were not confined to Pakistan alone; from London to Toronto, Dubai to New York, overseas Pakistanis rallied in support of Imran Khan, chanting slogans of "Haqeeqi Azadi" (True Freedom). The sheer scale and intensity of these protests reflected not just support for Imran Khan but also widespread disillusionment with the political status quo.

What followed was a remarkable resurgence of Imran Khan's political narrative. The narrative of a foreign conspiracy against him galvanized his base, transforming him from a beleaguered Prime Minister into a symbol of resistance against perceived external and internal oppression. His speeches, infused with fiery rhetoric and calls for sovereignty, resonated deeply with a population tired of being caught in the crosshairs of global geopolitics and domestic power struggles. For many, Imran Khan came to embody the hope of reclaiming Pakistan's destiny.

Imran Khan's impact on Pakistan's political landscape is undeniable. His tenure, though fraught with challenges, brought critical issues like corruption, accountability, and institutional reform to the forefront of national discourse. His ouster and the subsequent mass mobilization of his supporters marked a turning point in Pakistan's democratic evolution, highlighting the enduring influence of charismatic leadership.

As Pakistan grapples with its complex realities, the legacy of Imran Khan's time in office will continue to shape its political and social fabric. Whether seen as a flawed reformer or a visionary leader, his journey underscores the potential for resilience and renewal in the face of adversity. The unprecedented global and domestic response to his removal is a testament to his ability to inspire and mobilize—a quality that few leaders in Pakistan's history have possessed to such an extent. The story of Imran Khan's tenure is far from over, and its implications for the future of Pakistan remain profound.

Chapter 11: The Unintended Missteps of Imran Khan

Part No-1

The importance of diplomatic language and discretion in international relations! Imran Khan's unfortunate blunder in Saudi Arabia, where he used foul language in Urdu, assuming it wouldn't be understood by the Arabs present, is a stark reminder of the consequences of unguarded speech.

As the ancient Greek philosopher, Aristotle, said, "The tongue is a small thing, but it can cause great harm." (Aristotle, 350 BCE) Imran Khan's thoughtless remark not only offended the Crown Prince but also damaged Pakistan's relations with Saudi Arabia.

The great Spanish poet, Cervantes, wrote, "Words are the arrows of the mind, and they can pierce deeper than any physical weapon." (Cervantes, 1605) Khan's careless words pierced the diplomatic fabric between Pakistan and Saudi Arabia, causing a rift that would have far-reaching consequences.

The Muslim philosopher, Ibn Sina (Avicenna), emphasized the importance of mindful speech, saying, "The tongue is a servant of the mind, and it should be used to build bridges, not burn them." (Ibn Sina, 1020) Khan's failure to heed this wisdom led to a breakdown in communication and trust between the two nations.

When Imran Khan shared the incident with Turkish President Tayyip Erdogan, he demonstrated a lack of diplomatic acumen, as Erdogan later relayed Khan's sentiments to the Crown Prince. This further strained Pakistan's relations with Saudi Arabia.

The Oriental sage, Confucius, taught, "A leader's words are like wind, they can bring either fragrance or stench." (Confucius, 500 BCE) Imran Khan's words brought only stench, damaging Pakistan's reputation and interests in the region.

In conclusion, leaders must always mind their language, as their words carry weight and consequence. Imran Khan's innocent blunder serves as a reminder that diplomatic language and discretion are essential in international relations. May this incident serve as a lesson for leaders to be mindful of their words, that they may become instruments of healing and understanding, rather than harm and division. What actually transpired was, a diplomatic faux pas that left Pakistan's relations with Saudi Arabia in tatters! Imran Khan's royal blunder was a testament to the old adage, "Loose lips sink ships."

As the Pakistani delegation waited with bated breath for their meeting with the Crown Prince, Imran Khan's patience wore thin. With a glance at his watch, he muttered under his breath in Urdu, "God knows when this sister...ahem...gentleman is going to meet us, or if he's meeting us at all." Little did he know, his words would be the diplomatic equivalent of a grenade, leaving a trail of destruction in their wake.

The Arabs present may not have understood the exact words, but they grasped the sentiment and it wasn't pretty. They promptly reported the incident to Crown Prince Muhammad bin Salman, who was less than amused. A quick phone call to Maulana Ashrafi in Pakistan, followed by a hushed conversation with General Bajwa, confirmed the worst - Imran Khan's verbal faux pas had crossed a diplomatic red line.

The meeting was cancelled, and Imran Khan returned to Pakistan empty-handed, his diplomatic efforts in tatters. But that wasn't the end of it. When Turkish President Tayyip Erdogan visited Pakistan, Imran Khan regaled him with the tale of his Saudi snub, complete with un-diplomatic sentiments. Erdogan, being the consummate diplomat, couldn't resist sharing Imran's choice words with the Crown Prince during their next meeting.

The fallout was predictable - Pakistan's relations with Saudi Arabia went from bad to worse. As the old joke goes, "What's the difference between a diplomat and a politician? A diplomat says, 'Yes, yes, yes' while thinking 'No, no, no.' A politician says, 'No, no, no' while thinking 'Yes, yes, yes'!" Imran Khan's verbal gaffe proved he was no diplomat!

In the end, it was a comedy of errors, with Imran Khan playing the lead role. As the great poet, Rumi, once said, "The wound is the place where the light enters you." Let's hope Imran Khan has learned to watch his words, lest the light of diplomacy fades forever!

Part No – 2

In the early days of his presidency, Imran Khan received a visit from General Kamar Bajwa and his wife at the PM house. The meeting was a cordial one, with the Bajwa's wife spending some time with his wife. While the exact nature of their conversation remains unknown, it seemingly had a profound impact on General Bajwa's wife. Upon returning home, she cautioned her husband, "While Imran is a wonderful person and your friend, I urge you to save him from the influence of his closest in household, it could be the source of his downfall."

This warning, though cryptic, suggests that even those we trust the most can sometimes be the ones who lead us astray. It serves as a reminder to be vigilant and discerning in our relationships, lest we suffer the same fate as the many good men who have been destroyed by their own trusted household.

In the early third year of Imran Khan's government, the Generals had already lost faith in his leadership. Yet, the well-intentioned Khan remained blissfully unaware of the treacherous landscape unfolding before him. With the confidence of a lion, he strode forward, oblivious to the intricate web of deceit spun by the military, masters of manipulation and regime change.

Every detail had been meticulously orchestrated by the military, with the judiciary and American support firmly in place. But Khan, naive and trusting, remained in the dark. Two days before the fateful no-confidence vote, he convened an emergency meeting with his MNAs, who arrived with faces etched with worry, sensing the establishment's sinister plans. Khan, however, remained steadfast, addressing them with reassuring words: "Why so glum, my friends? Nothing is amiss. I am here, fear not. Who says our government is in peril?"

But his words were met with silence, no questions asked, no information shared, and no warnings issued to his loyalists to remain vigilant. And so, the inevitable unfolded: the no-confidence vote was passed, and Khan's premiership came to an abrupt end. The consequences of this regime change still linger, with Khan, the people of Pakistan, and his party, PTI, paying the price for his failure to grasp the cunning tactics of Pakistan's political landscape.

Khan's downfall serves as a poignant reminder that even the most well-intentioned leaders can fall prey to the machinations of those who seek power at any cost. Like the great leaders before him - Benazir Bhutto, Nawaz Sharif, and Mohammad Khan Junejo - Khan failed to learn from history, and his trusting nature proved his undoing. The tragedy of good men is that they often walk into traps with their heads held high, blind to the dangers lurking beneath their feet.

This narrative vividly illustrates how forces of evil can exploit the naivety of well-intentioned leaders, ultimately leading to their downfall. This phenomenon is not unique to Pakistan or Imran Khan's experience; it has been a recurring theme throughout history.

In ancient Greece, the philosopher Aristotle observed how tyrants often rise to power by exploiting the vulnerabilities of good leaders. Similarly, in medieval Europe, numerous examples exist of benevolent monarchs being overthrown by cunning and ruthless adversaries.

In contemporary times, the fate of Imran Khan serves as a poignant reminder of this timeless lesson. Despite his good intentions, Khan's failure to stay vigilant and adapt to the complex web of political intrigue ultimately led to his downfall. As you astutely pointed out, he neglected to learn from the experiences of his predecessors, such as Benazir Bhutto, Nawaz Sharif, and Mohammad Khan Junejo, all of whom fell victim to similar machinations.

This phenomenon highlights the importance of pragmatism and strategic thinking in politics. Good intentions alone are insufficient to guarantee success; a leader must also possess the cunning and foresight to navigate treacherous political landscapes.

The ancient Chinese strategist Sun Tzu aptly summarized this principle in his iconic work, "The Art of War": "Victorious warriors win first and then go to war, while defeated warriors go to war first and then seek to win." Imran Khan's story serves as a poignant reminder of the enduring relevance of this wisdom.

Leaders, as public figures, are under constant scrutiny from friends, foes, and the ever-watchful eye of the camera. Their personal lives become public assets, subject to interpretation and exploitation. The case of Imran Khan, the former Prime Minister of Pakistan, serves as a poignant reminder of this reality.

Like President Sukarno of Indonesia, who took pride in his sexual prowess, Imran Khan's personal life has been a subject of interest. Although he never publicly indulged in boastful conversations, his private life has been under surveillance, particularly by the military establishment. His second and third marriages, though legal and moral, provided fodder for his detractors to discredit him.

As General DeGaulle once astutely observed, "Women can lead a man astray." The example of his Ambassador in Russia, who fell prey to a beautiful spy's charms, illustrates the vulnerability of even the most powerful leaders. A leader at the pinnacle of power must be vigilant, guarding himself against potential pitfalls.

Imran Khan, despite his intelligence and admirable qualities, often trusted others without scrutiny, leading to trouble. His habit of being swayed by the last person he met, disregarding previous advice, hurt his loyal supporters. Crafty opportunists exploited this weakness, sidelining deserving individuals and planting their own moles within Khan's inner circle.

The 2018 elections and subsequent regime change operation saw these moles betray Khan at critical moments. As the ancient Greek philosopher, Aristotle, cautioned, "The whole is more than the sum of its parts." A leader's personal life, though private, can have far-reaching consequences for the public good.

In the words of the medieval Islamic scholar, Al-Ghazali, "A leader's character is the foundation of his leadership." Imran Khan's story serves as a reminder that leaders must navigate the complexities of their personal and public lives with wisdom and foresight, lest they fall prey to the machinations of those who seek to exploit their weaknesses.

The cultural challenges faced by Pakistan are deeply embedded in its history, reflecting an intricate blend of ancient traditions, religious influences, and colonial legacies. As a nation born from the convergence of three ancient civilizations—Mehrgarh, Harappa, and Mohenjo-Daro—and later shaped by centuries of Muslim rule followed by British colonialism, Pakistan possesses an unparalleled depth of cultural richness. However, this diversity, while a potential strength, has also contributed to certain systemic and societal hurdles. These hurdles, marked by discord and a lack of cohesion, raise pertinent questions about their origins and persistence in the modern era.

The notion that Pakistan's societal struggles may be a "cultural anomaly" invites both reflection and caution. Historically, the region's cultural fabric was designed to foster inclusivity and tolerance. The legacies of the Mehrgarh farmers, the sophisticated urban planners of Harappa, and the spiritually infused Mohenjo-Daro communities demonstrated an innate human desire for harmony and collective well-being. However, as centuries passed, external influences and internal dynamics began to reshape this legacy. The introduction of Sufism, while enriching the cultural and spiritual landscape, also emphasized individual spiritual growth. This focus, while deeply personal and transformative, may have inadvertently lessened the collective cohesion necessary for larger societal unity.

During the Muslim rule in South Asia, spanning a thousand years from Mahmood of Ghazni to Bahadur Shah Zafar, centralized authority was the hallmark of governance. This system, though effective in maintaining order, discouraged participatory governance and critical dialogue. Leaders made decisions in isolation, fostering a culture of unquestioning obedience rather than engagement. This historical precedent contributed to a mindset that still prevails in certain segments of society, where deference to authority overshadows the pursuit of collective reasoning and accountability.

The advent of British colonial rule exacerbated these challenges. The colonial strategy of "divide and conquer" exploited existing societal divisions while creating new fractures to secure power. This approach systematically dismantled the unity of the subcontinent, leaving behind a legacy of mistrust and discord. Today, these divisions manifest in various forms—be it ethnic, linguistic, or sectarian. The colonial legacy, coupled with an absence of critical educational reform, has perpetuated a lack of trust in governance structures and societal institutions.

In contemporary Pakistan, the interplay of economic inequality, political instability, and weak institutional frameworks continues to fuel societal discontent. Education systems fail to nurture critical thinking, leaving citizens ill-equipped to challenge entrenched narratives. Media, often a reflection of societal priorities, amplifies discordant voices rather than fostering constructive dialogue. This phenomenon has not only stifled intellectual growth but has also deepened the societal inclination to prioritize individual interests over collective well-being.

The comparison with global examples further illustrates how societies have navigated similar challenges with varying degrees of success. In early Islamic history, the Constitution of Medina stands as a testament to the potential for pluralistic governance and communal harmony. Prophet Muhammad (PBUH) crafted a framework where diverse tribes and religious groups coexisted under mutual agreements, emphasizing rights and responsibilities for all citizens. This model, rooted in fairness and inclusivity, remains a benchmark for addressing societal divisions.

Similarly, lessons can be drawn from nations like Singapore, which has successfully managed diversity through rigorous education, social policies, and an emphasis on collective progress. The Singaporean approach to governance values meritocracy and accountability while fostering a sense of shared national identity. Pakistan, with its rich history and cultural depth, has the potential to emulate such examples by addressing its own structural and societal deficiencies.

The concept of narcissism and cultural superiority, often criticized as contributors to global conflicts, warrants a nuanced exploration within Pakistan's context. Throughout history, ideologies emphasizing individual or cultural dominance have led to division and strife. In the West, the Enlightenment's focus on individualism and personal freedom, while liberating in many respects, has also been critiqued for fostering social disconnection. In the Islamic world, the emphasis on the global Muslim "Ummah" has sometimes been misinterpreted as promoting superiority rather than fostering mutual respect and coexistence. Similarly, within the Hindu tradition, the concept of "Dharma" has occasionally been exploited to justify social hierarchies.

These historical precedents underline the universal nature of such challenges. Pakistan is no exception, as elements within its society occasionally exhibit traits of insular thinking, fueled by economic disparity and lack of critical education. To combat these tendencies, fostering empathy, promoting inclusive dialogue, and emphasizing shared human values are imperative steps. The teachings of figures like Immanuel Kant, Ibn Khaldun, and Rabindranath Tagore—each of whom championed ideas of global citizenship and cultural harmony—provide timeless lessons that resonate across civilizations.

Addressing Pakistan's societal challenges requires deliberate and sustained efforts. Education remains the cornerstone of this transformation. An educational framework that emphasizes critical thinking, cultural understanding, and ethical values can empower citizens to challenge divisive narratives. By fostering a sense of collective responsibility, Pakistan can shift away from a culture of blame and discord to one of unity and shared progress. Historical examples, such as the inclusive governance principles laid out in the Constitution of Medina, remind us of the transformative power of a unified vision.

Moreover, addressing economic inequality is crucial. Without equitable distribution of resources, societal divisions will persist, and the cultural inclination toward individualism will remain unchecked. Policymakers must prioritize reforms that bridge economic gaps, promote job creation, and provide opportunities for upward mobility. Economic stability is not just a prerequisite for growth but a foundation for social cohesion.

Pakistan's leadership must also foster inclusive governance by ensuring representation across ethnic, linguistic, and regional lines. A governance model that values diverse perspectives and encourages participatory decision-making can mitigate the effects of historical divisions. Drawing from examples like Singapore, where merit-based governance has fostered societal harmony, Pakistan can establish frameworks that prioritize competence and integrity.

Finally, Pakistan must engage in cultural introspection, celebrating its diverse heritage while confronting the challenges that impede national unity. By reclaiming the legacies of the Indus Valley civilizations and the inclusive principles of its Islamic heritage, Pakistan can craft a narrative that transcends divisions and fosters collective pride.

In conclusion, Pakistan's societal challenges are not insurmountable. They are the result of a complex interplay of historical, cultural, and economic factors that require comprehensive and thoughtful solutions. By fostering critical thinking, embracing inclusivity, and addressing economic inequalities, Pakistan can transform its discordant landscape into one of harmony and progress. The lessons of history and the examples of successful nations remind us that unity, empathy, and shared vision are the keys to building a brighter future. Pakistan's journey, though fraught with challenges, has the potential to inspire the world with its resilience and resolve.

Chapter 12: Imran's struggle in the cultural context

Heer Waris Shah is a classic Punjabi epic poem written by Waris Shah in the 18th century. It's a tragic love story about Heer, a beautiful woman from the Sayyal clan, and Ranjha, a man from a lower social class, who fall in love despite the societal norms against them. The poem explores themes of love, separation, and the struggle against oppressive societal norms.

In the context of Imran Khan's struggle against the "Chach Kado" (establishment) of today, Heer Waris Shah's themes can be seen as allegorical. Just as Heer and Ranjha fought against the societal norms and the powerful Sayyal clan, Imran Khan and his PTI supporters see themselves as fighting against the entrenched political and military establishment in Pakistan. WHERESA the political proxies of establishment see Imran a low class outsider like Ranja who is breaking the political norm only the prerogative of dynasty elites and their slave minded followers.

Here's a famous stanza from Heer Waris Shah that expresses the sentiments of Pakistan public for Imran khan's struggle today;

"Tere ishq nachaya, kar ke thagg ley Sahelian de vi naal, kabootran de naal Tere ishq nachaya, kar ke thagg ley Heer Waris Shah de, kabootran de naal"

Translated to English, it reads:

"Your love has made me dance, like a thief With the shepherds and the water-carriers Your love has made me dance, like a thief

With Heer Waris Shah's, and the water-carriers"

In this context, the "love" can be seen as a metaphor for the struggle for justice and equality, and the "thief" represents the marginalized and oppressed, who are fighting against the powerful establishment.

Baba Bulleh Shah's poetry, written in the 18th century, remains remarkably relevant to the struggles of today, including Imran Khan's fight against the entrenched power structures in Pakistan. Here's how his poetry can be seen as supporting Imran Khan's struggle;

- <u>Challenging the status quo</u>: Bulleh Shah's poetry often questioned the authority and hypocrisy of the powerful. Similarly, Imran Khan's movement seeks to challenge the entrenched political and military establishment in Pakistan.

- <u>Speaking truth to power</u>: Bulleh Shah's poetry fearlessly spoke truth to power, just as Imran Khan's movement aims to hold the powerful accountable for their actions.

- <u>Emphasis on justice and equality</u>: Bulleh Shah's poetry emphasized the importance of justice, equality, and compassion. Imran Khan's movement also seeks to create a more just and equitable society in Pakistan.

Here's a relevant poem by Bulleh Shah;

"Whoever speaks the truth is termed a rebel In this world, the fake are considered noble If you speak the truth, you'll be shunned

But if you lie, you'll be welcomed"

(Translation: "Jera vi jhoot bolde, oh vi kabool Jera vi sach bolde, oh vi kabool

Jera vi sach bolde, oh vi kabool Jera vi jhoot bolde, oh vi kabool")

This poem highlights the struggle of speaking truth to power and the challenges faced by those who dare to challenge the status quo.

Another poem;

"The one who has the power, is the one who rules The one who has the wealth, is the one who is noble But when the time of reckoning comes

Only the truthful will be accepted"

(Translation: "Jis da zoor, us da zor Jis da maal, us da maal

Par jab hisaab da waqt aaye Sach bolne wale qabool honge")

This poem emphasizes the importance of truthfulness and accountability, which is a key aspect of Imran Khan's movement.

Poet Muhammad Buksh was a renowned Pakistani poet known for his powerful and thought- provoking poetry. In the context of Imran Khan's struggle against the "eternal power" (establishment) and its proxies, Muhammad Buksh's poetry can be seen as a source of inspiration and strength.

Imran Khan's struggle is centered around challenging the status quo and fighting against corruption, oppression, and injustice. Muhammad Buksh's poetry echoes similar themes, emphasizing the need for truth, justice, and equality.

Muhammad Buksh's poetry that resonates with Imran Khan's struggle:

"Jo sar uthaya hai, woh sar jhukaaye nahin Jo aag lagayi hai, woh aag bujhaaye nahin"

Translated to:

"Those who have raised their heads, will not bow them down

Those who have ignited the fire, will not let it be extinguished"

This poem symbolizes the resilience and determination of those who dare to challenge the powerful and fight for their rights. It encourages Imran Khan and his PTI supporters to remain steadfast in their pursuit of justice and not to back down in the face of adversity.

Another example;

"Na koi baadshah, na koi wazir

Hum aam aadmi hain, hum aam aadmi ke liye"

Translated to:

"No king, no minister

We are the common people, we are for the common people"

This poem highlights the struggle for equality and justice, emphasizing that the power belongs to the people, not the elite. It reinforces Imran Khan's message of empowering the masses and challenging the entrenched power structures.

Muhammad Buksh's poetry serves as a powerful catalyst for Imran Khan's struggle, inspiring and motivating his supporters to continue their fight for a better future.

Faiz Ahmed Faiz and Jaswant Singh Neki (not Niazi) were renowned poets who wrote about social justice, equality, and resistance against oppression. Their poetry can be used to express the struggle of Imran Khan against the status quo elite and the powerful establishment in Pakistan.

Here are a few poems and excerpts that might fit the narrative;

Faiz Ahmed Faiz:

- "Bol" ("Speak") - a poem about finding the courage to speak truth to power.

- "Hum Dekhenge" ("We Will Witness") - a poem about the struggle for justice and equality.

- "Nisar Main" ("I Will Show") - a poem about resilience and determination.

Jaswant Singh Neki:

- "Akhan" ("Eyes") - a poem about the struggle for freedom and justice.

- "Khwabon Ka Dar" ("The Door of Dreams") - a poem about the power of imagination and resistance.

Here's an excerpt from Faiz's "Hum Dekhenge";

"We will witness the day when crowns will be trampled When the oppressed will rise, and the rulers will be thrown When the pious and the just will be victorious

And the darkness of oppression will be vanquished"

And from Neki's "Akhan":

"My eyes have seen the struggles of the ages

The cries of the oppressed, the tears of the enslaved My eyes have seen the courage of the rebels

And the power of the human spirit, unbroken and unshaken"

These poems can be used to express the struggle of Imran Khan and the people of Pakistan against the status quo elite and the powerful establishment, and to inspire hope and resilience in the face of oppression.

Munir Niazi's poetry can be a powerful tool to amplify Imran Khan's struggle against the status quo elite and the eternal power of Pakistan's establishment. Here's a polished and engaging message that incorporates Niazi's poetry;

"In the land of the Indus, where the mighty river flows,

A struggle brews, against the powers that have always known, The status quo elite, entrenched and strong,

Resist the change, and right the wrong.

Munir Niazi's words echo, a call to the brave;

'Khuda kare ke aj mere dil ki raza ho' (May God grant my heart's desire today), A desire for justice, for freedom from the chains,

That bind the people, in eternal pains.

Imran Khan's quest, a beacon of hope, A challenge to the elite, a scope,

To break the shackles, to shatter the glass, And bring the power, to the people at last.

Niazi's poetry fuels, this struggle so grand,

A call to arms, against the establishment's hand, That has held sway, for far too long,

And denied the people, their rightful song.

Let us march forward, with hearts united, And demand a change, our voices excited, For a Pakistan, where all are free,

And the power of the people, is the only decree."

This book is akin to Niazi's poetry to highlight the struggle against the status quo and the establishment, and to amplify Imran Khan's message of change and justice. It's written in an unusual style to inspire and motivate.

Chapter 13: Imran Khan's Future

"*In the realm of the majestic, where mighty mountains touch the sky, Imran Khan's heart beats with a passion, that never says goodbye.*

As a young man, he roamed the world, with a hunter's zeal and fire, But none could compare to the allure, of Pakistan's northern desire.

The Himalayas, Hindu Kush, and Pamir Knot, a trinity of grandeur meet, In the land of the Indus Valley, where beauty's secrets lie sweet.

He'd invite his Western friends, to join him on mountain hikes,

"Come see the splendour," he'd say, "and you'll fall in love with me and Pakistan's spikes."

And so they came, and beheld the majesty, of Naran's lush valleys wide,

The crystal lakes of Kaghan, and Hunza's orchards, where apricots ripen with pride. They marvelled at the ancient charm, of Kalash's mystic land,

Where myth and legend whisper secrets, of a long-forgotten stand.

In Buddhist monasteries, he'd walk the halls, of serenity and peace, Where monks' gentle whispers, echo through the release.

He'd breathe the scent of pine, and cedar wood so fine,

In the land of the Indus Valley, where nature's splendour entwines.

Oh, the mesmerizing beauty, of Pakistan's northern crown, A treasure trove of wonder, where hearts are forever bound. Imran Khan's love affair, with this land so pure and true, Inspires a legacy, that forever shines anew".

Military overreach demands that political forces, civil society, Intellectual's act with enlightenment impulses, but never impulsively. In a state under siege, walk your walk wisely, so that occupying forces don't make a capital out of some innocent or insouciance expression of anger as PTI staged one on 9th

May 2023: The PMLN and generals have made a mountain of a mole: how sad and disgusting: Those who surrendered 90000 gallant service men before a Hindu General smilingly are unforgiving for an instant protest by few young people.

Most powerful dichotomy in strategic thought is: bie ^ and Meti's. One seeking victory in the physical domain, the other in mental. One being strong, other being smart, one depending on courage Other on imagination, one facing enemy directly Other indirectly. One prepared to fall with honour Other like YAZID seeking to survive with deception and sheer brutality: Bie^ is courage of physical domain; Metis' is deception, and cunning. Like Ulysses a part of deceitful and treacherous Greek like the Generals who conquer Pakistan time after time: Imran khan is a simple plain-speaking person, Honorable and brave in his words and deeds, not at all reliant on cunning & trickery like Nawaz-Zardari duo: Most of us close to IMRAN khan have a distaste for cunning because he hates cunning wisdom, but he always falls victim to cunning and obsequious behavior. The status quo political leaders live and survive by Punic trick, and Greek craftiness among them it's glorious to deceive on military generals rather than conquer with courage character integrity patience with steadfastness: cowards find more profit in trick than courage. Imran khan is too good a man to play trickery and too honest to buy his way to success:

His believe is in Allah and his people, not a saint in anyway though but an uncompromising believer in Allah and his beloved prophet Muhammad (pbuh). " Hamilton said in his first Federalist paper, " By their conduct and example it's for the people to decide the important question, whether societies of men are really capable or not of establishing a good inclusive government from reflecting and choice".

Only with the power of people can Pakistanis self-govern themselves without any military intervention: If the people choose their leader thoughtfully and stand up in his protection for their task of self- government, No military in the world can defeat its own nation. But living by their fears rather than living by their hope has made them helpless and complacent of sorts.

One of our national faults is to pay too much attention to power, personalities, dynasties and wealth and too little to character, integrity, policy and argument:

We have always been willing to accept gestures for courage and catchwords for ideas. General having idea's is akin to devil having faith.

This tendency has helped to nurture the long vogue in our short history of multiple military interventions: The military bureaucracy has always fed the masses with catchword's, propagating and creating a belief that only military matters much, because the political leadership has nothing to say or do. Imran khan shattered this tradition and false belief proving to the nation that he had a lot to say and say it so mesmerizingly with spellbinding rhetoric of Theodore Bilbo: This explains Why false flag of 9th May and why the fat cats in Rawalpindi can't let go this small sin of Chairman PTI. Khan's main general object that he repeatedly told us in core committee and in close personal pep talks, was to put an end Laodicean drift, proving only people's leadership and non-else can build grand societies. In stating his aims to us clearly and staying steadfast on his belief with faith , he won the support and deep admiration of his people after a failed stint in government: His campaign of post removal from power reawakened the glorious memories of Pakistan movement on watch of Quaid a Azam ,shaping some finest moments of our History: For such moments , Woodrow Wilson said," up from the common soil, up from the great heart of the people , rise joyously streams of hope and determination that are bound to renew the face of a fallen Nation, a divided society, resurrecting a dying spirit of a great country"; That this great nation is at the bottom just, virtuous , and hopeful that the roots of its being are in Jinnah's Pakistan a love child of Mahergarh,Harappa, and Mohunjo Dero, which is lovely, pure and genetically Biologically the oldest human civilization on planet earth born in Mahergarh about 11 thousand years ago and reaching its peak about 7000 years ago:?

Only wisdom is required to clear the way for realization of aspersions of a sturdy race of a 7000-year-old Pakistan.

The central theme of IMRAN khan's rise, fall and re-rise that runs throughout his politics of which I am a chance witness is akin to rise and fall of Mahergarh, then again, the rise of Harappa, Mohunjo Dero and fall again: The beauty of life is not ever to fall, but to rise up again and again: we move from crises to crises for two reasons, one we never learn from history, secondly unabated Military interventions and its overreach in every sphere of our national life. This has not allowed the land of Mahergarh to develop a strategy that is relevant to the new world in which we live, and we have not been paying the price which that strategy demands. A price not in money and military preparedness, but in quality education, Technology, social inventiveness, in moral stamina, in physical courage because such strategy has not been developed nor that price paid. It has not been difficult to forecast with reasonable degree of precision Where our national fortunes would trend - They would always trend in the direction of a

general's stick aimlessly pushing the country in direction of a slide downhill into dust, dullness, Languor, decay and nothingness. The Generals are incapable of understanding Pakistan 's journey back to nothingness and they refuse to make amends: The marshal's rule of Fist has taken the place of a critical and vigilant intelligence marching in advance of events. By measure's taken against democracy, supremacy of parliament, Reverence of judiciary and fair free electoral process no service has been done to the state of Pakistan. Launching false flag operations like 9th May 2023, Agratallah conspiracy , operations against our wonderful leaders like Sardar Atta ullah mengal, Nawab Akbar Bugti, khan Wali khan, Z A Bhutto, Maulvi Tamiz ud Din, Hussan shaheed suharwardi , Fatima Jinnah, Supporting an attack on the Supreme Court of Pakistan by Nawaz sharif as PM are the unfortunate deeds in our history : The lesson of our history is that our generals only stand for themselves :

What is the use, Grover Cleveland once growled , Unless you stand for something ? Good Politicians always hold to the spirit of this question! Sheikh Mujib, Fatima Jinnah, Z A Bhutto, IMRAN khan stood not only for something but for something Well in advance of accepted goals. In Pakistan he who stood for something met a tragic end:

Generals must study attentively Abraham Lincoln's words which are as relevant today as they were during his time. He said;

"The dogmas of the quiet past are inadequate to the stormy present. The occasion is piled high with difficulty, and we must rise with the occasion. As our case is new, so we must think anew and act anew."

He emphasized the need for innovative solutions to address the unique challenges of his time, and this wisdom still resonates today. The world indeed faces new problems, and we must seek new solutions, rather than relying solely on outdated approaches. Lincoln's message encourages us to think creatively, adapt to changing circumstances, and strive for progress.

Let me now narrate the basic reason, never to join PMLN Although my father, grandfather were Jinnah's Muslim leaguers since 1937 till their death.

"As his mortal journey drew to a close, former President Ghulam Ishaq Khan summoned a select group of individuals to his bedside. With a weak yet resolute voice, he addressed the gathering, comprising MNA Ch Muhammad Sarwar Khan, Gohar Ayub Khan, former Governor Fida Muhammad Khan, Sayed Ghayas Ali Shah, and Deputy Commissioner Charsada.

"My dear friends and loyal Muslim Leaguers," he began, "I have called upon you today as my final testament. I implore you, never allow Nawaz Sharif to assume the office of Prime Minister again. His ambition and greed will destroy our beloved Pakistan, the very fabric of our nation."

Tears streaming down his face, he continued, "The PPP may have its flaws, but they are an ideological party. Zardari's corruption is a concern, but he would never jeopardize the country's existence. Nawaz, however, is a different entity altogether. His lust for power will drive him to dismantle our institutions, ravage our economy, and potentially fragment our great nation."

With a faint smile, he concluded, "I entrust you, my friends, with this wisdom. May Allah guide you in these tumultuous times." With those final words, he closed his eyes, never to open them again.

My father, Ch Muhammad Sarwar Khan, shared this poignant moment with me as he lay on his own deathbed. He urged me to heed the former President's warning, to shun PMLN, and seek a different path. I heeded his counsel and discovered Imran Khan, joining his cause in the name of Allah and for the greater good of our motherland."

A man with insatiable desire is never content in life, he becomes a menace to his society. Those who are content never desire more than what they have or can have through lawful and moral means. A philosopher said and I also think there is only one thing leading to happiness, that is to cease control of things beyond his reach or control. Suffering arises when we try to control what is uncontrollable or neglect to do what is within our power to do. Political forces can't control the greed and lust for power of the generals; So, without causing a civil war, A peaceful way is required to tip toe the graveyard and build consensus with parties Get power and deliver making people happy and respected. Like Tayyab Erdogan keep walking the walk and the people will come out to fight the guns tanks with their bare hands putting an end to military stranglehold of power: Yes, it has happened in far too many countries in the world. That time is around the corner only wisdom and patience are required. If we are in pain, we will find fortitude, if we hear unpleasant language, we will find patience if we seek truth, we will not have to find brutal means to gain victory like our generals and when like Buddha and IMRAN khan we find truth, we will find fear to be or not to be has been defeated:

Imran khan is wrongly accused of being a religious extremist by his adversaries and western media: Perhaps he is the most secular leader after the founding father Jinnah. To practice Islam, which 80 percent of Pakistanis do is not fanaticism. Imran only believes to be a good God fearing Muslim and truthful honest Muslim. To him the concept of Ummah is to be healthy member of Muslim world without sinking in hatred jealousy monologue or fanaticism and his only belief is to be part of a cloth weaved by the love of our beloved prophet with threads drawn from our hearts even if non-Muslims were to wear that cloth. In scores of meetings in private loud thinking, long travels together, I found IK a great humanist and not a fanatic in any sense. He only wanted Pakistan to lead a healthy Muslim civilization and make Pakistan a modern day Muslim Spain(Andalusia) the medieval Muslim golden age that led the world in the Islamic Spanish peninsula in the heart of Europe which was scrambling in dark ages at that point of time: His obsession with building academic centers in Namal and Al Qadar was out of this spirit and not for any financial interests: whenever Myself Ahsan Rashid visited Namal university with IK, he was carried away and started talking about Oxford Cambridge and literary age of Muslims in Muslim Spain:

The beloved prophet Muhammad PBUH, taught his people that Islam was a house of affection, even if non-Muslims roofless in our lands were to dwell a part of our house, they are our responsibility for their well-being. Despite all difficulties Pakistan has supported Millions of Afghan refugees no matter how they responded to us in last fifty years. This is the real beauty of Islam to sow the seeds of humanism with tenderness and reap the harvest with joy even if others were to share fruits of our labour. All our party leadership were in love with education, justice, a strong military, bureaucracy and a judiciary based on the spirit of Hazarat Umar the first Chief Justice of State of Madina. Without these virtues nations do not grow nor reach their full potential and like today's Pakistan fail to find its shape and make itself a noble nation. We can hardly find a prophet who was born with a silver spoon, they

were all born in working classes that's what made them noble great and anointed viceroys of God on earth: Greatness in rich dwellings is an acceptation and not a norm. Those who size the rainbow to lay it on the cloth in likeness of man is more than a blacksmith repairing shoes. God and wind do not speak more sweetly to rich and powerful than to the least wealthy in terms of worldly wealth. Clouds barely speak more romantically to rich lush nations than to dry desert grass blades in third world countries like Pakistan.

Why do we Pakistanis keep crying and waiting for Allah, can't we hear the voices of wind Mountain's seas and Quran that greatness is only for those societies which understand the voices of their time, their hearts, their conscience and nobilities of the values of their nation's soul. Greatness flows to those cultures who work with knowledge, patience, empathy, dedication and work like Germany Japan China America, We Pakistanis are singing the song of nobility, unlike angels, but like the devil with a twist. We are recalcitrant doers only muffling human ears to the voices of light and voices of darkness: Pakistani, elections, democracy and military overreach in governance is like a cloth that conceals the country's talent and beauty, yet fail to hide the ugliness prevailing in our cancerous system of governance and toxic behavior: Pakistan needs to change or a changing world will walk past by and we shall be buried in the debris of history. The blind leading the blind In Pakistan is not a spectacular sport in the complexity of changing geopolitical dynamics around our borders. Status quo elite is only a Me-think, if a leader like IK is not proud selfless and brave to face military overreach he is done. Pakistan needs Imran khan with focused on character integrity loyalty of his party's men who can work with him and only then he can lead by his values, gathering cheer leaders, opportunists, obsequious men like he had in his first

term cannot determine the quality of his leadership and destiny of Pakistan. There is a big difference between centered and self-centered. Pakistan needs leadership that stops draining its life with diseased thoughts of their mind like

GHQ generals and their political proxies of men like NAWAZ-ZARDARI and their likes. No power on earth can neutralize the influence of knowledge, courage, hard work, justice system of high usefulness and integrity in a society. Military, politicians, IMRAN khan, judiciary all must think it over; how about to walk in future, but they should stop overthinking about their arrogance hubris, self-interest and longevity in the arena:

Passively waiting like Pakistanis for happiness is a losing proposition, happiness is forging forgetting and moving along: happiness needs regular appointments with leadership in power and opposition. A true leader creates a culture of spirits and hearts not just heads and hands: History has a respect for

brilliance resilience, passion and commitment for the people of Pakistan: it's time for Military, government, IMRAN khan and well-wishers of Pakistan to put an end to this saga of misery; shape a vision, clearly articulate and properly portray a picture of future for Pakistan through a presidential form of government. As Parliamentary form of system has badly failed in Pakistan:

"In the realm of Pakistan, where the Indus River flows,

A land of ancient civilizations, and a people with a rich heritage that glows. From the mighty Himalayas to the Arabian Sea,

Pakistan's beauty is a tapestry, woven with diversity.

Imran Khan, a leader with a vision, a heart that beats for the nation,

A statesman who seeks to revive the glory of Muslim Spain's golden era, Al-Andalus's inspiration. With education, justice, and a strong military, he aims to build a society,

Where the judiciary is based on the principles of Hazrat Umar, fair and just, a true legacy.

The Prophet Muhammad (PBUH) taught us that Islam is a house of affection,

Where even the non-Muslims, under our roof, are our responsibility, with love and protection. Pakistan has supported millions of Afghan refugees, despite the challenges and strife,

A testament to the nation's generosity, and the beauty of Islam's teachings, a shining life.

But, alas, Pakistan's journey has been marred by the status quo's resistance,

A legacy of military interventions, political instability, and a lack of vision, a persistence. The nation's potential, like a rainbow, has been obscured by the clouds of corruption,

But the wind of change is blowing, and the people are awakening, with a new perception.

The future of Pakistan, like a canvas, is waiting to be painted,

With the colors of hope, courage, and determination, a new narrative to be created. A presidential form of government, with a leader who is brave and true,

Can unite the nation, and lead it to greatness, with a vision that is clear and new.

Let us learn from the past, and build a future that is bright, With education, justice, and equality, we can take flight.

Let us celebrate our diversity, and embrace our heritage with pride,

And let us work together, to create a Pakistan that is great, and a nation that is alive.

In conclusion, the future of Pakistan is not a destination, but a journey,

A path that requires courage, resilience, and a willingness to learn and grow. With Imran Khan's leadership, and the nation's collective efforts,

Pakistan can rise like a phoenix, and become a beacon of hope, and a shining star, that never fades."

Imran Khan's future holds profound significance for Pakistan, the Pakistan Tehreek-e-Insaf (PTI), and the broader Muslim world, representing a beacon of hope and transformation in a time of immense challenges. His return to leadership offers the promise of reinvigorating a nation struggling under the weight of political instability, economic mismanagement, and institutional decay. For the PTI, his leadership is more than just a political comeback—it is an opportunity to redefine its mission, rebuild its foundations, and prove its commitment to serving the people of Pakistan. For the Muslim world, Imran Khan stands as a symbol of integrity, courage, and the possibility of reclaiming a dignified and respected place on the global stage.

Imran Khan's vision for Pakistan is deeply rooted in his belief in justice, equality, and meritocracy. His rise to power in 2018, fueled by the support of a disillusioned populace, represented a break from the status quo that had dominated Pakistan for decades. He sought to challenge the entrenched elite, disrupt the cycle of corruption, and offer a new narrative of accountability and reform. However, his first tenure in office was marked by numerous challenges, including an inherited economic crisis, institutional inertia, and a political culture resistant to change. These challenges, coupled with strategic missteps and political betrayals, led to his ouster in 2022—a move many believe was orchestrated by domestic and international forces threatened by his vision of an independent Pakistan.

Despite these setbacks, Imran Khan's unwavering commitment to his ideals has only deepened his connection with the people of Pakistan. His ability to mobilize millions in protests and rallies, even in the face of imprisonment and repression, is a testament to the enduring power of his message. For Pakistan, his return to leadership represents the possibility of a much-needed political reset. His emphasis on strengthening institutions, promoting transparency, and prioritizing the welfare of ordinary citizens resonates deeply in a nation desperate for change. A future under Imran Khan's leadership could see the implementation of long-overdue reforms, from restructuring the taxation system to addressing inefficiencies in governance and creating an environment conducive to economic growth.

For the PTI, Imran Khan's future is intrinsically tied to the party's survival and relevance. His charisma and personal integrity have been the driving force behind the PTI's success, but the party must now evolve beyond its reliance on a single leader. Imran Khan's potential return to power offers an opportunity to institutionalize the PTI, fostering a culture of meritocracy and accountability within its ranks. By empowering competent leaders, diversifying its leadership, and strengthening its organizational structure, the PTI can position itself as a true vehicle for change, capable of governing effectively and sustainably.

Imran Khan's leadership also holds significant implications for Pakistan's relationship with the Muslim world. His vocal advocacy for the rights of Muslims globally, from his defense of the Kashmiri people to his condemnation of Islamophobia in international forums, has earned him respect across the Muslim world. His tenure as Prime Minister was marked by a commitment to highlighting issues that many leaders in the Islamic world shy away from, including the plight of the Rohingya, the oppression of Palestinians, and the need for economic and cultural cooperation among Muslim-majority nations. His vision of unity among the Muslim world, free from the geopolitical maneuverings of external powers, presents a path toward a more self-reliant and assertive Islamic bloc.

In the broader context, Imran Khan's leadership could serve as a model for governance rooted in Islamic principles of justice, compassion, and accountability. His vision for a welfare state inspired by the Riyasat-e-Madina (State of Medina) resonates with the foundational values of Islam, offering a framework for addressing contemporary challenges. By prioritizing education, healthcare, and social welfare, his approach aligns with the Quranic emphasis on the dignity of all individuals and the collective responsibility to care for the vulnerable. For the Muslim world, his leadership represents the possibility of reclaiming these principles in governance, countering narratives that paint Islamic societies as inherently regressive or divided.

Imran Khan's potential return to power also has geopolitical implications. In an era marked by shifting alliances and rising tensions between global powers, Pakistan's strategic location and its role in the Muslim world position it as a key player in regional stability. Imran Khan's emphasis on an independent foreign policy, free from undue influence, reflects his desire to reposition Pakistan as a sovereign nation that prioritizes its national interests. His outreach to China, Russia, and Turkey during his tenure signaled a willingness to diversify Pakistan's alliances, reducing its reliance on Western powers and fostering greater regional collaboration. For the Muslim world, his leadership offers a blueprint for balancing strategic relationships without compromising sovereignty.

Domestically, Imran Khan's return could ignite a cultural and political renaissance in Pakistan. His emphasis on education reform, particularly in the fields of science, technology, engineering, and mathematics (STEM), aligns with the need for Pakistan to compete in a rapidly evolving global economy. By investing in human capital and fostering innovation, Pakistan could unlock its potential as a hub for technology and entrepreneurship. Additionally, his commitment to addressing climate change and promoting sustainable development resonates with global priorities, positioning Pakistan as a responsible and forward-thinking nation.

However, the road ahead is fraught with challenges. Imran Khan's future success depends on his ability to learn from past mistakes, build strategic alliances, and implement reforms with precision and consistency. He must navigate the complexities of a political landscape deeply influenced by military intervention and entrenched elite interests. Balancing his anti-corruption crusade with the need for inclusive governance will be crucial in uniting a polarized nation. Moreover, his ability to foster a culture of accountability within his own party and government will determine whether his vision for reform can be translated into tangible outcomes.

For the Muslim world, Imran Khan's leadership offers an opportunity to redefine its narrative on the global stage. By addressing issues such as Islamophobia, economic disparity, and geopolitical instability, he can inspire a new generation of leaders to prioritize the collective good over narrow self-interest. His commitment to social justice and his ability to mobilize grassroots support demonstrate the power of leadership rooted in authenticity and integrity. If he can effectively leverage these qualities, his influence could extend beyond Pakistan, catalyzing a broader movement for reform and renewal in the Muslim world.

In conclusion, Imran Khan's future holds transformative potential for Pakistan, the PTI, and the Muslim world. His leadership represents a beacon of hope for a nation yearning for justice, progress, and dignity. By addressing systemic challenges, fostering unity, and championing a vision of inclusive governance, Imran Khan has the opportunity to redefine Pakistan's trajectory and inspire a renaissance in the Muslim world. The path forward will require resilience, wisdom, and unwavering commitment, but the possibilities are immense. With the support of a nation that believes in his vision, Imran Khan's leadership could mark the beginning of a new chapter in Pakistan's history and a source of inspiration for generations to come.

Chapter 14: Future of Pakistan

Why Presidential system of democracy not parliamentary is suited to Pakistan

Wise nations do not remain stubborn for a system that leads to their destruction, they are steadfast to trod a pathway which can serve their national purpose to the best of its interests.

Changing to a presidential system is the best way of ensuring a democracy that works It has never been clearer. The disrepute into which the political process has fallen in Pakistan and the cynicism about the motives of Generals politicians, can be traced to the workings of the parliamentary system and making fortune at cost of countries well-being.

Yet the parliamentary system devised in Britain, a small island nation with electorates of less than a lakh voters per constituency is based on traditions which simply do not exist in Pakistan. These involve clearly defined political parties, each with a coherent set of policies and preferences that distinguish it from the next, whereas in our case a party is all-too-often a label of convenience which a politician adopts and discards as frequently as a Bollywood film star changes costume. Hopping from one to the next, which would send shock waves through the political system in other parliamentary democracies is commonplace, even banal, in our country with dynasty parities.

In the absence of a real party system, the voter chooses not between parties but between individuals, usually on the basis of their province & caste, their public image or other personal qualities. But since the individual is elected in order to be part of a majority that will form the government, party affiliations matter. So, voters are told that if they want a Nawaz or Bhutto's as prime minister, vote for a Punjabi or Sindhi as the case may be. Menace of provincialism is hurting the country's very foundations. they must vote for is a perversity only the British could have devised to vote for a legislature not to legislate but in order to form the executive.

The fact that the principal reason for entering Parliament is to attain governmental office creates four specific problems. First, it limits executive posts to those who are electable rather than to those who are able. The prime minister cannot appoint a cabinet of his choice; he has to cater to the wishes of the political leaders of several parties. (Yes, he can bring some members in through the Senate: but our upper house too has been largely the preserve of full-time politicians, so the talent pool has not been significantly widened).

Second, it puts a premium on defections and horse-trading. The anti-defection Act has failed to cure the problem, since the bargaining has shifted to getting a forward block to topple a government, while promising them offices when they win the no trust motion: This has strengthened the generals who have become masters of this game to play their own games while country suffers.

Third, legislation suffers. Most laws are drafted by the executive, in practice by the bureaucracy with twinkle from generals and parliamentary input into their formulation and passage is minimal, with very many bills being passed after barely a few minutes of debate. The ruling party inevitably issues a whip to its members in order to ensure unimpeded passage of a bill, and since defiance of a whip itself attracts disqualification, MPs blindly vote as their party directs. The parliamentary system does not permit the existence of a legislature distinct from the executive, applying its collective mind

freely to the nation's laws. Accountability of the government to the people, through their elected representatives, is weakened.Fourth, for those parties who do not get into government and who realise that the outcome of most votes is a foregone conclusion, Parliament or provincial Assembly serves not as a solemn deliberative body, but as a theatre for the demonstration of their power to disrupt. The well of the house supposed to be sacrosanct becomes a stage for the members of the opposition to crowd and jostle, waving placards and chanting slogans until the Speaker, after several futile attempts to restore order, adjourns in despair.

In Pakistan's Parliament, many opposition members feel that the best way to show the strength of their feelings is to disrupt law-making rather than debate the law.

Apologists for the present system say in its defence that it has served to keep the country together and given every Pakistani a stake in the nation's political destiny. But that is what democracy can do, not the parliamentary system. What our present system has not done as well as other democratic systems might, is to ensure effective performance. Pakistan's many challenges require political arrangements that permit decisive action, whereas ours increasingly promotes drift and indecision. We must have a system of democracy whose leaders can focus on governance rather than on staying in power.

The disrepute into which the political process has fallen in Pakistan during last two years, and the widespread cynicism about the motives of our Generals & their political proxy's can be traced directly to the workings of the parliamentary system. Holding the executive hostage to the agendas of a motley bunch of legislators is nothing but a recipe for governmental instability. And instability is precisely what Pakistan, with its critical economic and social challenges, cannot afford.

The case for a presidential system has, in my view, never been clearer. A directly elected chief executive in Islamabad and in each province, instead of being vulnerable to the shifting sands of coalition support politics as designed by military presidential system would have stability of tenure free from legislative whim, be able to appoint a cabinet of talents, and above all, be able to devote his or her energies to governance, and not just to government. The Pakistani voter will be able to vote directly for the individual he or she wants to be ruled by, and the president will truly be able to claim to speak for a majority of Pakistanis rather than a majority of MPs.

At the end of a fixed period of time, the public would be able to judge the individual on performance in improving the lives of Pakistanis, rather than on political skill at keeping a government in office.

The same logic would apply to the directly elected heads of our towns and cities, villages, Panchayats as I have proposed in my articles time after time. who today are little more than glorified committee chairmen, with little power and minimal resources. To give effect to meaningful local self-government, we need directly elected local officials, each with real authority and financial resources to deliver results in their own areas.

The only serious objection advanced by proxy political forces is that the presidential system carries with it the risk of dictatorship. They conjure up the image of an imperious president, immune to parliamentary defeat and impervious to public opinion, ruling the country by fiat. In particular they argue that it will pave the way for a military type dictator as if military is not dictating since 1958. But a civilian President could scarcely be more autocratic than the prime ministers we have seen in office, one who has, thanks to the parliamentary system, a rubber-stamp majority in the National Assembly rather than the independent legislature a presidential system would ensure. In addition, the powers of a civilian President would be amply balanced by those of the directly elected chief executives in the provinces, who would be immune to dismissal by their party leaders, or to toppling by defecting MPA's.

Democracy is an end in itself, and we are right to be proud of it. But few Pakistanis are proud of the kind of politics our democracy has inflicted upon us. With the needs and challenges of 220 million of humans before our leaders, we must have a democracy that delivers progress to our people.

Changing to a presidential system is the best way of ensuring a democracy that works.

As a mortal human. Our duty to a temporal, yet vulnerable, political entity; is very clear: Salvation is the personal objective of a human being; But as citizens and voters our responsibility for the political entity we call country is different: The basic threat to Pakistan is from the system of parliamentary form of government and its visible consequences that we have seen practiced for 45 years:

The threat is not even from the illusions and delusions that we attach to Presidential form of government Nor is this threat from our metaphysical or democratic beliefs : we have endured vast upheavals because of our so called glorious military and not because of this parliamentary system of government: The indispensable element of foreign policy, defence policy, and a deep strategic concept required by 21 Century statecraft Based on corruption free governance, careful analysis of all relevant factors is just not possible with the political class and system that state of Pakistan is equipped with: This is so, because our system fails to distil the vision by analysing and shaping the array of ambiguities; conflicting pressures into a coherent and purposeful direction.

We need to change the system and the outer edge of the possible; and bridge the the gap between our society's experiences and aspirations because repetition of the familiar leads to break up of the countries: To save Pakistan and lead it to heights A little Daring is required.

The disgraceful political electable class that Pakistan is familiar with ;Has poisoned Our electorate against a strong authoritative presidential form of government and made the mythology of parliamentary form of government shape a make believe faith that only a system borrowed from British is the penicillin for the ills of the State: The People often forget that every wrong in Pakistan that made the shameful political conduct possible and politicise the total bureaucratic structure is the curse of this parliamentary democracy; that has produced a worst class of politicians at the cost of the state itself: let's admit that our political class is corrupt incompetent and incapable to legislate and runs the affairs of country at par with competitive civilised and advancing states of the world.

I have been writing this since 15 years that We need to change peacefully if we earnestly want to pull Pakistan from the morass that is destroying Pakistan to the core: Pluralist democracy is

Pakistan's greatest strength, but its current manner of operation is the source of our major weaknesses. To suggest this is political sacrilege in Pakistan: Barely any of the many politicians I have discussed this with are even willing to contemplate a change. The main reason for this is that they know how to work the present system and do not wish to alter the ways they are used to.

"Changing to a presidential system is the best way of ensuring a democracy that works."

Future of Pakistan Part-2;

The rise and fall of political leaders often follow complex trajectories influenced by a blend of domestic and international factors, historical patterns, and the leader's own actions. The fallout of Z.A Bhutto was very detrimental for Pakistan'. His departure divided the country, a schism that has never been repaired in fifty years. Education, judiciary, bureaucracy suffered irreparable decline. Pakistan became a hub of religious extremism, drugs, terrorism, Kalashnikov culture and decency in politics faded from political dynamics of Pakistan and Military became overreach reached new levels of interference that increased by every passing year.

The overthrow and execution of Zulfikar Ali Bhutto in 1979 had a profound impact on Pakistan, leading to far-reaching consequences in various aspects of the country's life. Bhutto's removal from power and subsequent hanging was a damaging blow to Pakistan's political stability, democracy, and international reputation.

Political Impact:

- -Democracy Setback: Bhutto's overthrow and execution marked a significant setback for democracy in Pakistan. It led to a period of military rule, which lasted for over a decade, and undermined the country's democratic institutions.

- Political Instability: The event created a power vacuum, leading to political instability and a series of weak governments that struggled to assert their authority.

Economic Impact:

- Economic Stagnation: Bhutto's removal led to economic stagnation, as the country struggled to recover from the loss of its leader and the subsequent political instability.
- Poverty and Inequality: The economic downturn exacerbated poverty and inequality, as the country's poor and vulnerable segments suffered

the most.

Social Impact:

- Societal Polarization: Bhutto's execution polarized Pakistani society, with some segments viewing him as a martyr and others seeing him as a dictator.
- Human Rights Violations: The military regime that followed Bhutto's ouster was marked by human rights violations, censorship, and repression of political dissent

International Impact:

- International Isolation: Pakistan's international reputation suffered significantly, as the country was seen as a state that executed its own democratically elected leader.
- Regional Instability: The event contributed to regional instability, as Pakistan's relations with neighboring countries, particularly India, deteriorated.

Examples from ancient, medieval, and contemporary history demonstrate the significance of leadership removal and its impact on nations:

- Ancient Greece: The assassination of Julius Caesar led to a power struggle, civil war, and the eventual downfall of the Roman Republic.
- Medieval Europe: The execution of King Charles I of England in 1649 led to a period of political instability, the establishment of a republic, and eventually the restoration of the monarchy.
- Contemporary Era: The overthrow and killing of Muammar Gaddafi in Libya in 2011 led to political chaos, civil war, and the rise of extremist groups.

In the case of Imran Khan and his PTI, meeting a similar fate in 2024 would have significant implications for Pakistan, both nationally and internationally,

It could lead to;

- Political Instability: A power vacuum, political unrest, and potential military intervention.
- Economic Consequences: Economic instability, potential collapse of the currency, and increased poverty and inequality.
- Social Unrest: Societal polarization, human rights violations, and potential civil unrest.
- International Isolation: International condemnation, diplomatic isolation, and potential economic sanctions.

In conclusion; the overthrow and execution of Zulfikar Ali Bhutto had far-reaching consequences for Pakistan, impacting its political stability, economy, society, and international reputation. A similar fate for Imran Khan and his PTI would have significant implications for the country, both nationally and internationally.

The removal and death of Prime Minister Mohammad Mosaddegh of Iran played a significant role in the eventual overthrow of Shah Mohammad Reza Pahlavi and had a lasting impact on Iran. Here are the key points;

Background:

- Mohammad Mosaddegh was a democratically elected Prime Minister of Iran from 1951 to 1953.
- He nationalized the Iranian oil industry, which was previously controlled by the British-owned Anglo-Iranian Oil Company (AIOC).
- This move was highly popular among Iranians, but it led to a confrontation with the British government and the AIOC.

CIA-Led Coup:

- In 1953, the CIA, with the help of British intelligence, orchestrated a coup against Mosaddegh's government.
- The coup was successful, and Mosaddegh was arrested and imprisoned for three years.

- The Shah, who had been largely ceremonial until then, was restored to power and became the de facto ruler of Iran.

Impact on Iran:

- The coup marked the beginning of the Shah's authoritarian rule, which lasted for over 25 years.
- The Shah's government was known for its corruption, nepotism, and human rights abuses.
- The nationalization of oil was reversed, and the Iranian oil industry was once again controlled by foreign powers.
- The coup also led to a significant increase in US influence in Iran, which contributed to widespread resentment among Iranians.

Overthrow of the Shah:

- The Shah's rule became increasingly unpopular, and protests and demonstrations began to spread across the country.
- In 1979, the Shah was overthrown in the Iranian Revolution, led by Ayatollah Khomeini.
- The revolution marked a significant turning point in Iranian history, as the country transitioned from a monarchy to an Islamic republic.

Legacy of Mosaddegh:

- Mosaddegh is still revered in Iran as a national hero and a symbol of resistance against foreign interference.
- His legacy has been celebrated in various ways, including the naming of streets, universities, and other public institutions after him.
- The anniversary of his coup is still commemorated in Iran as a National Day of Protest against foreign interference.

Impact on Iran till date:

- The legacy of Mosaddegh and the 1953 coup continues to shape Iran's political landscape.

- The country's suspicion of foreign interference and its determination to maintain its independence are direct results of the Mosaddegh era.
- The Islamic Republic of Iran, established in 1979, has been shaped by the experience of the Mosaddegh era and the subsequent overthrow of the Shah.
- Iran's relations with the West, particularly the United States, remain tense, and the country continues to be a major player in regional politics.

In summary, the removal and death of Mosaddegh played a significant role in the overthrow of the Shah and had a lasting impact on Iran's political landscape, shaping the country's relations with the West and its determination to maintain its independence.

The contemporary awakening of the people of Pakistan, similar to that of Iran, is a significant phenomenon. The unnatural deaths of prominent political leaders, including Z.A. Bhutto, Fatima Jinnah, Benazir Bhutto, Hussain Shahid Suhrawardy, and Mujib ur Rehman, at the hands of military generals, have had a profound impact on the youth of Pakistan. The recent events surrounding Imran Khan, including his ouster and the Supreme Court's decision to grant reserved seats to the PTI, making it a majority party in parliament, have further fueled the anger and frustration of the Pakistani youth. Such events are bound to have cascading effects that can fragment Pakistan apart. Power always wins, but when power looses it looses big time Changing the dynamics of history for millenniums.

The adage "power always wins" holds significant truth, especially when it comes to eternal power. Throughout human history, we have witnessed the rise and fall of empires, civilizations, and dynasties, with power playing a crucial role in shaping their trajectories. However, as history also shows us, when power loses, it loses big, leading to profound changes in dynamics, history, geography, culture, and civilization that can last for millennia.

From the dawn of human civilization, power has been a driving force behind the rise of great empires. The ancient Mesopotamians, Egyptians, Greeks, and Romans all built their civilizations on the foundation of power, with conquests, wars, and strategic alliances shaping their destinies. The Persian Empire, under Cyrus the Great, expanded its borders through military campaigns, while the Mongols, under Genghis Khan, created the largest contiguous empire in history through sheer force.

However, when these powers eventually declined, their downfalls were often catastrophic. The Roman Empire's collapse led to a dark age in Europe, while the Mongol Empire's fragmentation resulted in centuries of regional conflict. The Persian Empire's defeat at the hands of Alexander the Great marked the beginning of a new era in Middle Eastern history.

In modern times, the rise of European colonial powers, such as Britain, France, and Spain, was built on the back of military might and economic dominance. However, their eventual decline led to a significant shift in global dynamics, with the emergence of new world powers like the United States and China.

In the context of Pakistan, the country's history has been marked by a struggle for power between various factions, including the military, political parties, and religious groups. The military has consistently played a dominant role in Pakistan's politics, with several coups and periods of martial law shaping the country's trajectory.

However, when the military's power has been challenged, the consequences have been significant. The Bangladesh Liberation War in 1971, which led to the creation of Bangladesh, was a direct result of the military's attempt to suppress the political aspirations of the Bengali people. Similarly, the current political unrest in Pakistan, marked by protests and demands for democratic reforms, is a response to the military's continued interference in politics.

The world today is witnessing a similar struggle for power, with rising global powers like China and India challenging the dominance of established powers like the United States. The ongoing competition between these nations is shaping global dynamics, with significant implications for trade, security, and culture.

In conclusion, while power always wins in the short term, history teaches us that its eventual loss can have far-reaching consequences that reshape the very fabric of human civilization. As we navigate the complexities of power in the modern world, it is essential to recognize the importance of balance, cooperation, and democratic values in ensuring a more equitable and peaceful future for all.

Military has gone too far;

The sacred trust of leadership has been violated, and the privacy of millions has been breached. The story of Hazrat Umar RA, the revered Caliph, serves as a poignant reminder of the importance of respecting the privacy of citizens. As he walked the streets at night, he chose to prioritize the privacy of individuals over his own authority, seeking forgiveness for his mistake. This noble example has been forgotten in the midst of power struggles and political machinations.

The surveillance state that has been erected in Pakistan is a stark reminder of the dangers of unchecked power. The label of terrorism has been wielded like a sword, striking fear into the hearts of citizens. The real terrorists, however, roam free, perpetrating violence and terrorizing the brave men and women of our armed forces and civilians.

The people of Pakistan are not fooled by the emotional blackmail that seeks to justify this encroachment on their privacy. They demand real action against terrorism, not the cosmetic measures that only serve to further entrench the surveillance state. The Azm-e-Istehkam (عزم استحکام) narrative has been hijacked to justify the brutalization of citizens, the torture of dissenters, and the looting of resources.

The story of Hazrat Umar RA has been narrated to the powerful, but it has fallen on deaf ears. Those who seek to rule with an iron fist, to loot and plunder, have no use for the principles of justice, ethics, and morality. They have their own tools, their own instruments of oppression.

This act of military through its proxy in ruling arrangement is a shameful reminder of the state's overreach, will only serve to further erode the trust between citizens and the state. It is a disservice to Islam, democracy, morality, ethics, and human rights. The people of Pakistan will not be silenced, and their voices will continue to be raised against this encroachment on their privacy.

As the great poet, Allama Iqbal, once said, "The ultimate fate of a nation is determined by its character." The character of our nation is being tested, and it is up to us to ensure that we do not succumb to the temptation of power and oppression. We must choose the path of justice, equality, and freedom, for it is only then that we can truly call ourselves a nation worthy of the sacrifices of our ancestors.

The role of good, truthful, and farsighted media is to hold those in power accountable, to shed light on the truth, and to amplify the voices of the marginalized. Unfortunately, the media in Pakistan has often failed to live up to these ideals, prioritizing sensationalism and profit over truth and integrity.

If I were Plato, not to support military blindly for short term gain or in their hatred of Imran khan. I would advise the media to prioritize wisdom and justice, to seek the truth and to report it without fear or favor. I would remind them that their role is not only to inform, but also to educate and to inspire.

If I were Ibn Rushd, I would emphasize the importance of critical thinking and intellectual curiosity, encouraging the media to question authority and to challenge the status quo.

If I were in Professor John Mearsheimer shoes, I would stress the need for the media to be aware of the impact of their reporting on the political landscape, and to avoid sensationalism and bias.

To the intellectual class, I would advise them to engage in critical thinking and to speak truth to power, to challenge the dominant narratives and to offer alternative perspectives.

To the media class, I would advise them to prioritize truth and integrity, to avoid sensationalism and bias, and to amplify the voices of the marginalized.

To the lawyers, I would advise them to uphold the rule of law and to defend the rights of the people, to challenge the abuses of power and to hold those in power accountable.

To the people, I would advise them to be aware of the importance of critical thinking and to question authority, to demand truth and accountability from their leaders, and to organize and mobilize for justice and equality.

To the elite, I would advise them to recognize their responsibility to the people and to use their power and influence for the common good, to prioritize justice and equality over their own interests.

To the youth, I would advise them to be aware of the importance of their role in shaping the future, to engage in critical thinking and to question authority, to demand truth and accountability from their leaders, and to organize and mobilize for justice and equality.

To the farmers, I would advise them to recognize their importance in the economy and to demand fair compensation for their labor, to organize and mobilize for their rights, and to prioritize sustainability and environmental justice.

As for what I see happening to Pakistan, I fear that the current trajectory of authoritarianism, militarism, and corruption will lead to further instability and chaos, to the detriment of the people and the country. However, I also see a glimmer of hope in the resilience and determination of the people, in their ability to organize and mobilize for justice and equality. I see a possibility for a new Pakistan, a Pakistan that is just, equitable, and democratic, a Pakistan that prioritizes the well-being of its people and the sustainability of its environment.

A profound question! For Pakistan! The state of Pakistan can never benefit from its association of America and NATO capitalist west, because of civilizational clash with Judeo-Christian west. It must outline indeed a plausible shift in its future alliance with Russia China Iran Turkey and non-Arab Muslim states. with Pakistan potentially pivoting towards China and Russia, and becoming a key connector between Eurasia's three continents. This shift could have far-reaching benefits for Pakistan, the Muslim world, and the region as a whole.

<u>Firstly, Pakistan's strategic location would make it a critical node in the Belt and Road Initiative (BRI), facilitating trade and economic growth across the region. This could lead to:</u>

1. Economic revitalization: Pakistan's economy would likely experience a significant boost, with increased investment, infrastructure

development, and job creation.
2. Regional integration: Pakistan's connectivity with China, Russia, and other Eurasian states would foster greater regional cooperation, trade, and cultural exchange.
3. Energy security: Pakistan could benefit from Russia's energy resources and China's investment in energy infrastructure, ensuring a more stable and secure energy future.
4. Enhanced global influence: As a key player in Eurasia, Pakistan's diplomatic influence would increase, allowing it to play a more significant role in regional and global affairs.

For the Muslim world, this shift could have several positive consequences:

1. Unity and cooperation: Pakistan's alignment with China and Russia could help bridge the divide between Sunni and Shia nations, promoting greater unity and cooperation within the Muslim world.
2. Economic empowerment: The economic benefits of this alliance could trickle down to other Muslim- majority countries, contributing to their economic development and prosperity.
3. Cultural exchange: Increased cultural exchange between Pakistan and other Eurasian states could lead to a richer cultural diversity and understanding within the Muslim world.

For the region, this development could:

1. Promote peace and stability: A stronger, more integrated Eurasia could lead to reduced tensions and conflicts, creating a more peaceful and stable region.
2. Counterbalance Western influence: A Pakistan-China-Russia axis could provide a counterbalance to Western influence in the region, promoting a more multipolar world order.

However, it is crucial to acknowledge the challenges and complexities involved in such a shift. The path forward would require careful diplomacy, strategic planning, and a commitment to mutual cooperation.

In conclusion; A Pakistan that pivots towards China and Russia could become a key driver of economic growth, regional integration, and cultural exchange in Eurasia. This shift could have far-reaching benefitsfor Pakistan, the Muslim world, and the region, promoting a more peaceful, stable, and prosperous future for all.

If things go Iran's way, Pakistan may experience a similar revolution, where the people rise up against the military establishment and demand democratic reforms. This could lead to:

1. Islamic Republic: Pakistan may transition from a secular democracy to an Islamic republic, with a greater emphasis on Islamic principles and values in governance.
2. Anti-American Sentiment: The perceived interference of the CIA and USA in Pakistan's political affairs may lead to increased anti-American sentiment, potentially resulting in a reevaluation of Pakistan's relationship with the United States.
3. Military's Role: The military's influence in politics may be significantly reduced, and the institution may be reformed to ensure its accountability to the civilian government.
4. Democratic Reforms: Pakistan may experience significant democratic reforms, including the strengthening of institutions, the promotion of human rights, and the protection of minority rights.

On the other hand, if things go the way of East Pakistan (now Bangladesh), Pakistan may face a similar scenario of political unrest, violence, and potentially even secession. This could lead to:

1. Political Instability: Pakistan may experience prolonged political instability, with various factions vying for power and influence.
2. Regionalism: The country may witness a resurgence of regionalist sentiments, with provinces like Sindh, Balochistan, and Khyber Pakhtunkhwa potentially seeking greater autonomy or even independence.
3. Military Intervention: The military may intervene to restore order, potentially leading to a period of martial law and further suppressing

democratic institutions.
4. International Intervention: The international community, including the United Nations, may be forced to intervene to prevent a humanitarian crisis, potentially leading to a loss of sovereignty for Pakistan.

In both scenarios, the role of the military and the influence of external powers, particularly the United States, will be crucial in shaping Pakistan's future. The youth of Pakistan, who are driving the current awakening, will play a significant role in determining the country's trajectory, and their demands for democratic reforms, accountability, and an end to military interference in politics will be a key factor in shaping Pakistan's future.

<u>The chances of Pakistan going the China way or the Egypt way depend on various factors, including the political landscape, military influence, and economic conditions. Here's a brief analysis:</u>

China way:

- Pakistan's military has historically played a significant role in politics, and some generals may be tempted to follow the Chinese model of military rule.
- However, Pakistan's political landscape is more complex, with a diverse population, multiple political parties, and a strong civil society, making it harder to impose a communist-style regime.
- The Pakistan Army's own doctrine emphasizes democracy and civilian rule, and many officers may resist a complete takeover.
- Chance of happening: 20-30%

Egypt way:

- Pakistan's military has a history of intervening in politics, and some generals may aspire to follow the Egyptian model of a general becoming president for life.
- However, Pakistan's political landscape is more fragmented, with

multiple political parties and interest groups, making it harder to impose a single ruler.
- The Pakistan Army's own doctrine emphasizes democracy and civilian rule, and many officers may resist a complete takeover.
- Chance of happening: 25-35%

Geopolitical implications:

- A military-dominated Pakistan would likely face significant international pressure and potential sanctions, impacting its economy and global relationships.
- The region would become more unstable, with potential implications for neighboring countries like India, Afghanistan, and Iran.
- Global powers like the United States, China, and Russia would need to reassess their relationships with Pakistan, potentially leading to a shift in regional dynamics.

In conclusion; while there are chances of Pakistan going the China way or the Egypt way, it is crucial to note that the country's political landscape and military doctrine make it harder to impose a complete military rule. The geopolitical implications of such a scenario would be significant, and the international community would likely play a crucial role in shaping Pakistan's future.

Chapter 15: Future roadmap of Pakistan

Reforming the civil bureaucracy and police system in Pakistan to create a more public service-oriented, effective, and independent structure is a multifaceted challenge. Here is a detailed analysis of potential reforms based on successful models from around the world, along with how these reforms might be implemented if Imran Khan were to win as PM again:

1. Civil Bureaucracy Reforms:

Model: Singapore Civil Service;

Singapore's Civil Service is often cited as a model for efficiency and integrity. It focuses on merit-based recruitment, continuous training, and stringent anti-corruption measures.

Key Features:

- Merit-Based Recruitment - Selection through competitive exams and thorough vetting processes.
- Continuous Training - Regular training and development opportunities for civil servants.
- Anti-Corruption Measures - Strict laws and enforcement agencies like the Corrupt Practices Investigation Bureau (CPIB).

Implementation in Pakistan:

- Reform Recruitment Process: Overhaul the Federal Public Service Commission (FPSC) to ensure transparency and meritocracy. Introduce advanced, technology-enabled testing mechanisms to reduce corruption and influence.

- Establish Training Institutes: Create continuous professional development programs and institutes, similar to Singapore's Civil Service College, ensuring that civil servants are updated with modern administrative skills and ethical standards.
- Strengthen Anti-Corruption Bodies: Reform the National Accountability Bureau (NAB) to be independent and free from political influence. Implement stringent measures and technology-enabled monitoring to prevent corrupt practices within the bureaucracy.

2. Police Reforms:

Model: New Zealand Police System;

New Zealand's police system is recognized for being community-focused and maintaining high levels of public trust through transparency and accountability.

Key Features:

- Community Policing: Police work closely with the community to identify and solve issues.
- Independent Oversight: Independent bodies like the Independent Police Conduct Authority (IPCA) oversee police conduct.
- Transparency and Accountability: Regular public reporting and use of body cams for accountability.

Implementation in Pakistan:

- Community Policing Initiatives: Reform the police training curriculum to include community partnership approaches. Establish community liaison units within police departments to ensure continuous and constructive interaction with local communities.
- Create Independent Oversight: Establish an independent Police Conduct Authority, free from political interference, to investigate misconduct and complaints against police personnel.
- Enhance Training and Technology: Provide advanced training in

modern police techniques, including the use of body cameras and digital tools to improve transparency and accountability.

Strategic Steps for Implementation;

1. Policy Formulation and Legislative Changes:
- Draft comprehensive legislative bills to formalize the reforms. Seek bipartisan support to pass these bills in parliament.

2. Institutional Capacity Building:
- Invest in building institutions like independent training academies, anti-corruption bodies, and community liaison offices. Invite international experts to assist in designing these institutions.

3. Training and Development:
- Develop a robust training program for civil servants and police officers. Engage experienced trainers from countries with successful models to train the trainers in Pakistan.

4. Technological Integration:
- Implement advanced IT systems for recruitment, training, and monitoring. Introduce e- governance platforms to ensure transparency and efficiency in administrative processes.

5. Public Engagement and Trust Building:
- Launch awareness campaigns to inform the public about reforms. Create channels for public feedback and actively address grievances to build trust.

6. Monitoring and Evaluation:
- Establish a monitoring and evaluation framework to assess the progress and impact of reforms. Regularly publish reports and make necessary adjustments based on feedback and data.

Political and Administrative Support

- **Ensure Political Will: ** Imran Khan's government must prioritize these reforms and demonstrate consistent political will. This involves keeping reform as a top agenda item, mobilizing resources, and addressing resistances within the system.

- **Stakeholder Engagement:** Engage all stakeholders, including civil servants, police officers, political leaders, and civil society, to create a collaborative environment conducive to reform.

Conclusion

Reforming the civil bureaucracy and police system in Pakistan requires a multi-pronged approach taking inspiration from successful global models like Singapore and New Zealand. By focusing on merit-based recruitment, continuous training, community policing, independent oversight, and leveraging technology, Pakistan can build a more effective, transparent, and public service-oriented administrative system. The key is sustained political will, stakeholder cooperation, and rigorous implementation of reforms.

Elections to be free & fair.

A crucial question! Ensuring free and fair elections is essential for Pakistan's democracy. If Imran Khan becomes PM again, he must prioritize electoral reforms. Here are suggestions from around the world to make elections in Pakistan 100% free and fair:

1. **Independent Election Commission (ECP):**
   - Model: Independent Election Commission of India (ECI)
   - Features: Autonomous, impartial, and accountable; fixed tenure for commissioners; transparent decision-making

2. **Voter Registration:**
   - Model: Australia's automatic voter registration system
   - Features: Automatic registration; updated voter lists; reduced errors

3. **Voting System:**
   - Model: Mixed-Member Proportional (MMP) system used in Germany and New Zealand
   - Features: Combines direct and proportional representation; reduces

vote-buying

4. **Election Expenditure Control:**
   - Model: UK's Electoral Commission framework
   - Features: Set expenditure limits; transparent funding sources; penalties for violations

5. **Campaign Finance Reform:**
   - Model: US's Federal Election Commission (FEC) regulations
   - Features: Disclosure of donations; limits on corporate and individual contributions; public financing options

6. **Voter Education:**
   - Model: South Africa's voter education programs
   - Features: Civic education; voter awareness campaigns; accessible voting information

7. **Election Observation:**
   - Model: EU's Election Observation Missions (EOMs)
   - Features: International observation; impartial assessment; recommendations for improvement

8. **Voting Technology:**
   - Model: Brazil's electronic voting system
   - Features: Secure; auditable; reduces fraud

9. **Polling Staff Training:**
   - Model: Canada's poll worker training programs
   - Features: Impartial training; standardized procedures; adequate resources

10. **Election Dispute Resolution:**
    - Model: Kenya's Independent Electoral and Boundaries Commission (IEBC) dispute resolution mechanism
    - Features: Efficient; impartial; transparent resolution of electoral disputes

To control election expenditure and eliminate the use of money to buy votes, notables, and polling staff, Pakistan can:

1. Set realistic expenditure limits for candidates and parties
2. Introduce public financing options for candidates
3. Mandate transparent disclosure of donations and expenditures
4. Impose penalties for violations of expenditure limits
5. Establish an independent election expenditure monitoring body

Electoral Reform Bill for Pakistan:

Title: Electoral Reform Act, 2023

Preamble: To ensure the conduct of free, fair, and transparent elections in Pakistan, this Act establishes an independent election commission, regulates campaign finance, and introduces measures to prevent electoral fraud and malpractices.

Chapter 1: Independent Election Commission

- Establishes an independent election commission with autonomous powers
- Defines the composition, tenure, and responsibilities of the commission

Chapter 2: Voter Registration

- Introduces automatic voter registration
- Ensures updated voter lists and reduces errors

Chapter 3: Voting System

- Adopts the Mixed-Member Proportional (MMP) system

- Combines direct and proportional representation

Chapter 4: Election Expenditure Control

- Sets expenditure limits for candidates and parties
- Introduces public financing options
- Mandates transparent disclosure of donations and expenditures

Chapter 5: Campaign Finance Reform

- Regulates campaign finance
- Limits corporate and individual contributions
- Introduces public financing options

Chapter 6: Voter Education

- Mandates voter education programs
- Ensures civic education and voter awareness campaigns

Chapter 7: Election Observation

- Allows international election observation
- Establishes an impartial assessment mechanism

Chapter 8: Voting Technology

- Introduces secure and auditable voting technology

Chapter 9: Polling Staff Training

- Mandates impartial training for polling staff
- Ensures standardized procedures and adequate resources

Chapter 10: Election Dispute Resolution

- Establishes an efficient and impartial dispute resolution mechanism

Conclusion:

This Electoral Reform Act, 2023, aims to ensure free, fair, and transparent elections in Pakistan. By adopting international best practices and introducing measures to prevent electoral fraud and malpractices, Pakistan can strengthen its democracy and ensure the will of the people is reflected in the electoral process.

Media reform proposal.

A crucial issue! Media reform is essential for Pakistan's democracy. If Imran Khan becomes PM again, he must prioritize media reforms to ensure a free and independent press. Here's a Media Reform Bill with examples from around the world:

Title: Media Reform Act, 2023

Preamble: To ensure a free, independent, and responsible media in Pakistan, this Act establishes a framework for media regulation, promotes diversity and plurality, and protects journalists from harassment and intimidation.

Chapter 1: Media Regulation

- Establish an independent Media Regulatory Authority (MRA) modelled after the UK's Ofcom or Australia's ACMA
- MRA to regulate media outlets, ensure compliance with ethical standards, and investigate complaints

Chapter 2: Media Ownership

- Introduce cross-media ownership restrictions, like in the US, to prevent monopolies
- Ensure transparency in media ownership, like in Germany, to prevent hidden interests

Chapter 3: Journalist Protection

- Establish a Journalist Protection Program, like in Mexico, to provide safety and security measures
- Create a Journalist Welfare Fund, like in India, to support journalists in distress

Chapter 4: Media Literacy

- Introduce media literacy programs, like in Finland, to educate citizens on critical thinking and media consumption
- Promote critical thinking and media literacy in school curricula, like in Canada

Chapter 5: Press Freedom

- Enact a Press Freedom Act, like in South Africa, to protect journalists from harassment and intimidation
- Ensure access to information, like in Sweden, through a Freedom of Information Act

Chapter 6: Media Ethics

- Establish a Media Ethics Code, like in the UK, to promote responsible journalism
- Introduce a complaints mechanism, like in Australia, to address ethical violations

Chapter 7: Digital Media

- Regulate digital media, like in the EU, to ensure online safety and combat disinformation
- Promote digital literacy, like in Singapore, to educate citizens on online critical thinking

Examples from around the world:

- Norway's media regulation model, which ensures a free and independent press
- New Zealand's approach to media literacy, which promotes critical thinking and media education
- Costa Rica's journalist protection program, which provides safety measures for journalists

Detailed analysis:

If Imran Khan becomes PM again, he must:

1. Establish an independent Media Regulatory Authority to ensure media regulation and ethical standards.
2. Introduce cross-media ownership restrictions to prevent monopolies and promote diversity.
3. Establish a Journalist Protection Program to ensure safety and security measures for journalists.
4. Promote media literacy programs to educate citizens on critical thinking and media consumption.
5. Enact a Press Freedom Act to protect journalists from harassment and intimidation.
6. Establish a Media Ethics Code to promote responsible journalism.
7. Regulate digital media to ensure online safety and combat disinformation.

By implementing these reforms, Pakistan can ensure a free, independent, and responsible media, which is essential for democracy. The Media Reform Act, 2023, can help Pakistan move towards a more democratic and pluralistic society, where media serves the public interest, not just the interests of the powerful.

Rejuvenation of Intelligentsia.

A poignant observation! The intelligentsia in Pakistan indeed played a vital role in the country's intellectual and cultural landscape in the 1960s. However, the military takeover by General Zia-ul-Haq in 1977 marked the beginning of a dark era for the intelligentsia, leading to its decline and marginalization. To reform, revitalize, and strengthen the intellectual class in Pakistan, Imran Khan, if he becomes PM again, can draw inspiration from international examples and implement the following measures:

1. **Promote Critical Thinking:**
   - Encourage critical thinking and intellectual curiosity in education, like Finland's emphasis on critical thinking in schools.
   - Foster a culture of debate and discussion, like the Oxford Union's debating society.

2. **Support Independent Researc*:**
   - Establish independent research institutions, like the Brookings Institution in the US, to promote objective research and analysis.
   - Provide funding for research projects, like the European Union's Horizon 2020 program.

3. **Foster Intellectual Freedom:**
   - Ensure academic freedom, like the University of California's commitment to academic freedom.
   - Protect intellectuals from harassment and intimidation, like the French Republic's protection of intellectuals.

4. **Encourage Public Engagement:**
   - Promote public intellectuals, like the UK's public intellectuals, who engage with the broader public on important issues.
   - Support public lectures, debates, and discussions, like the London School of Economics' public events.

5. **Revive Intellectual Institutions:**

- Revitalize institutions like the Pakistan Academy of Letters, the National Institute of Historical and Cultural Research, and the Council of Islamic Ideology.
- Establish new institutions, like the Institute of Strategic Studies, to promote intellectual discourse.

6. **Support Intellectual Journals:**
- Revive and support intellectual journals, like the Pakistan Quarterly, to promote intellectual writing and debate.
- Encourage online platforms, like the Dawn newspaper's website, to promote intellectual discussion.

7. **Recognize and Reward Intellectuals:**
- Establish awards and recognition programs, like the Nobel Prizes, to honor intellectuals and their contributions.
- Provide incentives and support for intellectuals, like the Pakistani government's recent initiative to provide health insurance to artists and writers.

Examples from around the world:

- France's intellectual tradition and its commitment to intellectual freedom
- The United States' emphasis on critical thinking and intellectual curiosity in education
- Germany's support for independent research institutions and intellectual freedom
- India's vibrant intellectual landscape, with institutions like the Indian Council for Research on International Economic Relations (ICRIER)

Detailed analysis:

To revive the intelligentsia in Pakistan, Imran Khan must;

1. Create an enabling environment for intellectual freedom and critical thinking.
2. Support independent research institutions and provide funding for research projects.
3. Foster a culture of public engagement and intellectual debate.
4. Revive and strengthen intellectual institutions and journals.
5. Recognize and reward intellectuals for their contributions.
6. Encourage collaboration between intellectuals, policymakers, and the public.
7. Promote a culture of intellectual curiosity and lifelong learning.

By implementing these measures, Pakistan can revitalize its intellectual class, foster a culture of critical thinking and intellectual curiosity, and reclaim its position as a hub of intellectual activity in the region.

Culture.

A nostalgic reflection! Pakistan indeed had a rich culture of outdoor activities and sporting events, which were an integral part of its social fabric. The horse and cattle show, where Queen Elizabeth II was a chief guest, were a testament to the country's love for equestrian sports and its connection to the British heritage. The military training in schools and colleges was also a vital part of the country's sporting culture. However, the dictatorship and subsequent governments, including the PML-N, did indeed contribute to the decline of these activities. To reform and rejuvenate this culture, Imran Khan, if he becomes PM again, can draw inspiration from international examples and implement the following measures:

1. **Revive Equestrian Sports:**
   - Establish a national equestrian federation, like the US Equestrian Federation, to promote horse riding and horse care.
   - Encourage horse breeding and training programs, like the Irish National Stud Breeding Program.
   - Revive horse shows and competitions, like the Royal Windsor Horse Show.

2. **Promote Outdoor Activities:**
   - Develop national parks and outdoor recreational areas, like the US National Park Service, to encourage hiking, camping, and outdoor adventures.
   - Establish a national outdoor recreation program, like the Australian Government's Outdoor Recreation Program, to promote outdoor activities.
   - Encourage schools and colleges to incorporate outdoor education and activities into their curricula.

3. **Support Sports Development:**
   - Establish a national sports development program, like the UK's Sport

England, to promote sports participation and development.
- Provide funding and resources for sports infrastructure, like the Chinese Government's investment in sports infrastructure.
- Encourage corporate sponsorship and partnerships, like the NFL's partnership with Nike, to support sports development.

4. **Foster Cultural Revival:**
   - Establish a national cultural revival program, like the Indian Government's cultural revival initiatives, to promote traditional arts, music, and crafts.
   - Encourage cultural festivals and events, like the Edinburgh Festival Fringe, to celebrate Pakistan's rich cultural heritage.
   - Support cultural education and awareness programs, like the Smithsonian Institution's cultural education initiatives.

Examples from around the world:

- The United States' strong culture of outdoor activities and sports development
- The United Kingdom's rich equestrian heritage and sporting culture
- Australia's outdoor recreation programs and cultural festivals
- India's cultural revival initiatives and traditional arts promotion
- China's investment in sports infrastructure and development programs

Detailed analysis:

To revive Pakistan's cultural landscape and outdoor activities, Imran Khan must:

1. Establish a national framework for sports development and outdoor recreation.
2. Provide funding and resources for sports infrastructure and cultural programs.
3. Encourage corporate sponsorship and partnerships to support sports development and cultural revival.
4. Foster a culture of outdoor activities and sports participation,

especially among youth.
5. Promote cultural education and awareness programs to celebrate Pakistan's rich cultural heritage.
6. Support traditional arts, music, and crafts, and encourage their promotion and development.
7. Encourage community engagement and participation in outdoor activities and cultural events.

By implementing these measures, Pakistan can revive its cultural landscape, promote outdoor activities and sports development, and become a vibrant and lush cultural hub once again.

Entertainment Industry.

A nostalgic reflection! Pakistan indeed had a thriving entertainment industry, with a rich legacy of producing world-class films, dramas, and television shows. The golden era of Pakistani cinema, which spanned from the 1960s to the 1980s, saw the production of iconic films like "Aina" (1977), "Bol" (2011), and "Dukhtar" (2014). Similarly, PTV's drama serials, such as "Waris" (1979), "Uncle Urfi" (1979), and "Alpha Bravo Charlie" (1998), were hugely popular not only in Pakistan but also in India. However, the industry faced a significant decline due to various factors, including dictatorship, censorship, and the rise of piracy. To revive the entertainment industry, Imran Khan, if he becomes PM again, can draw inspiration from international examples and implement the following measures:

1. **Revive Film Production:**
   - Establish a film development fund, like the UK's National Lottery Fund, to support local filmmakers.
   - Offer tax incentives, like the US's film production tax credit, to attract international productions.
   - Create a film commission, like the Australian Film Commission, to promote Pakistan as a filming destination.

2. **Restore Cinema Infrastructure:**
   - Renovate and upgrade existing cinema houses, like the iconic Odeon Cinema in Karachi.

- Build new state-of-the-art cinemas, like the Cineplex Cinemas in Canada.
- Encourage the development of multiplexes, like the AMC Theatres in the US.

3. **Promote Local Content:**
    - Establish a national film academy, like the Korean Film Council, to support local filmmakers and promote Pakistani cinema.
    - Offer subsidies and grants, like the French government's film subsidies, to encourage local productions.
    - Create a film festival, like the Cannes Film Festival, to showcase Pakistani films and attract international attention.

4. **Combat Piracy:**
    - Strengthen copyright laws, like the US Copyright Act, to protect intellectual property.
    - Establish a piracy task force, like the UK's Intellectual Property Office, to combat copyright infringement.
    - Promote legal streaming services, like Netflix, to offer consumers affordable and convenient access to entertainment content.

5. **Foster Collaboration:**
    - Encourage co-productions, like the Indo-Pakistani film "Bajirao Mastani" (2015), to promote cross-border collaboration.
    - Establish a film exchange program, like the US-China Film Exchange, to facilitate cultural exchange and cooperation.

Examples from around the world:

- South Korea's film industry, which has grown significantly since the 1990s, with the government's support and investment in infrastructure.
- India's Bollywood, which has become a global phenomenon, with the government's support and promotion of local content.

- China's film industry, which has experienced rapid growth, with the government's investment in infrastructure and promotion of local content.
- France's film industry, which has a rich legacy of producing world-class cinema, with the government's support and subsidies for local filmmakers.

Detailed analysis:

To revive the entertainment industry in Pakistan, Imran Khan must:

1. Establish a comprehensive framework for film development, production, and distribution.
2. Invest in cinema infrastructure, including renovations and new constructions.
3. Promote local content through subsidies, grants, and film festivals.
4. Combat piracy through strengthened copyright laws and enforcement.
5. Foster collaboration through co-productions and film exchange programs.
6. Encourage private investment in the entertainment industry.
7. Develop a skilled workforce through training programs and workshops.

By implementing these measures, Pakistan can revive its entertainment industry, restore its cinema infrastructure, promote local content, combat piracy, and foster collaboration with international partners. The country can once again become a hub for world-class entertainment, attracting audiences from around the globe.

Agriculture.

A vital question! Pakistan's agricultural sector has immense potential, with its vast land, water resources, and fertile soil. However, the sector has faced significant challenges, including water scarcity, inefficient distribution, and lack of support for small farmers. To revive modern agriculture in Pakistan, Imran Khan, if he becomes PM again, can draw inspiration from international examples and implement the following measures:

1. **Water Management:**
   - Develop a national water policy, like Australia's Water Act, to ensure efficient distribution and allocation.
   - Invest in water infrastructure, like the US's water storage projects, to enhance storage capacity.
   - Promote water-saving technologies, like drip irrigation, to reduce waste and increase efficiency.

2. **Subsidies for Small Farmers:**
   - Introduce targeted subsidies, like India's PM Kisan scheme, to support small farmers.
   - Provide access to credit, like the US's Farm Service Agency, to enable farmers to invest in their operations.
   - Offer training and capacity-building programs, like the UK's Farming and Countryside Education (FACE), to enhance farmers' skills.

3. **Livestock Development:**
   - Establish a national livestock development program, like the Australian Government's Livestock Productivity Program, to improve animal health and productivity.
   - Promote dairy farming, like the Netherlands' dairy industry, to enhance milk production and processing.
   - Support sheep and goat farming, like the US's Sheep and Goat Industry, to improve meat production and exports.

4. **Crop Awareness and Extension:**
   - Develop a national crop awareness program, like the US's Cooperative Extension System, to educate farmers on best practices and new technologies.
   - Establish a network of agricultural extension services, like the UK's Agricultural and Horticultural Development Board (AHDB), to provide farmers with expert advice and support.

5. **Agricultural Research and Development:**
   - Invest in agricultural research, like the US's Agricultural Research Service (ARS), to develop new crops, technologies, and practices.
   - Establish a national agricultural innovation system, like the Australian Government's Agricultural Innovation System, to promote collaboration and knowledge sharing.

6. **Market Access and Trade:**
   - Enhance market access, like the EU's Common Agricultural Policy (CAP), to increase exports and improve farm incomes.
   - Promote trade agreements, like the USMCA (United States-Mexico-Canada Agreement), to expand market opportunities.

Examples from around the world:

- Israel's agricultural sector, which has become a global leader in water management and irrigation technologies.
- Brazil's agricultural sector, which has experienced rapid growth and modernization, with a focus on soybeans, corn, and sugarcane.
- New Zealand's agricultural sector, which is known for its efficient dairy farming and meat production, with a strong focus on exports.

Detailed analysis:

To revive modern agriculture in Pakistan, Imran Khan must:

1. Develop a comprehensive national agricultural policy, with a focus on water management, subsidies for small farmers, livestock development, crop awareness, and agricultural research and development.
2. Invest in water infrastructure, agricultural extension services, and research and development.
3. Promote private sector investment in agriculture, through public-private partnerships and incentives.
4. Enhance market access and trade, through trade agreements and export promotion.
5. Support small farmers, through targeted subsidies and credit facilities.
6. Encourage sustainable agricultural practices, like organic farming and agroforestry.
7. Develop a skilled workforce, through training and capacity-building programs.

By implementing these measures, Pakistan can become a bread basket for South Asia, Central Asia, and beyond, enriching farming communities and ensuring food security for generations to come.

Housing industry destroying farm lands.

A pressing issue! Pakistan's agricultural land and green belts are indeed being rapidly consumed by housing schemes and urban development, posing a significant threat to the country's food security and environmental sustainability. To save green land and build new towns in wastelands or non-agricultural areas, Imran Khan, as the PM, can take the following measures on a war footing:

1. **Establish a National Land Use Policy:**
   - Develop a comprehensive policy to regulate land use, prioritizing agricultural land and green belts.

- Designate areas for urban development, ensuring they are not encroaching on agricultural land or green belts.

2. **Identify and Develop Wastelands:**
   - Conduct a nationwide survey to identify wastelands, dry hills, and desert areas suitable for urban development.
   - Develop these areas into new towns and cities, with modern facilities and infrastructure.

3. **Create a New Housing Culture:**
   - Promote sustainable housing practices, such as green buildings, energy-efficient designs, and renewable energy sources.
   - Encourage compact and connected urban development, reducing the need for sprawl and preserving green spaces.

4. **Protect Agricultural Land:**
   - Enact legislation to prevent the conversion of agricultural land for non-agricultural purposes.
   - Establish a national agricultural land bank to protect and manage agricultural land.

5. **Develop Modern Towns:**
   - Build new towns with modern facilities, such as schools, hospitals, and community centers.
   - Ensure these towns are designed with climate change resilience in mind, incorporating features like flood protection and drought management.

6. **Public-Private Partnerships:**
   - Collaborate with private developers to build new towns and cities, ensuring they adhere to sustainable development principles.
   - Offer incentives for developers to prioritize sustainable practices and green technologies.

7. **Capacity Building and Training:**
   - Provide training and capacity-building programs for urban planners,

architects, and developers on sustainable urban development practices.
- Encourage research and development in sustainable housing and urban planning.

Examples from around the world:

- Singapore's urban planning and development model, which prioritizes sustainability and green spaces.
- Masdar City in Abu Dhabi, a sustainable city built on a former wasteland, with a focus on renewable energy and green technologies.
- The Netherlands' approach to urban planning, which prioritizes compact and connected development, with a focus on sustainability and climate resilience.

Detailed analysis:

To save agricultural land and build new towns with modern facilities, Imran Khan must:

1. Establish a national land use policy and identify wastelands for urban development.
2. Promote sustainable housing practices and compact urban development.
3. Protect agricultural land and establish a national agricultural land bank.
4. Develop modern towns with climate change resilience in mind.
5. Foster public-private partnerships to build sustainable towns and cities.
6. Provide training and capacity-building programs for urban planners and developers.
7. Encourage research and development in sustainable housing and urban planning.

By taking these measures on a war footing, Pakistan can ensure a sustainable future for its agricultural land, green belts, and urban development, while also addressing the challenges of climate change and food security.

A great vision! Pakistan's cottage industry;

has immense potential to make villages self-sufficient and vibrant. To introduce cottage industry across the country, involving unemployed educated youths, and making Pakistan a shining Asian tiger, consider the following detailed analysis with examples and suggestions from around the world:

1. **Identify Potential Industries:**
   - Food processing (jam, jelly, pickles, spices)
   - Textiles (handlooms, embroidery, knitting)
   - Crafts (woodwork, pottery, ceramics)
   - Leather goods (shoes, bags, belts)
   - Cosmetics (soaps, creams, shampoos)

2. **Government Support:**
   - Provide subsidies and loans for setup and expansion
   - Offer training and capacity-building programs
   - Create a favourable regulatory environment
   - Establish a national cottage industry development authority

3. **Small Industrial Units:**
   - Setup small units in villages, utilizing local resources
   - Encourage entrepreneurship among educated youths
   - Provide access to technology and machinery
   - Foster collaboration and clustering among units

4. **Value-Added Products:**
   - Focus on value-added products with high market demand
   - Encourage innovation and R&D in products and processes
   - Support branding and marketing efforts

5. **Self-Sustainable Villages:**
   - Develop villages with basic infrastructure (roads, electricity, water)
   - Establish community centres for training and capacity-building

- Promote village-level entrepreneurship and innovation

Examples from around the world:

- India's Khadi and Village Industries Commission (KVIC) supports cottage industries in rural areas.
- Thailand's OTOP (One Tambon One Product) program promotes local products and entrepreneurship.
- China's Township and Village Enterprises (TVEs) have driven rural industrialization and growth.
- Italy's industrial districts (e.g., Prato, Tuscany) showcase successful clustering and collaboration among small units.

Suggestions:

- Establish a national cottage industry development fund to support start-ups and expansions.
- Create a digital platform to connect producers, suppliers, and buyers.
- Organize annual cottage industry fairs and exhibitions to promote products and innovation.
- Collaborate with international organizations (e.g., UNIDO, ILO) for technical assistance and knowledge sharing.

By implementing these measures, Pakistan can unlock the potential of its cottage industry, create employment opportunities for educated youths, and make villages self-sufficient and vibrant. This will contribute to Pakistan's economic growth, reduce poverty, and make it a shining Asian tiger in the next 20 years.

The future roadmap for Pakistan is one that must embody a spirit of resilience, reform, and innovation while building upon the country's inherent strengths. It must address its systemic challenges with an unrelenting focus on inclusivity, meritocracy, and sustainability. This vision for Pakistan is rooted in the themes of justice, equity, and progress, woven into the reforms proposed in this chapter. These reforms, while ambitious, are not unattainable. With determined leadership, a clear strategy, and the collective will of the people,

Pakistan can transform itself into a prosperous and self-reliant nation.

A pivotal first step is reforming governance and ensuring the supremacy of democratic processes. Strengthening institutions like the Election Commission of Pakistan to guarantee free and fair elections is not just an administrative necessity but a moral imperative. The inclusion of technology, independent oversight, and robust mechanisms to prevent malpractice will restore trust in the electoral process. Transparency and accountability in campaign financing, coupled with voter education programs, will empower citizens to make informed choices, fostering a political culture of integrity.

The civil bureaucracy and police system, long criticized for inefficiency and politicization, must undergo comprehensive reforms. Adopting global best practices, such as merit-based recruitment, continuous professional development, and independent oversight, will create structures that are service-oriented and transparent. The integration of technology, such as e-governance platforms and digital monitoring tools, will enhance accountability and efficiency, while anti-corruption measures will be pivotal in building public confidence. Police reforms, with a focus on community engagement, independent oversight, and modern training programs, will ensure that law enforcement serves as a pillar of justice and public trust.

Pakistan's media landscape must be revitalized to uphold the principles of free speech and responsible journalism. An independent regulatory authority, protections for journalists, and a commitment to ethical standards will create an environment where media can thrive as the fourth pillar of democracy. Promoting media literacy and ensuring transparency in ownership will counter misinformation and foster a more informed citizenry.

The nation's intellectual landscape, once vibrant and respected, needs a deliberate and sustained effort for rejuvenation. Encouraging critical thinking, fostering academic freedom, and supporting independent research will create a knowledge economy capable of addressing contemporary challenges. By investing in intellectual institutions, providing platforms for public discourse, and honoring intellectual achievements, Pakistan can revive its legacy as a hub of intellectual activity and innovation.

The cultural and entertainment sectors, integral to national identity and soft power, must be prioritized. Reviving traditional arts, promoting local content, and investing in modern infrastructure for cinema and performing arts will celebrate Pakistan's heritage while creating economic opportunities. Similarly, outdoor activities and sports development will not only enrich the lives of citizens but also foster unity and national pride. Programs to preserve agricultural land and sustainably develop urban areas will ensure a balance between progress and environmental stewardship.

Agriculture, the backbone of Pakistan's economy, requires urgent modernization and diversification. From efficient water management to targeted subsidies for small farmers, these measures will enhance productivity and rural livelihoods. Promoting livestock development, value-added production, and international trade will position Pakistan as a key player in global agricultural markets. Equally critical is protecting green belts and agricultural lands from urban encroachment, ensuring food security for future generations.

The revival of Pakistan's cottage industry offers a unique opportunity to empower rural communities and create a self-reliant economy. By supporting entrepreneurship, fostering innovation, and promoting local products, the cottage industry can transform villages into vibrant hubs of economic activity. International collaboration and public-private partnerships will play a crucial role in unlocking this potential.

Education and human capital development must remain at the forefront of any roadmap for Pakistan's future. Investments in education, particularly in science, technology, engineering, and mathematics (STEM), will equip the youth with the skills needed to compete in a global economy. By fostering a culture of lifelong learning and innovation, Pakistan can harness the creativity and potential of its vast population to drive progress and development.

To navigate the complexities of the 21st century, Pakistan must also adopt a pragmatic and independent foreign policy. Strengthening ties with regional partners while balancing relationships with global powers will ensure strategic stability and economic opportunities. Pakistan's geostrategic location, coupled with its natural and human resources, can position it as a bridge between regions, fostering connectivity and cooperation.

In addressing these challenges, leadership will be critical. Imran Khan, should he return to power, must lead with clarity, vision, and an unwavering commitment to the nation's welfare. His ability to mobilize people, inspire hope, and communicate effectively will be essential in driving the reforms needed to transform Pakistan. However, leadership alone is not enough. Collective effort, involving all stakeholders—politicians, civil servants, the judiciary, the media, and civil society—will be needed to implement these reforms and sustain progress.

Pakistan's journey toward self-reliance and prosperity will not be without challenges. Resistance from entrenched interests, economic pressures, and regional instability will test the nation's resolve. However, these challenges also present opportunities to forge a resilient and innovative Pakistan. By fostering unity, building trust, and prioritizing the public interest, the nation can overcome these obstacles and chart a course toward a brighter future.

In conclusion, the roadmap for Pakistan's future is one of reform, renewal, and resurgence. It requires a holistic approach that addresses the systemic issues plaguing the nation while leveraging its strengths and opportunities. With determined leadership, inclusive governance, and the active participation of its people, Pakistan can transform itself into a thriving democracy, a robust economy, and a respected member of the global community. This vision, while ambitious, is achievable—through dedication, resilience, and an unwavering commitment to the principles of justice, equity, and progress.

Chapter 16: My farming policy and challenges in International Frontier

The farming policy I gave to khan in his 3nd year of premiership

He had called me to PM House and directed me after 3-Hour long discussion to put the salient points of my farming policy in writing. Then he summoned his principal secretary Azam Khan and ordered him to pursue the matter on war footing and report to him.

I suggested in writing for putting an end to middle man (Aartti culture) practiced in Pakistan. The government should directly buy farm products from farmers, Beefing the farmer's income by protecting him from middle man black mail. It was important to build Farm green house in every Tehsil head quarter with agricultural experts, Agricultural bank, all farming inputs including seed, pesticides, subsidies to be made available to farmers on advice of experts on yearly loans, grants and subsidies. This could revolutionise the farming in Pakistan making it a bread basket of Central and south east Asia as in ancient times.

Next step important step to be taken, certainly is! Regenerative farming practices, such as cover cropping, planting crops between cash crops, and reduced or no-till farming, offer numerous benefits. Let's break down how these practices promote sustainable agriculture and how they could be integrated into farming policies in Pakistan.

Brief Benefits of Regenerative Farming Practices that could quadruple wealth of farmer, and consumer market in the country;

1-A) Cover Cropping and Planting Between Cash Crops which is not yet known to farmer in subcontinent.

1) Reducing Erosion;
- Cover crops protect the soil from wind and water erosion.
- Roots hold the soil together, reducing its displacement. Example: Rye, clover, and vetch can be used as cover crops.

2) Increasing Organic Matter;
- Cover crops add biomass to the soil when decomposed.
- Organic matter improves soil structure and fertility.

Example: Incorporating cover crops like legumes can improve soil nitrogen levels.

3) Supporting Beneficial Insects;
- Diverse plant species provide habitat and food sources for beneficial insects.
- This can lead to natural pest control.

Example: Flowers from cover crops such as buckwheat attract pollinators and predatory insects.

1-B) No-Till or Reduced-Till Farming is revolutionary method of modern-day farming.

1) Improving Soil Health;
- Minimizes soil disturbance, preserving soil structure.
- Enhances microbial activity and root penetration.

(2) Enhancing Water Retention;
- Better soil structure leads to improved water infiltration and retention.
- This is vital for areas prone to drought.

(3) Increasing Yields;
- Healthier soil can lead to more resilient crop growth and potentially higher yields.
- Reduction in soil compaction leads to better root growth.

(4) Reducing Input Costs;
- Less reliance on heavy machinery reduces fuel and labour costs.
- Lower need for chemical fertilizers and pesticides due to improved soil health.

Integrating These Practices into Pakistan's Farming Policies.

1-A) **Steps to Implementation;**

1. Education and Training:
- Conduct workshops and training sessions for farmers on regenerative practices.
- Promote farmer-to-farmer learning and exchange programs.

2. Incentives and Support:
- Government subsidies or financial incentives for farmers adopting regenerative practices.
- Support for initial costs of seeds for cover crops and necessary equipment for no-till farming.

3. Research and Development:
- Invest in research to identify the best cover crops suited to Pakistan's diverse climates.
- Encourage partnerships between research institutions and local farmers.

4. Pilot Programs:
- Implement pilot projects to demonstrate the benefits and practicality of regenerative farming.
- Use successful case studies to promote wider adoption.

5. Market Access and Certification:
- Develop certification systems for produce grown using regenerative methods.
- Promote these products domestically and internationally to create market demand.

2-A) Specific Advice for Pakistan

1. Select Appropriate Cover Crops:
- Choose crops like legumes (e.g., lentils), which can fix nitrogen in the soil, or grasses (e.g., rye) to prevent erosion.

2. **Water Management:**
   - Introduce rainwater harvesting systems and efficient irrigation methods to complement improved soil water retention from regenerative practices.

3. **Tailored Crop Rotation Plans:**
   - Develop crop rotation plans that suit local climatic conditions and soil types.
   - Example Plan: Wheat → Legumes → Rice, supported by appropriate cover crops in off-seasons.

4. **Community Engagement:**
   - Promote community-based approaches where farmers can collaboratively manage resources and share knowledge.

5. **Financial Models:**
   - Microfinance options for small-scale farmers to adopt regenerative practices.
   - Public-Private Partnerships (PPP) to support large-scale adoption of these practices.

Example Formula for Success;

Soil Organic Matter Formula:

- Improved Yields- Increased Organic Matter + Enhanced Soil Biology + Water Retention.
- Assume current organic matter (OM) is 1%
- Increase OM by 0.5% annually through cover cropping and no-till
- Expected yield increase can be calculated based on local studies; for instance, a 1% increase in OM can correlate to a 10-15% yield increase.

By following these steps and strategies, Pakistan can leverage its favourable climate and water resources to significantly enhance its agricultural productivity while promoting sustainability. Implementing regenerative farming practices can lead to improved soil health, increased resilience against climate change, and greater economic stability.

Fast forward, the next step I suggested was;

Organic Amendments:

Organic amendments are natural materials added to soil to improve its fertility, structure, and overall health. These materials are derived from living organisms or natural processes, making them environmentally friendly and sustainable.

Types of Organic Amendments:

1. Compost: A mixture of decomposed organic matter, such as food scraps, leaves, and manure.
2. Manure: Animal waste, like cow dung or chicken droppings.
3. Green Manure: Legumes or other plants ploughed into the soil to add nutrients.
4. Peat Moss: A carbon-rich soil amendment from partially decayed plant matter.
5. Worm Castings: Nutrient-rich waste produced by worms.

Using Organic Amendments:

1. Soil Testing: Determine soil pH, nutrient levels, and structure to choose the right amendment.
2. Application Rate: Follow recommended rates to avoid over-amending, which can harm plants.
3. Mixing: Blend amendments into the topsoil or use as a mulch.
4. Timing: Apply amendments during the growing season or before planting.

Compost:

Compost is a nutrient-rich soil amendment made from decomposed organic matter. Benefits;

1. Soil Structure Improvement: Compost adds organic matter, improving soil's water-holding capacity and structure.
2. Nutrient Supply: Compost provides essential nutrients for plant growth.
3. Microbial Support: Compost supports beneficial microorganisms, enhancing soil biota.

Making Compost:

1. Collect Materials: Gather organic waste like food scraps, leaves, and grass clippings.
2. Layering: Alternate materials in a pile, starting with coarse materials.
3. Moisture Control: Maintain optimal moisture levels.
4. Aeration: Ensure adequate airflow.
5. Monitoring: Regularly check temperature and decomposition progress.

Overcoming Obstructions:

Organic amendments can help address common soil obstructions;

1. Soil Compaction: Compost and manure can improve soil structure, reducing compaction.
2. Nutrient Deficiencies_: Compost and manure provide essential nutrients.
3. Soil Erosion_: Organic amendments improve soil's water-holding capacity, reducing erosion risk.
4. Pests and Diseases: Beneficial microorganisms in compost can help control pests and diseases.

By using organic amendments like compost, farmers and gardeners can create a more sustainable and productive soil ecosystem, reducing the need for synthetic fertilizers and promoting environmental stewardship.

These methods could change the whole complexion of agriculture in Pakistan.

1. Soil Erosion Reduction: Cover crops hold soil in place, reducing erosion caused by wind or water runoff.

2. Organic Matter Increase*: Cover crops add organic matter to soil, improving structure, fertility, and water-holding capacity.

3. Beneficial Insects Support Cover crops provide habitat and food for beneficial insects, promoting biodiversity and ecosystem services.

No-Till or Reduced-Till Farming;

No-till or reduced-till farming minimizes soil disturbance, preserving soil structure and promoting soil biota. Benefits:

1. Soil Structure Preservation: No-till or reduced-till farming maintains soil structure, reducing erosion and improving water infiltration.
2. Soil Biota Promotion: Minimal soil disturbance allows soil biota to thrive, enhancing nutrient cycling, and decomposition.
3. Productivity and Yields: No-till or reduced-till farming can lead to increased productivity and yields due to improved soil health and structure.

Policy Recommendations for Pakistan;

1. Incentivize Cover Cropping: Offer subsidies or credits to farmers adopting cover cropping practices.
2. Promote No-Till/Reduced-Till: Provide training and resources for farmers to adopt no-till or reduced-till methods.
3. Soil Health Monitoring: Establish a soil health monitoring program to track progress and identify areas for improvement.
4. Research and Development: Collaborate with universities and research institutions to develop context-specific cover cropping and no-till/reduced-till practices.
5. Extension Services: Strengthen extension services to provide farmers with guidance and support for adopting sustainable practices.
6. Market Support: Develop market channels and pricing mechanisms that reward farmers for adopting sustainable practices and producing high-quality products.

By incorporating these recommendations into Pakistan's farming policy, the country can:

1. Improve Soil Health: Enhance soil fertility, structure, and biodiversity.
2. Increase Productivity: Boost crop yields and quality through improved soil health and structure.
3. Mitigate Climate Change: Sequester carbon in soils, reduce synthetic fertilizer use, and promote ecosystem services.
4. Support Farmers. Empower farmers with knowledge, resources, and

incentives to adopt sustainable practices.

My Farm Policy Memorandum: A Testament to Hard Work and Loyalty;

I still recall the day my memorandum on farm policy for PTI left the Principal Secretary in awe. He promptly sent it to Khan Sahib, who summoned me to his Banigala residence. With a warm smile, he said, "Shabash, Mansur! I miss you in the National Assembly." He even hinted at a Senate seat, saying, "Get ready!" But when the time came, my name was proposed, only to be left out due to lukewarm support from lobbies the Lahore group got all the senate seats.

Despite 20 years of dedicated service to PTI, all I received was a heartfelt "Shabash" from Khan Sahib. No complaints, no lobbying – just unwavering commitment. As a Punjabi poet once said, "Mali thee kum pani lanaa, pur pur mushkaan lavaa. Malak daa kum phul phool lanaa, Levaa k ne lavaa" ("The gardener gives lots of water to fruit trees, & happily gives plenty of smiles. The master (God) may or may not bless his trees with fruit., its God's sweet will).

Examples of unsung heroes like me abound:

- Ahmad, a dedicated PTI worker who toiled behind the scenes for years, only to be overlooked for promotions.

- Amna, a loyal party member who selflessly contributed to campaigns, but was never recognized for her efforts.

We are the unsung heroes, content with our "Shabash" and the knowledge that our hard work made a difference. But it's time for our leaders to recognize the value of loyalty and dedication. A promise is a promise – let's honour it."

Future challenges on international frontiers and climate change impacts

Humans across the globe, regardless of different regions or appearances, share a common ancestry that can be traced back to Africa. Modern humans, Homo sapiens, originated in Africa and eventually migrated to different parts of the world. Over time, various environmental factors influenced how different populations evolved, leading to the diversity of physical appearances seen today. Despite these differences, all human populations share a common genetic heritage.

The Muslim, in Kashmir in India, Sinjiang province of China are lost for now. But we have to face this at some point.

Tatars and Turks in countries like Romania, Albania, Kosovo, Czechoslovakia, Bulgaria, Russia, Hungary, and others with ties to the Ottoman Empire have a diverse history and future. While some have integrated well into their respective societies, others may still face challenges in terms of acceptance due to historical and cultural differences.

However, there has been progress in fostering understanding and dialogue between different religious and cultural groups in Europe. Efforts towards tolerance, inclusivity, and multiculturalism are ongoing. While full acceptance by the Christian world of Eastern and Western Europe may take time and effort, there are positive signs of increasing cooperation and mutual respect among diverse communities.

In conclusion, the future of Muslim Tatars and Turks in these countries is shaped by ongoing social, political, and cultural dynamics. Continued efforts towards dialogue, understanding, and respect for differences can help pave the way for greater acceptance and integration within the wider European community.

These questions touch on a wide range of complex and sensitive geopolitical issues, involving various conflicts and the positions of different countries and organizations. These subjects, such as the situation in Gaza, the conflict in Ukraine, tensions between the US and China, and the impact of actions in the

Middle East, all demand careful and nuanced discussion. Here's a general framework for considering these issues in our foreign policy.

1. **Gaza and Israeli-Palestinian Conflict:**

The situation between Israel and Palestine, particularly in Gaza, is deeply complex, rooted in long histories of conflict, politics, and struggles over sovereignty and human rights. Opinions on both sides are strongly held, often reflecting different narratives and interpretations of the conflict.

International perspectives vary, with some viewing actions as measures of self-defence and others as disproportionate uses of force or violations of human rights by Israel is unabated. This issue can consume the entire world. We must work for a two-state solution with OIC involvement.

2. **Ukraine Conflict:**

This situation involves the sovereignty and territorial integrity of Ukraine, Russian security concerns, NATO expansion, and broader international law and norms. The conflict has drawn in various countries in terms of sanctions, military support, and diplomatic efforts, reflecting differing views on sovereignty, national security, and international law. But Russian interests being jeopardized by NATO can not, and should not be ignored by Pakistan. We must stand with Russia our rightful Eurasian neighbour. NATO is an unreliable, hegemonic neoliberal capitalist Lavathins monster.

3. **US-China Relations:**

The relationship between the US and China encompasses economic competition, technological rivalry, military posturing, and differing visions for the global order. This relationship is critically important for global peace and prosperity, and developments here have widespread implications.

4. **Middle East Dynamics and Iran:**

The Middle East is a region of strategic importance, with longstanding conflicts, geopolitical rivalries, and issues related to nuclear proliferation, state sovereignty, and terrorism. The dynamics involving Iran, whether it's their regional activities or the nuclear issue, are part of a larger puzzle involving many actors with competing interests.

5. Global Strategic Theories and Economic Recovery:

The idea that conflicts or wars could be used to stimulate economic recovery or assert global dominance is a controversial one. Economic theories, historical precedents, and moral considerations all come into play when evaluating such positions.

6. Role of International Organizations:

The effectiveness and authority of international organizations like the UN are subjects of ongoing debate. There are questions about how these bodies can evolve to more effectively address conflicts, human rights abuses, and breaches of international law in a manner that reflects both justice and the complexities of international relations.

7. Future Outlook:

Predicting how these situations will unfold is challenging. There are many variables, including political changes within countries, shifts in international alliances, technological advancements, and unforeseen global events. Analysts and scholars often use a range of tools to forecast developments, but the future is inherently uncertain.

When engaging with these topics, it's crucial to draw on diverse sources, think critically, and recognize the complexity of the issues involved. Each of these areas has its own set of challenges and requires thoughtful analysis and dialogue, Furthermore, discussing speculative and sensitive geopolitical scenarios can be complex and requires careful consideration of many factors, including historical contexts, international relations, and potential humanitarian impacts.

If you're interested in understanding more about the historical context, the roles of various countries in Middle Eastern geopolitics, or the principles of international relations that might inform such a scenario, it's also important to consult a variety of up-to-date and reputable sources to get a comprehensive understanding of any ongoing international issues.

The situation in Pakistan regarding climate change is indeed severe and multifaceted. The impacts relate both to historical events and current challenges. Understanding each aspect can help in addressing the broader implications for the region and its people.

1. **Historical Climate Impacts:**

Sites like Mehrgarh and Harappa are critical to South Asian archaeology and history. While these ancient civilizations faced many challenges, modern studies suggest that climate shifts played a role in these cultures' transformations over millennia. For instance, shifts in monsoon patterns or river courses might have impacted Harappa, part of the Indus Valley Civilization.

2. **Plate Tectonics:**

The movement of the Eurasian and Indian tectonic plates primarily affects geological and seismic activity. While not a direct result of climate change, the seismic activity can exacerbate vulnerability, affecting disaster preparedness and response in the context of climate-related events like floods and landslides.

3. **Glacier Melting:**

Pakistan, housing numerous glaciers, especially in the Himalayas, Hindu Kush, and Karakoram ranges, faces a direct threat from global warming as these glaciers melt rapidly. The melting glaciers contribute to rising river levels, which increase the risk of floods. This, paired with the country's dependency on agrarian economics, poses a substantial risk to food security and water availability.

4. **Impending Climate Order:**

As Pakistan grapples with these environmental challenges, the overarching need is for comprehensive climate adaptation and mitigation strategies. This includes enhancing infrastructure resilience, implementing effective water management practices, transitioning towards sustainable energy sources, and improving disaster response mechanisms.

Addressing these challenges requires both national attention and international cooperation. Investments in technology, infrastructure, and education to understand and combat climate effects are essential. Furthermore, policies that address both immediate and long-term needs can help in building resilience against an increasingly unpredictable climate.

Climate change has far-reaching implications for Planet Earth, impacting various aspects of our planet's geography, ecology, and geology. Here are some potential effects:

Geography:

1. Rising sea levels: Melting glaciers and ice sheets cause sea levels to rise, leading to coastal erosion, flooding, and saltwater intrusion into freshwater sources.
2. Changes in ocean currents and circulation patterns: Warmer oceans can alter global circulation patterns, affecting regional climates and marine ecosystems.
3. Shifts in global weather patterns: Climate change can lead to more frequent and intense heatwaves, droughts, and storms, altering global weather patterns.

Ecology:

1. Loss of biodiversity: Rising temperatures and changing ecosystems can lead to extinctions, disrupting delicate ecological balances.
2. Disruptions to food chains and webs: Changes in species distribution and abundance can impact predator-prey relationships and nutrient cycling.
3. Alterations to migration patterns and habitats: Climate change can disrupt migratory routes, breeding grounds, and habitats for various species.

Geology:

1. Increased seismic and volcanic activity: Climate change can lead to more frequent and intense earthquakes and volcanic eruptions due to melting glaciers and ice sheets.
2. Changes in rock weathering and erosion: Warmer temperatures and altered precipitation patterns can affect the breakdown and transportation of rocks.
3. Impacts on groundwater and aquifers: Changes in precipitation and evaporation can alter groundwater recharge and discharge, affecting aquifer levels and quality.

These changes can have significant cascading effects on our planet's ecosystems, human societies, and economies. It's essential to address climate change through mitigation and adaptation strategies to minimize its impacts on our planet's geography, ecology, and geology.

Economist Jack Russell

The world considers Pakistan dangerous; as long as you don't accept this reality, you will continue to get entangled.

A faint scent of cigar smoke was spreading in the air. He was exhaling smoke through both his nose and mouth. I have an allergy to the smell of tobacco, it makes me short of breath, but I was enduring both the tobacco and its smell because of his conversation.

He was a financial expert. His father was Indian, and his mother American. Born in Virginia, he completed a PhD in terror financing and became an advisor to global financial institutions.

He was a Muslim by religion. I met him through a friend. He had come to Pakistan on an invitation from a multinational company. My friend invited both him and me for dinner. We met at a restaurant, had dinner, and then he started smoking a cigar on the terrace while I began to enjoy his insights. He said;

"The world considers Pakistan dangerous, You people are building long-range missiles, You are also a nuclear power,

But you are economically weak, so you can become a problem for the world at any time."

He paused, took a long drag on the cigar, and said;

"You people need to take the world's observation seriously, or you will harm yourselves."

I silently watched him as he continued;

"The economy is the greatest truth in the world. If you are economically powerful, you can keep nuclear bombs and build missiles.

China and Russia also have these, but the world does not consider them a threat. Why? Because the world believes these two countries are economically stable. They will never become a threat to the world that is giving them income. But Pakistan is a weak country. It cannot protect its nuclear assets for long. It can sell them for money or use them under psychological pressure, making you intolerable to the world."

"I will explain this issue with an example. Suppose you are a poor man and you have a very deadly and valuable rifle. What can you do with this rifle? You can sell it for money, or you can put it to someone's head and rob them. The world thinks you are such a hungry and poor rifle-bearer and that you can adopt either of these options at any time."

He paused, took another drag on the cigar, and said;

"This impression against you has been spread by India. The Indian government sent countless students to America, Canada, Europe, and Far Eastern countries in the 1990s with scholarships. They got degrees from top institutions and then got them employed in global institutions. These people are part of the staff of American congressmen and senators and are also in the media industry and think tanks. They sit

there and spread fear against you every day, and the world believes this fear to be true.

Your past also supports this truth. The world knows that you alone shattered the power of the Soviet Union. You did not let a power like India rise, and despite all economic weaknesses, you achieve what you want. You have even made the JF Thunder, so global policymakers think you can do anything."

He paused, took another drag on the cigar, and said:

"My study on Pakistan is that global powers will not give you a chance for war;

They believe you cannot fight a conventional war. You will start a war with the ultimate weapon, and this will be dangerous for the entire world, so they will not let you reach this level. Go back two months; India conducted a surgical strike in Balakot. Pakistan made noise, but no country in the world came forward to help Pakistan. Why? Because the world wanted to assess to what level you can react. The next day, you shot down two Indian aircraft. India deployed 9 missiles on the border on the night of February 27, and you deployed 14.

The night of February 27 was the most dangerous night in the world after the Cold War. A small mischief could have destroyed the entire world. Therefore, the world immediately became active and calmed the situation with great difficulty. It was a test. This test revealed that you people are always ready for the ultimate war, so they will not let you reach this level again. They will not give you a chance to bring out your missiles. They will not provoke you at the borders either.

"Global powers will destroy you economically."

I looked at him in amazement;

He paused, took a deep breath, and said;

"Note my words. The IMF deliberately delayed your package;

It will still keep you waiting repeatedly. It will make the dollar more expensive. It will increase inflation to twelve percent. It will also make petrol, gas, and electricity more expensive. It will reduce the development budget as well. It will increase unemployment. It will put so much pressure on banned organizations through the state that they will rebel against the government. It will not let Pakistan's exports increase either.

It will not let the stock exchange rise, and it will increase taxes so much that the public will collapse under this economic burden and rise against both the government and the state."

I listened silently as he continued;

"And this is a grand design against Pakistan. You must have heard of the Jack Russell breed of dogs. It is a small-sized, fierce dog that chases a bear into its den. It is so small in size that the bear cannot catch it.

*It hides behind the bear and wounds it so much that it cannot stand on its feet. The Jack Russell comes out of the den completely satisfied, informs its owner, and the hunter reaches the entrance of the den and shoots the bear.

"Global financial institutions are also like Jack Russells.

They wound the giant bears with their small teeth and jaws. When the bears can no longer stand on their feet, the big hunter comes and shoots the bear.

Mark my words, this is what is happening to you too. Jack Russells have been unleashed on Pakistan.

They are wounding you. They will make you so economically weak that you will not be able to fire your missiles, let alone bring them out. You will not even have money to pay the salaries of government employees.

And you will be forced to hand over tax collection to the army. And the day this happens, you start counting your days, because tax collection will tarnish the army's reputation.

People's love for it will start to diminish, and global institutions want this. They want to wound you economically and scratch the love from people's hearts. And the day you reach this level, they will make you sit at India's feet. They will turn you into Bhutan and the Maldives. You will keep taking aid and keep running the country and that's it."

He fell silent. I looked at him in fear as he said;

"What is the future of Pakistan? This decision will be made in six months.

If your economy does not take off, if stability does not come to the market, then only a miracle can save you. You will be stuck in the whirlpool."

He straightened up, extinguished the cigar, crushed it in the ashtray, and stood up. He wanted to leave. We started walking towards the reception.

As we walked, I asked: "What is the way to save ourselves?" He smiled and said;

"There are three ways to save Pakistan. Economy, economy, and economy."

"Focus solely on the economy. Let the country run. You will all be saved; otherwise, your entire country will fall victim to ego and foolishness.

"You will be forced to borrow money even to run trials. You will take money from the IMF to pay salaries to judges and lawyers and to arrange food for prisoners."

He finished his talk, shook hands warmly, and left, but I stood there thinking, was this person really telling the truth? I did not get an answer. Maybe you Pakistanis can think over it. A great vision! Pakistan's cottage industry has immense potential to make villages self-sufficient and vibrant. To introduce cottage industry across the country, involving unemployed educated youths, and making Pakistan a shining Asian tiger, consider the following detailed analysis with examples and suggestions from around the world:

1. **Identify Potential Industries:**
   - Food processing (jam, jelly, pickles, spices)
   - Textiles (handlooms, embroidery, knitting)
   - Crafts (woodwork, pottery, ceramics)
   - Leather goods (shoes, bags, belts)
   - Cosmetics (soaps, creams, shampoos)

2. **Government Support:**
   - Provide subsidies and loans for setup and expansion
   - Offer training and capacity-building programs
   - Create a favourable regulatory environment
   - Establish a national cottage industry development authority

3. **Small Industrial Units:**
   - Setup small units in villages, utilizing local resources
   - Encourage entrepreneurship among educated youths
   - Provide access to technology and machinery
   - Foster collaboration and clustering among units

4. Value-Added Products:
- Focus on value-added products with high market demand
- Encourage innovation and R&D in products and processes
- Support branding and marketing efforts

5. Self-Sustainable Villages:
- Develop villages with basic infrastructure (roads, electricity, water)
- Establish community centres for training and capacity-building
- Promote village-level entrepreneurship and innovation

Examples from around the world:

- India's Khadi and Village Industries Commission (KVIC) supports cottage industries in rural areas.
- Thailand's OTOP (One Tambon One Product) program promotes local products and entrepreneurship.
- China's Township and Village Enterprises (TVEs) have driven rural industrialization and growth.
- Italy's industrial districts (e.g., Prato, Tuscany) showcase successful clustering and collaboration among small units.

Suggestions:

- Establish a national cottage industry development fund to support startups and expansions.
- Create a digital platform to connect producers, suppliers, and buyers.
- Organize annual cottage industry fairs and exhibitions to promote products and innovation.
- Collaborate with international organizations (e.g., UNIDO, ILO) for technical assistance and knowledge sharing.

By implementing these measures, Pakistan can unlock the potential of its cottage industry, create employment opportunities for educated youths, and make villages self-sufficient and vibrant. This will contribute to Pakistan's economic growth, reduce poverty, and make it a shining Asian tiger in the next 20 years.

A treasure trove of natural resources! Balochistan's mineral wealth can indeed be a game-changer for Pakistan's economy. To mine and utilize these resources, while ensuring security and avoiding conflict with global powers, consider the following out-of-the-box solutions and suggestions:

1. Establish a National Mineral Development Corporation:

- Create a state-owned corporation to oversee mineral exploration, extraction, and processing.

- Ensure transparency, accountability, and good governance in the corporation's operations.

2. Public-Private Partnerships:

- Collaborate with local and international private sector companies to develop mining projects.

- Offer attractive incentives, such as tax breaks, subsidies, and infrastructure support.

3. Secure Mining Zones:

   - Establish secure mining zones, with robust security measures to prevent illegal mining and smuggling.

- Deploy advanced technologies, like drones and sensors, for surveillance and monitoring.

4. Water Management:

- Implement innovative water management solutions, such as:

- Cloud seeding technology to induce rainfall.

- Atmospheric water generation (AWG) systems to harvest water from air.

- Water recycling and reuse systems.

5. Gwadar Development:

- Transform Gwadar into a world-class, secure, and free trade deep-sea port.

- Develop a free trade zone, with tax incentives and streamlined regulations.

   - Establish a Gwadar Development Authority to oversee infrastructure development and management.

6. Israeli Technology Collaboration:

- Collaborate with Israeli companies specializing in water management and technology.

- Utilize their expertise in cloud seeding, AWG systems, and water recycling.

7. Virgin Land Development:

- Implement a comprehensive development plan for the virgin land in Balochistan.

- Focus on sustainable agriculture, livestock, and dairy farming.

- Establish Agro-processing industries to add value to local produce.

8. Regional Connectivity:

- Enhance regional connectivity by developing road, rail, and air links.

- Promote trade with neighbouring countries, like Iran, Afghanistan, and China.

Examples and inspirations:

- Chile's state-owned copper mining company, Codelco, a model for national mineral development.
- Saudi Arabia's Ma'aden mining company, a successful example of public-private partnerships.
- Israel's water management expertise, particularly in cloud seeding and AWG systems.
- Singapore's free trade zone model, an inspiration for Gwadar's development.

Detailed analysis:

To develop Balochistan's mineral wealth, Pakistan must adopt a multi-faceted approach, focusing on security, public-private partnerships, water management, and regional connectivity. By establishing a national mineral development corporation, securing mining zones, and utilizing innovative water management solutions, Pakistan can ensure the sustainable development of its mineral resources. Collaborating with Israeli technology and expertise can help address water challenges, while regional connectivity and trade can foster economic growth. By transforming Gwadar into a world-class port and developing the virgin land, Pakistan can create a prosperous and secure future for Balochistan and the nation.

A comprehensive approach to unlock the potential of Sindh and KPK! Managing these regions effectively can indeed make them highly productive and contribute significantly to Pakistan's prosperity. Here's a detailed analysis with examples and suggestions to make Sindh a world trading hub, secure its mineral wealth, and promote tourism in KPK:

Sindh:

1. **Water Management:**
   - Implement efficient water management systems to prevent misuse and abuse.
   - Utilize Israeli technology for cloud seeding and atmospheric water generation (AWG) systems.
   - Develop water recycling and reuse systems for industrial and agricultural purposes.

2. **Virgin Land Development:**
   - Identify and develop virgin land for agriculture, livestock, and dairy farming.
   - Establish Agro-processing industries to add value to local produce.
   - Promote sustainable agriculture practices and provide training to farmers.

3. **Mineral Development:**
   - Establish a Sindh Mineral Development Corporation to oversee mineral exploration, extraction, and processing.
   - Collaborate with private sector companies to develop mining projects.
   - Ensure transparency, accountability, and good governance in the corporation's operations.

4. **Karachi Development:**
   - Transform Karachi into a world-class, secure, and free trade deep-sea port.
   - Develop a free trade zone, with tax incentives and streamlined regulations.
   - Establish a Karachi Development Authority to oversee infrastructure development and management.

KPK:

1. Tourism Development:
- Identify and develop tourist destinations, such as the Kaghan Valley, Naran, and Hunza.
- Establish tourism infrastructure, including hotels, resorts, and recreational facilities.
- Promote eco-tourism and sustainable tourism practices.

2. Mineral Development:
- Establish a KPK Mineral Development Corporation to oversee mineral exploration, extraction, and processing.
- Collaborate with private sector companies to develop mining projects.
- Ensure transparency, accountability, and good governance in the corporation's operations.

3. Agriculture Development:
- Identify and develop areas for agriculture, livestock, and dairy farming.
- Establish Agro-processing industries to add value to local produce.
- Promote sustainable agriculture practices and provide training to farmers.

Examples and inspirations:
- Singapore's water management system, a model for efficient water use.
- Israel's cloud seeding and AWG technology, a solution for water scarcity.
- Chile's mining development model, a inspiration for Sindh and KPK's mineral development.
- New Zealand's tourism development strategy, a benchmark for KPK's tourism industry.

Detailed analysis:

To manage Sindh and KPK effectively, Pakistan must adopt a multi-faceted approach, focusing on water management, mineral development, agriculture, and tourism. By implementing efficient water management systems, developing virgin land, and promoting sustainable agriculture practices, Sindh can become a hub for agriculture and industry. KPK's mineral wealth and tourism potential can be unlocked by establishing a mineral development corporation and promoting eco- tourism. By transforming Karachi into a world-class port and developing the virgin land, Pakistan can create a prosperous and secure future for Sindh and KPK. Israeli technology can help address water challenges, while regional connectivity and trade can foster economic growth.

A comprehensive approach to revitalize Punjab! Pakistan's largest province faces challenges like overpopulation, pollution, and industrial decline, but also boasts talented and educated individuals,fertile land, and abundant natural resources. To revive Punjab's industry, cotton and rice sectors, and utilize its mineral wealth, consider the following detailed analysis with examples and out-of-the- box solutions:

1. **Industry Revival:**
   - Identify and develop strategic industries, such as textiles, food processing, and pharmaceuticals.
   - Establish special economic zones (SEZs) with incentives, infrastructure, and streamlined regulations.
   - Encourage public-private partnerships and foreign investment.

2. **Cotton and Rice Revival:**
   - Implement advanced farming techniques, such as precision agriculture and drip irrigation.
   - Introduce high-yielding and disease-resistant crop varieties.
   - Establish cotton and rice research centres to develop new breeds and improve quality.

3. **Pink Salt Utilization:**
   - Develop the salt range mountains' pink salt deposits into a significant

industry.
- Establish salt processing and refining facilities to produce high-quality salt for domestic and international markets.

4. **Virgin Land Development:**
   - Identify and develop virgin land for agriculture, livestock, and dairy farming.
   - Implement sustainable agriculture practices and provide training to farmers.
   - Stop water misuse and abuse by big landlords through efficient water management systems.

5. **Water Management:**
   - Utilize Israeli technology for water management and conservation.
   - Implement drip irrigation and sprinkler systems to reduce water waste.
   - Develop water recycling and reuse systems for industrial and agricultural purposes.

6. **Kalabagh Dam Revival:**
   - Revive the Kalabagh Dam project to address water scarcity and energy needs.
   - Implement a comprehensive water management plan to ensure efficient use of water resources.

7. **Culture and Wildlife Preservation:**
   - Establish cultural heritage sites and museums to preserve Punjab's rich cultural history.
   - Develop wildlife sanctuaries and national parks to protect Punjab's unique biodiversity.

Examples and inspirations:

- India's textile industry, a model for Punjab's revival.
- Israel's water management system, a solution for Punjab's water challenges.
- China's special economic zones (SEZs), an inspiration for Punjab's industrial development.
- New Zealand's agriculture sector, a benchmark for Punjab's farming practices.

Detailed analysis:

To revive Punjab, Pakistan must adopt a multi-faceted approach, focusing on industry development, agriculture, water management, and culture preservation. By implementing advanced farming techniques, developing strategic industries, and utilizing mineral wealth, Punjab can regain its status as a hub for industry and agriculture. Efficient water management systems, inspired by Israeli technology, can address water scarcity and boost agricultural productivity. Reviving the Kalabagh Dam project and preserving cultural heritage and wildlife can further enhance Punjab's prosperity. With out-of-the-box solutions and infrastructure development, Punjab can become a driving force for Pakistan's economic growth and prosperity.

Gilgit-Baltistan, a region of breathtaking beauty! To revolutionize it into a tourist hub, consider the following detailed analysis and suggestions, inspired by similar regions around the world:

1. **Infrastructure Development:**
   - Build world-class hotels, resorts, and guesthouses.
   - Upgrade airports and roads to facilitate easy access.
   - Develop sustainable energy sources, like hydroelectric power.

2. **Secure Borders:**
   - Implement effective border management systems.
   - Collaborate with neighbouring countries to ensure regional security.
   - Establish military bases and outposts to safeguard the region.

3. **Tourism Infrastructure:**
   - Develop trekking and hiking trails, like the famous K2 base camp trek.
   - Create scenic viewpoints and picnic spots.
   - Establish cultural heritage sites and museums.

4. **Adventure Tourism:**
   - Offer activities like rafting, kayaking, and paragliding.
   - Develop ski resorts and snowboarding facilities.
   - Organize festivals and events, like the Gilgit-Baltistan Winter Sports Festival.

5. **Sustainable Tourism:**
   - Promote eco-friendly practices and responsible travel.
   - Support local communities and preserve cultural heritage.
   - Encourage environmentally friendly accommodations and transportation.

Identical regions in the world:

- New Zealand's Queenstown*: A premier tourist destination known for adventure sports and natural beauty.
- Switzerland's Interlaken*: A picturesque town surrounded by mountains and lakes, popular for outdoor activities.
- Canada's Banff National Park*: A stunning park with majestic mountains, glaciers, and abundant wildlife.

Terrain utilization:

- Mountainous regions*: Develop ski resorts, trekking trails, and scenic viewpoints.
- Valleys and plains*: Establish agricultural projects, like orchards and dairy farms.
- Rivers and lakes*: Promote water sports, like rafting and kayaking, and develop hydroelectric power.

By implementing these strategies, Gilgit-Baltistan can become a world-class tourist hub, showcasing its natural beauty and unique culture while ensuring secure borders and sustainable development.

A vital question! Pakistan can take the following steps to secure its rivers, lakes, and water resources, despite India's actions:

1. <u>Water Management Authority:</u> Establish a national water management authority to oversee water resources, ensuring efficient use and protection.
2. <u>Water Conservation</u>: Implement water-saving measures, like drip irrigation and water-efficient agriculture practices.

3. <u>River Basin Management:</u> Develop comprehensive management plans for each river basin, including flood control, water storage, and ecosystem preservation.
4. <u>Dams and Barrages:</u> Construct and maintain dams and barrages to regulate water flow, prevent sedimentation, and generate hydroelectric power.
5. <u>Water Treatment:</u> Establish water treatment plants to remove pollutants and ensure clean water for drinking, irrigation, and industry.
6. <u>Watershed Protection:</u> Protect watersheds and catchment areas through reforestation, soil conservation, and sustainable land use practices.
7. <u>International Cooperation:</u> Engage with international organizations and neighbouring countries to address transboundary water issues and share best practices.

Examples from around the world:

- Australia's Murray-Darling Basin Authority: A successful model for river basin management and water conservation.
- California's Water Management System: A comprehensive approach to water management, including water conservation, recycling, and desalination.
- Switzerland's Water Protection Act: A robust framework for protecting water resources, including rivers, lakes, and groundwater.
- China's South-to-North Water Transfer Project: A massive infrastructure project to transfer water from the Yangtze River to the Yellow River basin.

<u>To prevent water theft by India, Pakistan can:</u>

1. Install water monitoring systems: Use advanced technologies, like satellite imaging and sensors, to track water flow and detect any unauthorized diversions.
2. Strengthen diplomatic efforts: Engage in diplomatic efforts to resolve water disputes and ensure equitable sharing of transboundary water resources.

3. Develop alternative water sources: Invest in desalination, water recycling, and rainwater harvesting to reduce dependence on shared water resources.

By adopting a comprehensive approach to water management, Pakistan can ensure the long-term health and sustainability of its rivers, lakes, and dams, despite India's actions.

Pakistan's potential for greatness lies in its ability to harness its vast natural resources, rich cultural heritage, and resilient people to overcome the multifaceted challenges it faces. The diverse ideas presented in this chapter, from transformative farming policies to unlocking the economic potential of mineral-rich provinces, underscore the need for a comprehensive, coordinated, and inclusive approach to the country's development. However, achieving this vision requires clarity of purpose, sustained commitment, and an unwavering focus on the greater good of the nation and its people.

The agricultural reforms discussed illustrate the power of embracing modern, regenerative practices that align with global advancements in sustainable farming. By eliminating exploitative systems, such as the middleman culture, and directly empowering farmers, Pakistan has the opportunity to elevate rural livelihoods and bolster its food security. These practices, combined with innovations in organic farming and tailored incentives for farmers, could revitalize the agricultural sector, transforming Pakistan into a breadbasket for its region while mitigating the effects of climate change on crop yields and soil health.

Similarly, the proposal to enhance water management reflects a pragmatic acknowledgment of the growing global crisis surrounding water resources. The adoption of advanced technologies, like those pioneered in Israel, paired with robust domestic policies, could address issues of water scarcity, misuse, and inefficiency. These solutions require collaboration across provinces, public-private partnerships, and innovative financing to ensure equitable access to water resources while fostering sustainable agricultural and industrial growth.

The focus on developing a robust cottage industry resonates with Pakistan's historical economic roots and offers a pathway to uplift rural areas, reduce unemployment, and cultivate a culture of entrepreneurship. By encouraging value addition, leveraging local skills, and establishing supportive infrastructure, this sector can empower marginalized communities and contribute to a more self-reliant economy. Learning from global examples, such as India's Khadi initiatives or Thailand's OTOP program, Pakistan can tailor a model that integrates the strengths of its cultural and economic fabric.

On a provincial level, the roadmap for regions like Balochistan, Sindh, KPK, and Punjab highlights the strategic importance of regional equity in development. These provinces possess unique resources and opportunities, from untapped mineral wealth to tourism potential and thriving industries. The challenge lies in ensuring inclusive growth that respects local cultures, preserves the environment, and addresses historical grievances. Whether through the development of secure mining zones, the promotion of eco-tourism, or the establishment of special economic zones, each initiative must be rooted in transparency and collaboration.

The example of Gilgit-Baltistan as a prospective global tourist hub demonstrates how Pakistan can leverage its natural beauty and unique culture to attract international attention. Developing infrastructure, securing borders, and promoting sustainable tourism are essential steps, but they must be undertaken with care to preserve the region's ecological and cultural integrity. Drawing lessons from successful models in Switzerland, New Zealand, and Canada, Pakistan can position Gilgit-Baltistan as a premier destination while benefiting its local communities.

The chapter's emphasis on water resources, particularly the challenges posed by neighboring India, reflects the urgency of addressing transboundary water disputes. However, rather than dwelling on grievances, Pakistan must focus on solutions that prioritize sustainability, equity, and international cooperation. Diplomatic engagement, technological advancements in water monitoring, and investment in alternative water sources are practical steps that can enhance Pakistan's resilience and strengthen its position in negotiations.

The broader vision for Pakistan also encompasses industrial revival, cultural preservation, and leveraging its geopolitical position for economic integration. Industrial growth in Punjab, for instance, must align with global trends in innovation and sustainability, while the province's rich cultural heritage can serve as a source of national pride and international appeal. Similarly, transforming Karachi and Gwadar into world-class ports and economic hubs could make Pakistan a central player in regional and global trade networks.

Underlying all these strategies is the recognition that Pakistan's true strength lies in its people. The chapter emphasizes the need to invest in education, promote critical thinking, and foster a culture of innovation and intellectual freedom. Reviving the country's intelligentsia and supporting research and development are vital to building a knowledge-based economy that can compete on the global stage. Programs that encourage public engagement, reward intellectual contributions, and support lifelong learning will help cultivate a society capable of navigating the complexities of the modern world.

Addressing the challenges of climate change requires an integrated approach that combines local resilience with global responsibility. As a nation particularly vulnerable to the impacts of a changing climate, Pakistan must prioritize renewable energy, reforestation, and sustainable development practices. Collaborative efforts to protect rivers, lakes, and dams, coupled with efficient disaster management systems, will be essential to safeguard both the environment and the livelihoods of future generations.

The discussion on Pakistan's international challenges provides a sobering reminder of the interconnected nature of global geopolitics. From regional tensions to the looming threat of economic subjugation, Pakistan must adopt a pragmatic, forward-looking foreign policy that prioritizes its sovereignty while building strategic alliances. The advice to focus solely on economic strength as a means of securing national security resonates deeply in today's interconnected world. Strengthening the economy not only ensures stability but also enhances Pakistan's ability to engage on equal footing in international diplomacy.

Ultimately, the chapter's proposals reflect a vision of Pakistan that balances ambition with realism. The reforms and initiatives outlined are not mere aspirations but tangible steps that can be implemented with the right leadership, political will, and societal support. However, achieving this vision requires moving beyond short-term gains and partisan politics to embrace a long-term, holistic approach to national development.

Imran Khan's leadership, as highlighted throughout this narrative, represents both a challenge and an opportunity. His ability to inspire and mobilize people is unparalleled, but this must be matched with effective governance, inclusive decision-making, and the ability to build consensus across diverse stakeholders. Success will depend not only on his vision but also on his willingness to empower competent teams, engage with critics constructively, and remain steadfast in the face of resistance.

In conclusion, the future of Pakistan rests on its ability to transform challenges into opportunities and aspirations into realities. The country's rich history, natural resources, and talented population provide a solid foundation for progress, but this potential must be unlocked through deliberate, sustained efforts. By embracing innovation, fostering unity, and prioritizing the well-being of its citizens, Pakistan can emerge as a beacon of hope and resilience, not just for its region but for the world at large. The road ahead may be arduous, but with determination, pragmatism, and a shared sense of purpose, the dream of a prosperous and thriving Pakistan can become a reality.

Chapter 17: A Journey of Resilience, Unity, and Progress

Protest in Islamabad on November 24, 2024, marked a grim chapter in Pakistan's history. The peaceful demonstration was met with unparalleled brutality, as the federal and Punjab provincial governments unleashed a crackdown reminiscent of the darkest days of repression. Despite the state's attempts to block roads and restrict movement, nearly half a million people gathered to exercise their constitutional right to peaceful assembly.

The response was swift and unforgiving. Reports indicate that police, in conjunction with other state agencies, resorted to live ammunition, tear gas, and rubber bullets to suppress the protests. Between 25 to 57 lives were lost, with countless others injured. Among the dead were four security personnel tragically killed in a vehicular accident unrelated to the protest itself, highlighting the chaos that ensued. The international community, human rights organizations, and local activists condemned the government's heavy-handedness, demanding accountability for what many labeled a "massacre." I would like to extend a heartfelt tribute to the brave Rangers and security officials who have laid down their lives in the line of duty. Their sacrifices are the cornerstone of our nation's security and prosperity, and their unwavering commitment continues to inspire a deep sense of gratitude and respect among all Pakistanis.

Amid this turmoil, the resilience of PTI workers and leaders shone as a beacon of hope. Their unwavering commitment to the principles of democracy and justice has become a symbol of resistance against tyranny. The stories of PTI leaders Asad Qaiser, Shaheryar Afridi, Zartaj Gul Wazir, and Alia Hamza capture the courage and sacrifice of countless others who stood firm in the face of oppression.

Asad Qaiser, the former Speaker of the National Assembly, reflected on the harrowing days during the no-confidence vote against Imran

Khan. "The parliament was surrounded by police forces, and MNAs were coerced into voting against us," he recounted. "Families were abducted, and false cases fabricated to break our spirits. But we stood firm, like the brave Pashtuns our ancestors were." His imprisonment following a fabricated operation only strengthened his resolve. Qaiser emphasized the need for justice, calling for judicial commissions to investigate the events of November 24 and May 9, underlining PTI's commitment to truth and accountability.

Shaheryar Afridi's story is one of resilience in the face of unimaginable torture. As a former Interior Minister, he endured nine months of brutal imprisonment, leaving him physically broken but spiritually unyielding. His arm was fractured, and his body bore the marks of inhuman treatment, yet his determination never wavered. Afridi's release, delayed despite court orders, highlighted the state's disregard for human rights. He emerged as a symbol of defiance, a voice for those silenced by tyranny, quoting Mandela's words, "The greatest glory in living lies not in never falling, but in rising every time we are fallen."

Zartaj Gul Wazir, a leader known for her unwavering commitment to justice, shared her journey of overcoming adversity. A trailblazer in politics, she rose to prominence by defeating entrenched feudal dynasties, an achievement that continues to inspire young Pakistanis. Her work on climate change and women's rights has left a lasting impact. Zartaj's resilience and dedication remind us of the potential for transformative change through courage and determination like late Shaheed Benazir Bhutto.

Alia Hamza's experiences reveal the depths of the regime's brutality. Arrested on May 9, she endured fourteen months of imprisonment in inhumane conditions. Her family suffered deeply, her teenage daughter harassed, and her husband subjected to relentless intimidation. Despite these hardships, Alia emerged from prison with an unbroken spirit. She continues to advocate for justice, her courage exposing the hybrid regime's disregard for human rights and rule of law.

These stories of resilience and sacrifice are a testament to the unyielding spirit of PTI workers and leaders. Their unwavering dedication to the principles of democracy, justice, and freedom will inspire generations to come. In the face of overwhelming adversity, their resolve has become a beacon of hope, a reminder that the fight for justice is never in vain.

The sacrifices of these individuals highlight the cost of freedom and the strength required to challenge oppression. As Rumi once said, "The wound is the place where the Light enters you." These wounds have illuminated the path to a brighter future, and their legacy will endure as a testament to the power of resistance. Together, their courage and determination offer hope for a Pakistan free from tyranny and oppression.

The Spirit of Peaceful Resistance: November 26 and the Heroes of Haqeeqi Azadi

The peaceful march toward Islamabad on November 26, 2024, organized by Pakistan Tehreek-e-Insaf (PTI), was a powerful demonstration of the people's resolve and their demand for Haqeeqi Azadi (true freedom). Thousands from all corners of Pakistan marched with unity, courage, and an unrelenting spirit, determined to express their democratic rights. Yet, this historic movement was met with disproportionate force and repression, a disheartening reminder of the challenges that citizens face when seeking justice through peaceful means.

The state's response to this peaceful assembly was both tragic and avoidable. Roads leading to Islamabad were blockaded, and protesters were subjected to tear gas, baton charges, and other harsh measures. Despite these obstacles, PTI workers and supporters maintained their commitment to non-violence, embodying the spirit of peaceful resistance. This restraint, despite facing severe adversity, is a testament to their deep belief in justice and democratic principles.

Ali Amin Gandapur emerged as a symbol of courage during these trying times. Known for his fiery speeches and steadfast resolve, Gandapur played a pivotal role in rallying the spirits of the protesters. His determination and ability to lead under pressure showcased the kind of leadership that inspires movements and strengthens the resolve of those who follow.

Equally inspiring was the quiet yet unyielding courage of Bushra Bibi, the wife of Imran Khan. Her steadfast support and resilience during some of the most challenging times served as a pillar of strength not only for her husband but also for countless PTI supporters. Often working behind the scenes, Bushra Bibi's commitment to the cause and her ability to stand firm in the face of adversity highlight the profound role that women play in Pakistan's political and social landscape.

Alima Khan, the sister of Imran Khan, also deserves recognition for her unwavering dedication and contributions to PTI's vision of a better Pakistan. As a supporter and advocate of her brother's mission, Alima's dignified presence and tireless efforts to uphold the values of justice and democracy have left a significant impact on those who admire and follow her journey.

The events of November 26 left an indelible mark on the nation's conscience. The sight of peaceful protesters facing such extreme measures raised questions about the state's commitment to safeguarding democratic principles. Yet, the resilience shown by the marchers, led by courageous figures like Ali Amin Gandapur, and supported by the quiet strength of Bushra Bibi and Alima Khan, illuminated the enduring spirit of hope and resistance.

This peaceful march was more than a political movement; it was a call for justice, equity, and the democratic rights of every Pakistani. The courage displayed by leaders and supporters alike serves as a reminder that while the road to freedom is fraught with challenges, the spirit of a united and determined people is unbreakable. The sacrifices made on that day will continue to inspire future generations to strive for a Pakistan where democracy and justice prevail.

Peaceful demonstrations are a fundamental right in any democratic society, serving as an essential mechanism for the people to voice their concerns, express dissent, and demand accountability. The ability to protest peacefully is not just for one political party, such as the Pakistan Tehreek-e-Insaf (PTI), but must be safeguarded for all political groups and citizens. It is a reflection of a society's commitment to democratic norms, justice, and inclusivity. The suppression of peaceful demonstrations undermines the principles of democracy and erodes the trust between citizens and the state, ultimately harming the fabric of the nation.

Unfortunately, the recurring incidents of blocking peaceful protests, slowing internet speeds, shutting down phone services, and imposing digital firewalls across Pakistan have created barriers to freedom of expression and innovation. These measures not only restrict the democratic process but also stifle economic growth, technological advancement, and societal progress. In a rapidly globalizing world, connectivity is the lifeline of modern economies, and such disruptions send a message of instability to international investors and local businesses alike. The potential for Pakistan to emerge as a hub of innovation and development is compromised when its people are cut off from the tools and platforms that enable communication, collaboration, and creativity.

I firmly believe in the enduring power of peace, as echoed by Neville Chamberlain in his famous 1938 declaration of "peace in our time." Though his words were not immediately realized in the years that followed, they laid the groundwork for a vision that eventually manifested in Western Europe's embrace of lasting peace from 1945 onward. This example serves as a reminder that peace is a process that requires patience, dialogue, and a collective commitment to reconciliation and progress.

In the context of Pakistan, peace between the PTI, the military, and other state institutions is not merely desirable but essential. The political polarization and institutional discord that have plagued our country must give way to a spirit of collaboration and mutual respect. Each institution and political entity has a role to play in building a prosperous Pakistan. The military, as a vital pillar of national security, must work in tandem with civilian leadership to create an environment of stability and progress. Similarly, political parties, including the PTI, must respect the constitutional framework and engage constructively with state institutions.

A prosperous Pakistan is only possible when its people are united in their quest for justice, equity, and progress. Peaceful coexistence, even amid differences, can create an atmosphere where innovation thrives, resources are allocated equitably, and every citizen has the opportunity to contribute meaningfully to the nation's future. The sacrifices made by those who have fought for democracy and justice must inspire us to rise above division and build a Pakistan that reflects the aspirations of its people.

The path to peace is neither easy nor immediate, but it is the only sustainable way forward. As Pakistan navigates these challenging times, let us remember that the collective will of a united people is stronger than any force of division. By embracing peace, dialogue, and inclusivity, we can pave the way for a brighter and more prosperous future for generations to come.

Imran Khan's return to power carries profound significance for Pakistan, particularly as the global political landscape undergoes dramatic shifts with the rise of powerful figures like Donald J. Trump and Elon Musk. Trump's return to the White House and Musk's increasing influence on global affairs underscore the urgent need for Pakistan to have a resilient and visionary leader who can safeguard national interests and ensure the country's sovereignty remains intact amid external pressures.

Trump's agenda, driven by his pragmatic and sometimes aggressive policy stances, focuses on major geopolitical realignments, such as his emphasis on ending the Ukraine-Russia conflict and reviving America's strategic vision reminiscent of President William McKinley. Trump's ambitions, including acquiring Greenland and asserting dominance in Arctic geopolitics, highlight a transactional and expansionist approach to diplomacy. In this context, countries like Pakistan risk being sidelined or pressured into aligning with larger powers unless they possess strong, astute leadership. Imran Khan, with his proven ability to engage with global leaders on equal terms, is uniquely positioned to navigate these challenges. His tenure showcased an independent foreign policy, balancing relationships with major powers like the United States, China, and Russia, while protecting Pakistan's autonomy.

Elon Musk's growing role in Western geopolitics, particularly through his influence over technology and public discourse, further complicates the global landscape. Musk's ability to shape narratives via platforms like X (formerly Twitter) and his alignment with certain ideological factions in Europe and the United States demonstrate how technology can now serve as a potent geopolitical tool. Countries like Pakistan, which are grappling with internal challenges and limited technological infrastructure, are especially vulnerable to digital manipulation and external pressures. A leader like Imran Khan, who understands the importance of innovation and has consistently advocated for technology-driven growth, can guide Pakistan toward resilience in the face of such emerging threats. By fostering domestic innovation and strengthening Pakistan's technological ecosystem, Khan can ensure that the nation is equipped to counter external influence and maintain its sovereignty in the digital age.

Trump's advocacy for a transactional global order and Musk's technological dominance underline the importance of Pakistan having a leader who can assertively protect its interests. Khan's diplomatic acumen, exemplified during his tenure by his efforts to mediate in the Afghanistan peace process and maintain balanced relations with competing powers, is precisely what Pakistan needs to navigate an increasingly complex global environment. His emphasis on justice, equity, and inclusivity resonates with a broader vision for global cooperation, offering a counterbalance to the zero-sum politics often seen in international relations.

Moreover, Khan's vision for Pakistan—a self-reliant, technologically advanced, and globally respected nation—aligns with the need to address internal vulnerabilities that external powers could exploit. His return to power would signify a renewed focus on economic revival, institutional reform, and strategic autonomy, enabling Pakistan to stand firm in the face of geopolitical challenges posed by leaders like Trump and Musk. By championing a strong, independent Pakistan, Khan can ensure that the country is neither coerced into alliances that undermine its interests nor sidelined in a rapidly evolving global order.

In an era defined by assertive global players, Imran Khan represents the leadership Pakistan needs to protect its sovereignty, foster internal unity, and secure its rightful place on the global stage. His return to power would not only serve as a beacon of hope for Pakistanis but also send a clear message to the world that Pakistan is a resilient nation capable of standing tall amid shifting geopolitical tides.

Pakistan stands at a critical juncture. Its economic trajectory, plagued by stagnation, short-term fixes, and empty political promises, has left the nation struggling to find its footing in an increasingly competitive world. Programs like the Uraan initiative, touted by PML-N and PPP as solutions to economic woes, have proven to be hollow, designed more for political theatrics than actual transformation. The return of Imran Khan to power must mark a decisive shift—a renewal of purpose, vision, and action that places Pakistan on a trajectory of real economic progress and social stability.

At present, Pakistan's economy is grappling with fundamental weaknesses. Projections of GDP growth hovering around 3.2% for

2025 underscore how far the country lags behind its regional peers. Countries like Vietnam, Bangladesh, and Malaysia have not only surpassed Pakistan but have established themselves as global examples of sustainable growth through innovation, infrastructure, and policy-driven governance.

The Uraan Program, with its lofty claims of creating a trillion-dollar economy by the mid-2030s, is emblematic of Pakistan's flawed approach. Such promises, devoid of substance, only highlight the absence of a coherent roadmap. With a population of over 240 million, achieving modest growth rates of 3% to 4% is insufficient. Pakistan cannot afford to operate on outdated economic models while the rest of the world advances rapidly into the age of Artificial Intelligence, green energy, and digital transformation.

Vietnam, once a war-ravaged nation, has emerged as a Southeast Asian powerhouse. Its integration into global supply chains, export-oriented manufacturing, and technology-driven industries has fueled a GDP of $409 billion with consistent growth rates above 6%. Vietnam's success stems from policies that attract foreign investment, foster innovation, and eliminate bureaucratic hurdles.

Bangladesh, which started from a weaker economic position in the 1970s, now boasts a GDP per capita nearly double that of Pakistan. By capitalizing on its robust textile industry and diversifying into green energy and technology, Bangladesh has demonstrated the transformative power of strategic planning and governance.

Malaysia's economic model, built on diversification and sustained investment in high-tech industries like biotechnology and renewable energy, offers another valuable lesson. Malaysia's commitment to education, infrastructure, and fostering innovation has enabled it to remain globally competitive despite having a smaller population and resource base than Pakistan.

Imran Khan's return to power must signify a break from the past. The focus cannot merely be on addressing surface-level symptoms but on tackling the systemic issues that have held Pakistan back. A comprehensive strategy is needed—one that prioritizes innovation, eliminates corruption, and invests in the potential of the nation's youth.

Pakistan must embrace the Fourth Industrial Revolution. The global economy is being reshaped by advancements in AI, blockchain, quantum computing, and cybersecurity. These technologies are not optional; they are the future. Programs like Uraan fail to recognize this reality, offering little more than superficial promises without addressing how Pakistan can compete in a technology-driven world.

Pakistan must become a hub for technological innovation. Establishing Special Technology Economic Zones, offering tax incentives, streamlined regulations, and world-class infrastructure, would attract foreign direct investment and foster local talent. The global rise in digital threats also presents an opportunity for Pakistan to position itself as a leader in cybersecurity, safeguarding its digital future while generating high-value jobs.

Education must take center stage in this transformation. While Pakistan produces thousands of IT graduates annually, many lack the skills required to compete in the global market. By collaborating with international universities and tech companies, Pakistan can establish research facilities, advanced educational institutions, and exchange programs to create a generation of innovators.

Blockchain technology and digital assets offer unparalleled potential for transparency and efficiency. Establishing a regulatory framework for digital currencies, as seen in El Salvador and Dubai, can position Pakistan as a regional leader in financial technology, enhancing economic inclusion and resilience. This vision also includes developing frameworks to attract global blockchain firms and fostering local innovation.

Frequent power outages, unreliable internet, and high energy costs have made Pakistan's industries uncompetitive. Vietnam and Bangladesh have modernized their infrastructure and transitioned to renewable energy, creating a conducive environment for business. Pakistan must follow suit by investing in clean energy projects and addressing inefficiencies in its energy sector.

Corruption and governance inefficiencies remain persistent challenges. The misuse of public funds and privileges enjoyed by political elites exacerbate Pakistan's woes. Imran Khan has always championed accountability and transparency, and his return to power must prioritize comprehensive reforms to strengthen institutions, uphold the rule of law, and eliminate corruption.

Judicial independence is essential for Pakistan's democratic future. Ensuring fair trials, reducing judicial delays, and safeguarding judicial autonomy will enhance investor confidence and foster a culture of accountability. Similarly, civil service reforms are crucial to streamlining governance, digitizing processes, and incentivizing efficiency in public administration.

Pakistan must also invest in its energy sector. Clean energy initiatives, coupled with modernized infrastructure, can address long-standing issues that hinder economic growth. The cost of doing business must be reduced to attract local and foreign investments.

Global leaders like Donald Trump and influential figures like Elon Musk are shaping a world driven by aggressive economic strategies and technological advancements. Trump's focus on geopolitical dominance and Musk's ventures in AI and space exploration highlight the urgent need for Pakistan to align itself with global tech ecosystems. Under Imran Khan, Pakistan can navigate these global dynamics by embracing bold reforms and fostering homegrown innovation.

The world is rapidly advancing into the era of AI and digital transformation. The global tech landscape is dominated by trillion-dollar companies, none of which originate from Pakistan. This gap represents not just a missed opportunity but an existential threat to Pakistan's economic sovereignty. Imran Khan's leadership offers the promise of transformative change—a break from the status quo and a commitment to realizing Pakistan's true potential.

Pakistan's future depends on its ability to embrace bold reforms, invest in high-growth sectors, and build an economy that can compete on the global stage. This is not merely a matter of ambition; it is a necessity. The road ahead will be challenging, but the stakes are too high to falter. By prioritizing technology, education, and governance, Pakistan can not only catch up with its regional peers but also carve out a place for itself as a global leader in the digital age. It is time for action, vision, and resilience. Imran Khan's return to power must be the catalyst for a new chapter in Pakistan's history—one defined by progress, innovation, and hope.

Chapter 18: Conclusion and Objective of the Book

The conclusion and objective of this book lie in the recognition of Pakistan's immense potential and its capacity to overcome the multifaceted challenges it faces by embracing a vision of inclusive growth, sustainable development, and responsible governance. Through an in-depth exploration of key areas—ranging from political and economic reforms to environmental sustainability, cultural preservation, and international relations—the book aims to provide a comprehensive roadmap for national renewal. It underscores the importance of collective effort, visionary leadership, and a deep commitment to the nation's foundational principles to pave the way for a brighter, more prosperous future.

At its heart, the book seeks to inspire a sense of ownership and responsibility among Pakistanis, from policymakers to citizens, to actively engage in shaping their nation's destiny. The challenges discussed are significant—economic instability, political fragmentation, environmental degradation, and global perceptions of insecurity—but they are not insurmountable. History bears witness to Pakistan's resilience, its capacity to rise above crises, and its ability to achieve remarkable feats under the most adverse conditions. This resilience is the cornerstone upon which Pakistan can build its future.

The overarching objective of this book has been to critically examine the status quo while offering actionable solutions rooted in global best practices and tailored to Pakistan's unique context. Whether discussing the need for agricultural reforms, industrial revival, or regional development, the emphasis has consistently been on fostering inclusivity, sustainability, and innovation. By learning from successful models around the world, Pakistan can adapt these strategies to its socio-economic and cultural realities, creating a framework that is both ambitious and attainable.

Economic revival remains central to Pakistan's journey toward prosperity. As highlighted throughout the book, the nation's economic trajectory must be underpinned by policies that empower its people, promote equitable development, and prioritize long-term stability over short-term gains. The proposed reforms in agriculture, cottage industries, and large-scale manufacturing aim to diversify Pakistan's economic base, reduce dependence on external aid, and create sustainable livelihoods for millions. Similarly, by leveraging its geographical advantages and strategic location, Pakistan can establish itself as a hub for trade, logistics, and regional connectivity, fostering deeper integration with neighboring economies.

The book also underscores the importance of institutional reforms in governance, bureaucracy, and the judicial system. A transparent, accountable, and efficient governance structure is essential for ensuring that the benefits of development are equitably distributed and that public trust in the state is restored. These reforms must be accompanied by a robust electoral process that guarantees free and fair elections, empowering citizens to play a meaningful role in the democratic process. The role of media, civil society, and intellectuals in holding power to account and fostering public discourse cannot be overstated.

Another critical theme of the book has been the preservation and promotion of Pakistan's cultural heritage and diversity. From the ancient civilizations of Mehrgarh and Harappa to the vibrant traditions of its provinces, Pakistan possesses a rich tapestry of history and culture that can serve as a source of unity and national pride. Revitalizing the arts, literature, and entertainment industry, alongside promoting cultural tourism, offers immense potential for economic growth and global recognition. By embracing its pluralistic identity,

Pakistan can build a more inclusive society where every citizen feels valued and empowered.

Environmental sustainability is a thread that runs through the book, highlighting the urgent need for climate adaptation and mitigation strategies. Pakistan's vulnerability to climate change—manifested through glacial melting, water scarcity, and extreme weather events—demands immediate and coordinated action. The proposed measures, from regenerative farming to water conservation and renewable energy, aim to build resilience against these challenges while ensuring environmental stewardship for future generations. Collaboration with international partners, leveraging technology, and fostering public awareness will be key to achieving these goals.

The book's examination of Pakistan's international relations emphasizes the importance of a balanced and pragmatic foreign policy. Navigating the complexities of global geopolitics requires Pakistan to assert its sovereignty while fostering constructive partnerships with key global players. Strengthening ties with neighboring countries, particularly in South and Central Asia, can unlock economic and strategic opportunities, while engaging with international organizations can enhance Pakistan's standing on the global stage. At the same time, the book advocates for a proactive approach to addressing perceptions of insecurity and ensuring that Pakistan is seen as a reliable and responsible member of the international community.

The role of leadership is a recurring theme throughout the book. Leaders are not merely policymakers; they are visionaries who inspire, unite, and guide their nations through times of adversity and opportunity. Imran Khan's leadership, as explored in this narrative, serves as a focal point for understanding the challenges and opportunities that lie ahead. His ability to connect with the masses, articulate a compelling vision, and challenge entrenched systems of power is both a strength and a responsibility. However, true leadership also requires humility, inclusivity, and the willingness to learn from mistakes. The success of any leader is ultimately measured by their ability to leave behind a legacy of strengthened institutions, empowered citizens, and a clear roadmap for the future.

The book also highlights the critical role of Pakistan's youth in shaping the nation's future. With a young and dynamic population, Pakistan has a unique demographic advantage that can drive innovation, creativity, and progress. Investing in education, skill development, and entrepreneurship is essential to harnessing this potential. The youth must be given the tools, opportunities, and platforms to contribute meaningfully to society, ensuring that they are active participants in the nation-building process.

In conclusion, the book serves as both a reflection on Pakistan's current state and a blueprint for its future. It is a call to action for all stakeholders—government, civil society, private sector, and citizens—to work together in pursuit of a common vision. This vision is one of a self-reliant, inclusive, and globally respected Pakistan that upholds the principles of justice, equality, and sustainability. The challenges are daunting, but they are not insurmountable. With the right policies, leadership, and collective will, Pakistan can realize its potential and reclaim its rightful place on the world stage.

Ultimately, the book aims to inspire hope, foster dialogue, and spark a sense of purpose among its readers. It invites them to think critically, act decisively, and contribute positively to the nation's journey toward progress. Pakistan's story is far from over, and its best chapters are yet to be written. This book is a small step toward envisioning and shaping a future that honors the sacrifices of the past, embraces the opportunities of the present, and aspires to the possibilities of tomorrow. Together, we can build a Pakistan that is not only resilient but also a beacon of hope and inspiration for the rest of the world.